BEDA

A JOURNEY THROUGH THE SEVEN KINGDOMS
IN THE AGE OF BEDE

Henrietta Leyser is a historian specialising in the history of medieval England. An emeritus fellow of St Peter's College, Oxford, her previous books include *Hermits and the New Monasticism: A Study of Religious Communities in Western Europe, 1000–1150* (1984) *and Medieval Women: A Social History of Women in England 450–1500* (1995).

BEDA

A journey through the
SEVEN KINGDOMS
in the age of Bede

Henrietta Leyser

HEAD
♀ZEUS

To Timea, in memory of many journeys

With Bede was buried almost all historical record down to our own day; so true is it that there was no English competitor in his field of study, no would-be rivals of his fame to follow up the broken thread. A few, whom favouring Jesus loved, achieved a not discreditable level of learning, but spent all their years in ungrateful silence; while others, who had scarcely sipped the cup of letters, remained in idleness and sloth. So, as each proved more idle than the last, zeal for these studies languished long in the whole island. A good specimen of this decadence will be found in his verse epitaph, a shameful effusion, quite unworthy the monument of so great a man:

> The reverend Bede here buried is.
> Christ grant him everlasting bliss,
> At wisdom's well to drink his fill,
> For which he longed with loving zeal.

Can anything excuse this shameful state of affairs? In that same monastery where, while he lived, burgeoned a school of every branch of learning, could no one be found to enshrine his memory except in this piteous doggerel?

WILLIAM OF MALMESBURY, *Gesta regum Anglorum: The History of the English Kings* (ED. AND TRANS. R. A. B. MYNORS, COMPLETED BY R. M. THOMSON AND M. WINTERBOTTOM, 1998), BOOK I, p. 95.

...Anglo-Saxon sculpture lacks the immediate attractiveness of other forms of Christian art...This is material that has to be examined in the field; it is often set in some dark corner of a locked church, whose keyholder is unavailable; frequently it will be set behind an immovable pew, or beneath a flower arrangement which it would be tactless to disturb; it will sometimes be incorporated into later masonry far out of reach of available ladders, or it will form part of a jealously guarded rockery.

RICHARD N. BAILEY, *England's Earliest Sculptors*

(1996), p. 3.

CONTENTS

PREFACE

The seeds of this book were sown as long ago as January 2007 at 'Bede's World', the famous museum and mock Anglo-Saxon farm at Jarrow (close to Newcastle) built in honour of the great eighth-century monk and historian, Bede.

The place is deserted. Apart from my own hired car, the car park is empty. In alarm and dismay I turn to Timea, the friend whom I have lured from the States expressly to pay homage to Bede, for an explanation. She gives a wry smile: 'Last night's storm felled pylons and overturned trucks. Didn't they say back at our hotel that almost none of the employees made it in? No one in their right minds will have come out in this.'

I am sobered, but not for long. Bede himself suspected that the world might end at any time, but that would not have kept him in bed or deflected him from his purpose. How else to find the time to write over thirty works on subjects as diverse as calendrical calculations and the tides, saints' lives, biblical commentaries and the greatest source there is for the England of his day, *The Ecclesiastical History of the English People?*

★

A year later, my friend from New York is here again. We are now in Selsey, in Sussex, this time on the tracks of a contemporary of Bede's, that ostentatiously great abbot and bishop, Wilfrid,

who, during a stay in Sussex, converted the inhabitants to
Christianity by teaching them how to become better fishermen
and who then went on to establish a monastery at Selsey. Where,
I want to know, is Wilfrid commemorated? We stop to ask in the
local post office and receive blank looks. Can I perhaps buy a
guide to Selsey? Nothing available, not even a postcard. Once
again I am indignant at this seeming lack of interest in seventh-
century England.

Further enquiries mollify me a little: the parish church at
Selsey, I now gather, was until the mid-nineteenth century at
Church Norton, two miles away from the centre of the modern
town of Selsey, and it is here that Wilfrid perhaps had his headquarters and where a medieval chancel still stands that bears his
name. We drive there. The chancel is situated on a windswept
promontory. Inside, we find a faded copy of a poem by Rudyard
Kipling, 'Eddi's Service'. It captures both the desolation of the
site and its power:

> Eddi, priest of St Wilfrid
> In his chapel at Manhood End
> Ordered a midnight service
> For such as cared to attend.
>
> But the Saxons were keeping Christmas,
> And the night was stormy as well.
> Nobody came to the service
> Though Eddi rang the bell.
>
> 'Wicked weather for walking,'
> Said Eddi of Manhood End.

'But I must go on with the service
For such as care to attend.'

The altar-lamps were lighted, –
An old marsh-donkey came,
Bold as a guest invited,
And stared at the guttering flame.

The storm beat on at the windows,
The water splashed on the floor,
And a wet, yoke-weary bullock
Pushed in through the open door.

'How do I know what is greatest,
How do I know what is least?'
This is My Father's business,'
Said Eddi, Wilfrid's priest.

'But – three are gathered together –
Listen to me and attend.
I bring good news, my brethren!'
Said Eddi of Manhood End.

And he told the Ox of a Manger
And a Stall in Bethlehem,
And he spoke to the Ass of a Rider,
That rode to Jerusalem.

They steamed and dripped in the chancel,
They listened and never stirred,

While, just as though they were Bishops
Eddi preached them The Word,

Till the gale blew off on the marshes
And the windows showed the day,
And the Ox and the Ass together
Wheeled and clattered away.

And when the Saxons mocked him,
Said Eddi of Manhood End,
'I dare not shut His chapel
On such as care to attend.'

And it is finally here at Church Norton that my friend urges to me to make my own record of 'Bede's World'. For the sake of 'such who care', we plan to visit sites within each of the seven principal kingdoms of Anglo-Saxon England as named by Bede so as to create some sort of record, however partial, of the country he himself put on the map.

★

My first acquaintance with Bede was as an undergraduate at Oxford, at a time when the third book of Bede's History was a set text all undergraduate historians were expected to study during their first year. I cannot pretend it was love at first sight; the problem of the dating of Easter, which seemed to dominate the text, was bewildering and the calculations incomprehensible. However, later on in my degree I had the great good fortune to be tutored by James Campbell of Worcester College, Oxford, whose voice I still hear and whose acumen I have perceived ever since in all that he has written about Bede and the early church in England.

My next debt is to another great scholar of the conversion of England, Henry Mayr-Harting, who one term entrusted to me those of his St Peter's College students who were now facing, as I had done, Book III of *The Ecclesiastical History of the English People*. It was the first teaching of undergraduates I had ever done and it is not too much to say that Bede, and the reading of texts, became the bedrock of all my subsequent teaching. I have many further debts: my thanks are due in the first instance to Timea Szell, who gave up precious vacation time to spend long days with maps and copies of Nicholas Pevsner's guides in search of sites; to Anthony Cheetham and Richard Milbank of Head of Zeus, who have provided consistent encouragement and considerable help with the text, and to Jane Robertson for her exemplary copy-editing; to St Peter's College, Oxford, my primary academic home; to my family and to my friends, in particular Samuel Fanous, Geoffrey Fouquet, Lesley Smith and Eric Southworth, for their support and interest; to the Pontifical Institute of Medieval Studies in Toronto, where I was privileged to spend the spring of 2012, and for the warm hospitality there of James Carley and Ann Hutchison; and very particularly to Richard Shaw, once my pupil, whom I re-met in Toronto, and who is now in all things Bedan my mentor; his own forthcoming work on Bede will be essential to all future scholarship. Richard very generously read through the whole manuscript in its final stages, saving it from an alarming number of errors and infelicities. Those that remain are, of course, my own.

BISHOPRICS AND
SELECTED MINSTERS

KEY
Episcopal Sees
+ Notable monastery or minster

NORTH SEA

IRISH SEA

Abercorn
Coldingham
Melrose
Lindisfarne
BERNICIA
Whithorn
Carlisle Hexham Jarrow
Wearmouth
Hartlepool
Gilling Whitby
Catterick Lastingham
Ripon Hackness
NORTHUMBRIA
York
Leeds Beverley
ELMET Barrow
Chester
ANGLESEY
LINDSEY
Lincoln? Partney
Bardney
Breedon
Lichfield
MERCIA Leicester North
Castor Elmham
Peterborough Burgh
Leominster Oundle Castle
MAGONSAETE Worcester Ely Dunwich?
Hereford EAST
HWICCE ANGLIA
St. Albans EAST
Malmesbury Dorchester SAXONS
Bradwell-
London Barking on-Sea
Glastonbury Chertsey
WEST SAXONS SURREY Rochester Reculver
Winchester Canterbury
Exeter Sherborne Bosham SOUTH KENT
Selsey SAXONS
ISLE OF WIGHT

N
W E
S

INTRODUCTION

Everyone should know Bede's great work, The Ecclesiastical History of the English People. So thought King Alfred, and he was of course right, at least if you have an interest in England before 1066, in the England of Sutton Hoo, of Beowulf and the Staffordshire hoard, of how it was that England became Christianised and how this conversion shaped the development of the country, its landscape and its legends. But what do we know about Bede himself? Not very much. In 680, aged seven, he was sent away from his (possibly aristocratic) home to be educated by the monks of the newly founded monastery of Wearmouth on the banks of the Tyne, just as generations of English schoolboys would be dispatched at that same age to boarding school in later centuries.

A few years later, Bede was moved to the even newer monastery of Jarrow, which the Northumbrian king was building on the other side of the Tyne estuary, and it is here that he was to spend the rest of his life, delighting always (he tells us) 'in learning, teaching, writing'. His output was prodigious; to the end of the Ecclesiastical History he appended a bibliography of his works: it amounted to over thirty books. Nonetheless, he never forgot that his primary duty was the celebration of the monastic liturgy. His attendance became legendary. Alcuin of York (c.740–814), recording Bede's belief in the presence of angels during services, imagined Bede saying: 'And what if they should find me absent. Will they not say: "Where is Bede?"'

Despite the huge and long-lasting popularity of Bede's *Ecclesiastical History* (as many as 140 manuscripts have survived to this day), Bede would not have regarded himself primarily as a historian. First and foremost he was a teacher and a monk. He was concerned with the past only in as far as knowledge of it could help create a better future and save souls. He wrote at a time of considerable political turbulence and instability in Northumbria and with a gnawing sense that the end of the world might be imminent. His boyhood experience of plague, which pretty well wiped out the entire community at Jarrow in the epidemic of the mid-680s, will have added to his sense of the fragility of life. But before the final trumpet of the last days, knowledge of God and of his Creation must, Bede thought, be diffused. Even on his deathbed he was still at work. Cuthbert, later abbot of Wearmouth and Jarrow, was present at the time and in a letter to a colleague described the scene:

> During those days there were two pieces of work worthy
> of record, besides the lessons which he gave us every day
> and his chanting of the Psalter, which he desired to finish:
> the gospel of St John, which he was turning into our
> mother tongue to the great profit of the Church, from the
> beginning as far as the words 'But what are they among
> so many?' and a selection from Bishop Isidore's book *On
> the Wonders of Nature*; for he said 'I cannot have my children
> learning what is not true, and losing their labour on this
> after I am gone.'
>
> ('CUTHBERT'S LETTER ON THE DEATH OF BEDE', *Bede's
> Ecclesiastical History of the English People*, ED. AND TRANS.
> B. COLGRAVE AND R. A. B. MYNORS, P. 583)

Where and how Bede thought that his *Ecclesiastical History* related to the rest of his work has been much debated. In his Preface, he tells us that it had a moral purpose: 'Should history tell of good men and their good estate, the thoughtful listener is spurred on to imitate the good; should it record the evil ends of wicked men, no less effectually the devout and earnest listener or reader is kindled to eschew what is harmful and perverse, and himself with greater care pursue those things which he has learned to be good and pleasing in the sight of God' [p. 3]. To what extent Bede saw 'the English people' of his title as a chosen race, destined to form themselves one day into a single kingdom, is less certain. Bede's concern was not with political unity but with uniformity of Christian belief and practice. About this uniformity, he was passionate. In the closing chapters of his book, he triumphantly recorded the acceptance by the monks of Iona of what he believed to be the correct way to calculate the date of Easter, and the proper way to fashion a tonsure. At the same time a deep sense of foreboding hovers over his final pages:

In the year of our Lord 729 two comets appeared around the sun, striking great terror into all beholders. One of them preceded the sun as it rose in the morning and the other followed it as it set at night, seeming to portend dire disaster to east and west alike. One comet was the forerunner of the day and the other of the night, to indicate that mankind was threatened by calamities both by day and by night. They had fiery torch-like trains, which faced northwards as if poised to start a fire. They appeared in the month of January and remained for almost a fortnight. At this time a terrible plague of Saracens ravaged Gaul with

cruel bloodshed and not long afterwards they received
the due reward of their treachery in the same kingdom...
[S]oon after Easter... Osric, king of the Northumbrians,
departed this life... after appointing Ceolwulf... as his
successor. Both the beginning and the course of his
reign have been filled with so many and such serious
commotions and setbacks that it is as yet impossible to
know what to say about them or to guess what the outcome
will be. [Book V, Chapter 23]

Against such uncertainties, Christianity offered the hope of an
eternal kingdom in sharp contrast to eighth-century earthly
kingdoms which came and went. Territorial boundaries fluctu-
ated; dynasties were toppled. It was a lucky king who died in his
bed. Some, but not all, of this political turmoil can be detected
in Bede's work.

Bede himself liked order; he also liked numbers, and he did
what he could to impose some sense of order on the political map
of England by describing a country inhabited by three different
peoples (Angles, Saxons and Jutes), who between them occupied
a varying number of kingdoms. Of these, the ones that mattered
most to Bede were the kingdoms of Kent, Northumbria, Mercia,
the East Angles, the East Saxons, the South Saxons and the West
Saxons. But he was also well aware of other smaller kingdoms
(five at least), and it was only the attempt of twelfth-century
historian Henry of Huntingdon to simplify Bede that led to
the myth of 'seven kingdoms'. Henry was to prove enormously
influential in all subsequent accounts of Anglo-Saxon history, including those of the sixteenth century, when the term
'heptarchy' was first coined to describe these particular English

kingdoms before the period of the Viking invasions. Alongside this notion of a 'heptarchy' grew the idea that one king out of the seven could possess authority over all the others, even to the extent of being recognised as a *bretwalda* (or *brytenwalda*), a term meaning either 'Britain ruler' or 'wide ruler'. The names of these seven kingdoms still live on in many guises – from the names of local authorities to commercial companies – but in our post-imperial age the idea that there was ever a single ruler with any institutional power over seven neatly defined kingdoms has long been jettisoned. Power in pre-Conquest England is seen now as fluid and messy; if one king ever proved more powerful than his peers this was not because he held an official position; it was simply, and for the time being, a fact of life.

Nonetheless, Bede does name a number of kings whom he himself thought of as particularly powerful. In his obituary notice of Aethelbert of Kent (d. 616), Bede told his readers that while Aethelbert was the first English king 'to enter the kingdom of heaven' [11, 5], there were others before him who had exceptional power: Aelle, king of the South Saxons in the fifth century, heads the list, followed by Ceawlin, a sixth-century king of the West Saxons. Next comes Aethelbert; after him, Raedwald, king of the East Angles, then three Northumbrian kings, Edwin, Oswald and Oswiu. The attentive reader will notice both the role Bede gives to his native Northumbria and the fact that he mentions only five kingdoms, omitting Essex (never in Bede's eyes a particularly influential kingdom) and, more surprisingly, Mercia. When describing the state of England in the final pages of his work, Bede does, however, add a reference both to Essex ('the kingdom of the East Saxons') at the time of its conversion, as well as to Mercia during the period of its great king, Aethelbald. Rivalry

A NOTE TO THE READER

The guiding path in this 'journey' has been the places which Bede himself mentions and for which there are still physical remains, with here and there a stopping-off at places which, for whatever reason, do not feature in Bede's *History* but which seemed too important to pass by. Every attempt has been made to keep abreast of recent scholarship, but this is a fast-moving field and there may already be instances where an entry has become outdated because of new finds or new interpretations. The Further Reading section is necessarily selective, but it is hoped the works listed there will help readers undertake journeys of their own.

This journey begins with England's first two cathedrals, but however impressive places such as Canterbury and Rochester will have seemed, and however resonant their appeal to the city life of the Roman past, it was primarily minsters, not bishoprics, (even allowing for some overlap) which effected the conversion of England. A 'minster' in this context is not, or rather is not only, 'a monastery' in the accustomed sense of the word. In what follows, 'minster' and 'monastery' are words that have been used interchangeably, so no special significance should be attached to whichever term is used beyond an acknowledgement that precise definitions are for this period seldom, if ever, either possible or appropriate. Minsters in Anglo-Saxon England housed monks and nuns (and sometimes both) but they were never isolated from the outside world. They were both seminaries and centres of industry: they provided the king with a new literate class and they provided the new religion with its specialised needs – books, vestments and reliquaries. Their rules were eclectic. They were essential as mission-centres because in the time of Bede there was no such thing as a 'parish church'; the English parochial system was yet to come. Minsters were, moreover, important bulwarks of royal power, not least, as we shall see, because they offered status and security to royal women and provided the means whereby kings could establish cult centres. They also, quite incidentally, offered aristocratic patrons a way of amassing land, a development of which Bede was to take a very dim view.

Entries are by kingdom and within kingdoms by alphabetical order (except for Canterbury, Rochester, Lindisfarne and London, whose importance dictates that they should take precedence over all other locations within the kingdoms of Kent, Northumbria and Essex). References in square brackets are to the edition of *Bede's Ecclesiastical History of the English People*, edited and translated by B. Colgrave and R. A. B. Mynors (Clarendon Press, 1969; revised reprint, 1991).

Cross references to other entries in the book are indicated by a superscript abbreviation of the kingdom within which the target entry will be found (for example, [K] refers to an entry under Kent; [N] to an entry under Northumbria; [EA] to an entry under East Anglia and so on).

The shires have been given the names they had before their reorganisation in 1974. This is not meant to suggest that these shires were already in existence in Bede's day. Most shires are of late-Anglo-Saxon origin, though in some cases the chosen boundaries reflected earlier territorial divisions and identities.

SELECTED CHRONOLOGY †

449	Arrival in Britain of the English.
547	Accession of Ida, forefather of the Northumbrian royal house.
565	St Columba leaves Ireland and founds a monastery at Iona.
596	Mission to England under St Augustine, dispatched by Pope Gregory.
597	The start of Augustine's mission in Kent.
604	East Saxons accept Christianity.
625	Consecration of Paulinus as bishop of the Northumbrians.
627	Baptism of King Edwin of Northumbria.
633	Edwin killed (battle of Hatfield Chase). Paulinus returns to Kent.
633–4	Return of pagan rule in Northumbria.
635	Battle of Heavenfield: Christian victory in Northumbria for King Oswald.
	Aidan of Iona invited to Northumbria by King Oswald to be his bishop.
642	King Oswald killed. Oswiu and Oswine share Northumbrian rule.

† The Chronlogy is based in the main on dates and information in *Bede's Ecclesiastical History of the English People*, ed. and trans. B. Colgrave and R. A. B. Mynors, Book V, Chapter 24.

651	King Oswine killed. Death of Bishop Aidan.
655	Battle of the Winwaed: death of Penda; Mercians accept Christianity.
664	Synod of Whitby settles the dispute on the correct dating of Easter.
668	Theodore of Tarsus appointed Archbishop of Canterbury.
670	Death of King Oswiu of Northumbria.
674	Land granted to Benedict Biscop for the building of monastery of St Peter at Wearmouth.
678	Bishop Wilfrid (expelled from Northumbria); converts the South Saxons.
680	Bede becomes an oblate at Wearmouth under Biscop.
685	Dedication of the church at Jarrow.
687	Death of Cuthbert of Lindisfarne.
710	Death of Bishop Wilfrid.
716	Monks of Iona accept Synod of Whitby method for the dating of Easter.
c.731	*The Ecclesiastical History* completed.
735	Death of Bede.

BEDA

A JOURNEY THROUGH THE SEVEN KINGDOMS
IN THE AGE OF BEDE

KENT

At that time, Aethelberht, king of Kent, was a very powerful
monarch. The lands over which he exercised his suzerainty [sic]
stretched as far as the great river Humber, which divides
the northern from the southern Angles. [Book I, Chapter 25]

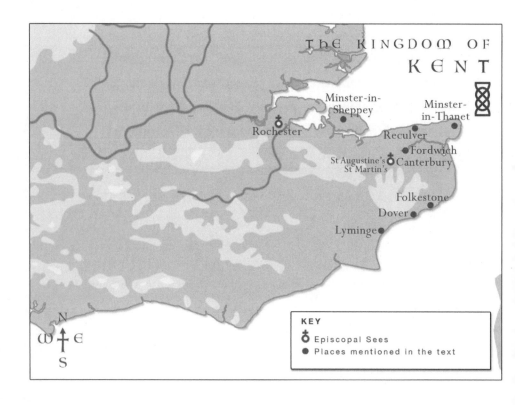

THE KINGDOM OF
KENT

Minster-in-
Sheppey

Rochester

Minster-
in-Thanet

Reculver

Fordwich

St Augustine's
St Martin's

Canterbury

Folkestone

Dover

Lyminge

N
W   E
S

KEY

Episcopal Sees
Places mentioned in the text

K ent is 'the land at the edge' or the 'cornerland of England': this is the etymology of its name and it was this position that made the region at times vulnerable, at times prosperous (and sometimes both) and explains why it was here that monks landed in 597 on their mission to restore Christianity to England.

By 409 or 410, when the Roman occupation of Britain came to an abrupt end, the elite of Kent had already accepted the Christian faith, but except in pockets here and there little of this new religion survived the arrival in England of those pagan newcomers we now call the Anglo-Saxons. According to Bede, the first of these peoples came at the invitation in the mid-fifth century of the Briton Vortigern in order to help him against attacks by Picts, and it was Vortigern who settled them in Kent. However, it was not long before further, now unwelcome, contingents arrived, so that 'the number of foreigners began to increase to such an extent that they became a source of terror to the natives who had called them in' [1, 15].

Bede calls the leaders of the original Kentish contingent the brothers Hengist and Horsa. Long consigned to the realm of legend, Hengist and Horsa remain an intriguing pair, since their names in Old English mean 'stallion' and 'horse'. Horses were important creatures in Germanic paganism and it is noticeable how, in the conversion of England to Christianity, a number of pagan traditions were appropriated rather than expunged. The genealogies of rulers are but one such example; in this instance, pagan gods with seeming ease become the forefathers of Christian rulers. Thus in Bede's genealogy for Kent, Hengist becomes the forefather of Eormenric, who himself fathered King Aethelbert, a key figure in the conversion story.

With Eormenric we may already have moved from legend to history: the Frankish component of Eormenric's name, 'Eormen', points to those connections which made Kent prosperous as well as politically vulnerable. Excavations of literally hundreds of sixth-century Kentish graves have revealed the new influences on the fashions of the well-dressed Kentish woman of the day, her jacket fastened with as many as four brooches, with accoutrements of great strings of beads and gold-brocaded veils. At the same time, excavations also suggest there were others in Kent who, less keen on such Frankish ostentation, buried their dead using boat planks to cover the body – a forlorn attempt to keep alive North Sea traditions threatened now by these new trends.

In the late sixth century and early seventh century, during the reign of King Aethelbert, cultural change was intensified and sharpened by the Christian challenge. How and why England again accepted the religion of Rome will be a constant theme in each of our seven kingdoms. At the same time we need to note how it was the adoption of Christianity that gave cohesion to these new kingdoms. Each was shaped from a patchwork of different peoples; some proved better than others in their stitching, but in every case it was the role of the new faith and the work of its missionaries that was crucial.

Let us move on to the year 596, to a place in what is now the south of France (but at the time was still called Gaul). A group of around forty monks have halted their journey. On the orders of Pope Gregory the Great, these monks had set out for England on a mission to convert its pagan inhabitants to Christianity, but they have somehow lost any enthusiasm they may once have had for the project. Bede offers an explanation for their change of mood: 'They... had already gone a little way on their journey when they were paralysed with terror. They began to contemplate returning home rather than going to a barbarous, fierce, and unbelieving nation whose language they did not even understand' [1, 23].

The long-held assumption that it was the thought of the English which so terrified the missionaries has in recent years been challenged; the convincing alternative is that it was the state of Gaul following the death of King Childebert which really unnerved Augustine and his men. But in any case, Gregory was adamant: the mission must proceed. Even before he became pope, Gregory had (so the story goes) set his heart on the conversion of the English after a chance encounter with English slave boys for sale in Rome; such boys, he had punned, are not English (Angli) but angels. Now, under the command of Augustine, future bishop of Canterbury (Augustine himself was never an 'archbishop'), the mission to England was ordered to proceed.

In 597, the party crossed the Channel, possibly embarking close to Boulogne in boats the monks themselves (possibly) help to row. But whatever the chosen route, we know the landing place was the Isle of Thanet in Kent. Here King Aethelbert detains the monks until he has had the opportunity to meet and interrogate them. Aethelbert is no stranger to Christianity. His wife, Bertha, is a Christian Frankish princess – but tolerating the creed of a foreign bride is of a different order from allowing into his kingdom preachers intent on subverting (as Bede puts

The meeting is thus presented as a risk. But it proceeds well: the missionaries approach with due ceremony. They pray for the king. At his command, they sit and give a sermon. The king is reassured; the missionaries are offered hospitality and they are allowed to preach. Pope Gregory's long-planned mission can now get underway.

But despite notable successes in the early years, the conversion of the whole country nevertheless takes time – kingdoms convert, relapse and convert anew. Old beliefs and customs die hard, and it would take many decades before England could be considered even nominally a Christian country.

The first record we have of laws demanding Christian practices and punishing heathen sacrifice comes from King Wihtred of Kent just under a hundred years after Augustine had first landed. By that time Kent had lost its pre-eminence as a kingdom, though even during its most troubled periods its possession (achieved, as we shall see, by chance) of the chief see of the country remained a source of strength.

It is here, then, with Canterbury that our journey should begin.

CANTERBURY • Kent

So he [King Aethelbert] gave them a dwelling in the city of Canterbury, which was the chief city of all his dominions; and, in accordance with his promise, he granted them provisions and did not refuse them freedom to preach. [1, 25]

Before the departure of the Roman legions in 409 and 410, Canterbury had been a magnificent walled city made up of fine

houses, baths and temple precincts. Excavations have shown
how quickly over the fifth century the infrastructure of the city
had crumbled and the extent to which buildings and streets had
fallen into disrepair. The sound and sight of the Christians as
they approached this now rather desolate settlement would have
been striking: Augustine and his party carrying before them (or
so Bede tells us) a silver cross 'as their standard' and an icon
of Christ painted on a board. It is likely that this novel-looking
party headed for some sort of reception in the old Roman theatre
– a huge building originally built to accommodate an audience of
around 7,000. Even in a dilapidated state the theatre would have
provided an impressive setting; possibly it is where Aethelbert
was used to holding court. We should nonetheless be wary
lest by following Bede we imagine that after some triumphant
meeting all Augustine needed to do was to convert the king,
restore Canterbury's former glory and confirm its foreordained
destiny as the chief see of the English church. The reality is not
so simple.

When Pope Gregory the Great dispatched his mission, it is
most unlikely that he could have imagined Canterbury as the
headquarters of his Christianised England. Gregory's conception of the country is likely to have been based upon knowledge
of the arrangements in place under the years of the Roman occupation. To Gregory's mind, the obvious centres were therefore
London and York. In his letter of 601 to Augustine, the pope is
very clear on this point. He expected the archbishops of London
and York each to have twelve bishops working under them;
whether London or York was the chief see would, he imagined,
depend on the relative seniority of the two archbishops at any
given time. The primacy which Canterbury finally came to enjoy

over York depends upon a tangled and complex story that rumbled on well into the twelfth century, but notably, at no point were claims by London ever part of the argument. From the moment of his arrival in England in 597, Augustine, in partnership with Aethelbert, had made Canterbury the centre of his mission. The case was perfectly straightforward: Aethelbert was at the time the most powerful king in the land and London was not part of his kingdom. Nonetheless, it is striking that Bede calls both Canterbury and London a 'metropolis' – an appellation he gives no other English town.

Canterbury Cathedral

Canterbury Cathedral, as built by Augustine, is hard now to reconstruct. Much extended throughout the Anglo-Saxon period, it was utterly burnt to the ground in 1067, and recent archaeology has posed as many questions about it as it has provided answers. However, it now looks as if the cathedral was erected on a new site (albeit using ancient stone) and that the intention was not to restore what was left of Romano-British Christianity but rather to recall the topography of Pope Gregory's Rome – hence the dedication to 'the holy Saviour, our Lord and God Jesus Christ' in imitation of the Lateran basilica, with a 'matching' church dedicated to St Peter and St Paul built (as at Rome) outside the city walls. In conformity with Gregory's instruction to Augustine (that he and his fellow missionaries should live together, following the precepts of Acts 4: 32), the cathedral was from the start intended to provide for a monastic community with a cloister, dormitory and refectory adjoining its north side, albeit with a supporting staff of married clergy and a separate house in the city for the archbishop. (On one notable occasion,

St Augustine's successor, Archbishop Laurence, while he was preparing to leave Kent to escape the pagan rule of Aethelbert's son, King Eadbald, slept overnight in the cathedral itself. A vision of St Peter woke him. Peter chided the archbishop for his cowardice and scourged him for dereliction. The episode made so great an impression on Laurence that he decided to stay in the country while King Eadbald, on seeing the wounds made by the scourge, was persuaded that the time had come for him to convert.) A further church, the church of the Four Crowned Martyrs, also echoed the topography of Rome, where a church of the Four Crowned Martyrs stood near to the Lateran. Tradition held that the four martyrs (victims of the Diocletianic persecution of the late third century) had been stonemasons, so honouring them in Canterbury at a time of energetic stone-building may have seemed particularly propitious, all the more so when their church withstood a raging fire (even as Bede attributes the miracle to Mellitus – then Canterbury's bishop – rather than to the martyrs' powers of protection).

Shortly after Bede's death, a free-standing baptistery was added to the eastern end of the cathedral by Archbishop Cuthbert (740–60), an unusual feature in England but which again had a parallel in the Lateran baptistery at Rome. Over time, the power and prestige of the cathedral enabled it to furnish the crypt (a ring-crypt of a type found in Rome) with the bodies of a number of the most famous of all Anglo-Saxon saints, including those of Fursey of Crowland[M] (whose life Bede describes with admiration) and Wilfrid of Hexham[N] (whom Bede seems to have viewed rather more critically.) In Bede's own day, however, Canterbury's lustre was provided by the legacy of Theodore, consecrated archbishop in 668. The choice of Theodore was as surprising as it was inspired. A Greek monk, born in what is now southeastern Turkey, Theodore was already in his sixties when he set out for England (and even then he was kept waiting four months on the far side of the Channel while his hair grew, so that he could be tonsured in a manner acceptable to the English.) It was Theodore who gave structure, doctrinal orthodoxy and learning to the embryonic English church. 'To put it briefly,' wrote Bede, 'the English Churches made more spiritual progress while he was archbishop than ever before' [v, 8].

St Martin's

What signs, if any, did Augustine find of the survival of British Christianity? This is a much-debated point, but in any case Christianity cannot have been an entirely unknown religion; for one thing, provision had had to be made for Aethelbert's queen, Bertha, to attend services. These were evidently conducted by her Frankish chaplain, Liudhard, in an old Roman church dedicated to St Martin that stood outside the city walls. This church was now offered to Augustine and his followers for their use while their new premises were being built. Today, St Martin's still contains some seventh-century work – it is possible that those parts of the south and north wall that are made of Roman brick could well have been there in Bertha's time. Certainly the church, situated to the east of the city, fits Bede's description of the place where Augustine and his monks met to say masses, to sing psalms, preach and baptise until such time as Aethelbert himself converted, whereupon they were allowed greater freedom of movement. The dedication of the church to St Martin gains interest when placed besides accounts of the devotion of Bertha's Frankish mother to St Martin at Tours itself, where

Martin (d. *c.*397) lay buried. It would seem highly probable that Bertha, sent away to marry 'a man from Kent' – in the words of Gregory, the sixth-century bishop of Tours – would have sought consolation in fostering in her new country the cult of a saint with familial associations, since saints in the Middle Ages were both 'the friends of God' and of those who prayed to them on earth.

A remarkable testimony to Bertha's Christianity and the wide-ranging implications of her Frankish connections is the gold 'medalet', a coin-pendant, dug up from a grave in Canterbury in the nineteenth century (and now in the World Museum, Liverpool). The obverse side depicts a man wearing a diadem, inscribed with the name of Bertha's priest, Bishop Liudhard; on the reverse is a cross, double-barred and wreathed. The inspiration for this unusual depiction of the cross may have come from the Byzantine reliquary containing a fragment of the true cross which, with considerable aplomb, Bertha's relative Radegund had been able to acquire for her convent at Tours. Radegund's thank-you letter, written on the occasion to Constantinople, recalls the finding of the true cross by Helena, British mother of the emperor Constantine. Was Helena seen as a role model for Bertha? Undoubtedly the idea appealed to Pope Gregory, who wrote to Bertha (in a letter Bede either did not know or chose not to quote): 'God once fired the hearts of the Romans for the Christian faith through Helena of holy memory, the mother of the most religious emperor Constantine; so now we believe that his mercy is at work in your majesty's zeal for the English.'

St Augustine's (St Peter and St Paul)

Visitors to Canterbury today are likely to make straight for the cathedral. Most never venture as far as the ruined abbey of

St Augustine (known originally as the monastery of St Peter and St Paul); ruins may be wonderful for children, dogs and picnics, but how can they compete for interest with the splendour of a cathedral? The judgement may seem fair enough; but to understand Augustine's mission, a visit to the ruins is essential.

Bede is very clear that it was with King Aethelbert's support that Augustine set about establishing – in addition to his cathedral – a separate monastery for himself and his fellow monks, built outside the city on northeastern side, so in fact not far from St Martin's. This was the planned burial place for both Augustine and subsequent archbishops, as well as for King Aethelbert and his wife, Bertha. In other words, the monastery can in some ways be seen as possessing greater importance for Aethelbert than did the cathedral. It was here that Christian kingship was to be affirmed, celebrated and strengthened.

But why was it the monastery and not the cathedral that was chosen for this function? The obvious model here is Rome, where St Peter's was built outside the city walls. In the late antique world, no church that was intended to act as a mausoleum would have been built inside the walls of any city; the deep-seated anxiety that the dead might pollute the living took time to disappear. A quite different, but no less important consideration is that to the northeast of Canterbury, close by St Augustine's but downstream by the river Stour, lay Fordwich.

By the eighth century, Fordwich had become a 'wic' – an important trading centre – and it is likely that the foundations for its prosperity were already being laid in the late sixth century. The new life Christianity brought to Roman towns was paradoxically sustained by the new levels of economic activity that lay outside them. Across England, as we shall see, Christianity stimulated trade, even if, sometimes, it was kept at arm's length (though no further) from its sacral sites.

Little now remains of St Augustine's – it was largely demolished after the Norman Conquest – but archaeologists have confirmed the account Bede gives of it. It had a principal church, dedicated to St Peter and St Paul (it was only in the tenth century that the name was changed from St Peter and St Paul to St Augustine), a further echo of Rome which housed the tombs of both these saints. On all sides of the main nave were a number of chapels (the word Bede uses is 'porticus'), akin in some ways to boxes in a theatre. Here were to be buried the special dead. A porticus on the north side was reserved for the prelates of Canterbury; at an altar here, dedicated to Gregory the Great, and to the achievements of St Augustine and his successors, a mass was celebrated every Saturday. A porticus on the south side was reserved for Aethelbert, together, possibly, with Bertha. An account of the late eleventh century (when the tombs were in the process of being moved to a new church) suggests that those buried here had first been embalmed and then laid in wooden coffins over which concrete was poured. An epitaph would have marked each tomb. Given the importance of these special dead, there is every reason to imagine that the original surroundings are likely to have been more sumptuous than this description may suggest. Death rituals had to commemorate glory in life, quite apart from signalling hopes of eternity. Aethelbert, as a Christian, cannot have wanted less splendour than his pagan forebears might have received.

When Aethelbert died, paganism was still alive and well. Eadbald, who succeeded his father in 616, had never accepted the new faith and, scandalously to Bede, he inaugurated his rule by marrying his stepmother. His eventual acceptance of Christianity (prompted, as we have seen, by the sight of those wounds which Bede claims St Peter had inflicted on the faint-hearted archbishop of Canterbury, Laurence) was marked by his building of a new mausoleum for himself, St Mary's, close to St Peter and St Paul's.

Finally, mention must be made of a church dedicated to St Pancras, situated further away from the main buildings but within the same purlieu, built on almost the same axis and lying between St Martin's and St Augustine's. It seems to have been standard practice for an Anglo-Saxon monastic complex to include several churches, but St Pancras has added interest since tradition held that formerly it had been King Aethelbert's heathen temple. If so, then here is an example of a pagan shrine being re-dedicated in accordance with Pope Gregory's instructions. The choice of St Pancras (a Roman martyr of the third century) is especially striking since it was precisely in the early decades of the seventh century that his cult was also fostered in Rome. Once again Canterbury can be seen as closely aligned to Roman fashion.

The site of St Augustine's Abbey thus recalls numerous layers in the story of the conversion: here is a former pagan temple; an altar dedicated to Pope Gregory; reminders of the saints of Rome; royal tombs; and a chapel founded by a king whose beliefs were typical of that period of apostasy that affected each kingdom before the conversion of England could be said to have been completed and secure.

The Canterbury School

By 601, just four years after Augustine's arrival, the mission was clearly proving a success, even as it was also desperately short of resources. Pope Gregory came to the rescue, dispatching, Bede tells us, not only more men but also 'all such things as were generally necessary for the worship and ministry of the church, such as sacred vessels, altar cloths, and church ornaments, vestments for priests and clerks, relics of the holy apostles and martyrs, and very many manuscripts' [1, 29]. From this impressive list, the most remarkable item is the last. Let us not forget that while Anglo-Saxon pagan priests will have had their own ceremonies, rituals and talismans, what they did not have were books. Of all the treasures brought by St Augustine to Kent, nothing will have surpassed the gift of a new literate culture. But for this to take root and to be maintained, both libraries and schools were urgently needed. Although we do not know exactly when the school at Canterbury was established, it seems to have been already sufficiently operative in the 630s to act as a model for King Sigeberht of East Anglia (cf. Dunwich[EA]).

The apogee of the Canterbury school, however, was undoubtedly reached during those years when Theodore was archbishop [d. 690] and Hadrian [d. 709] abbot. The reputation this pair shared is as remarkable as the curriculum they set up. Pupils (among whom one of the most illustrious was Aldhelm, abbot of Malmesbury[W] and later bishop of Sherborne[W]) were expected to become proficient not only in biblical studies but also in Greek, Latin, law, mathematics and astronomy. But despite the renown of Theodore's school, the learning it provided was also in certain respects idiosyncratic: for example, in the interest it took in the literal interpretation of texts. A Canterbury scholar of his day, writing about the 'cucumbers and melons' of Numbers 11:5, observes that 'cucumbers are called *pepones* when they grow large... in the city of Edessa they grow so large that a camel can scarcely carry two of them'. Exact observation of this kind has often been considered an English characteristic. Should we thank Theodore? Perhaps.

Theodore's and Hadrian's library has not survived, but there is one book associated with the earliest days of Christianity in Canterbury which warrants its own pilgrimage (though it requires a trip to Cambridge where it is now kept, in the Parker Library of Corpus Christi College). The book is the so-called Gospels of St Augustine, a generously illustrated manuscript of the sixth century, probably made in Rome. Although there cannot be any proof that this book belonged to Augustine, tradition has long held it to be so, and until the Reformation this is likely to have been the book which was displayed on the high altar as one of the cathedral's most precious relics. Today, it has again become a highly venerated volume. Since 1945, for the enthronement of a new archbishop, the manuscript has been taken from Cambridge to Canterbury so that the archbishop can be sworn into office upon it.

Theodore's contribution to the church in England lay, however, not only in his patronage of scholarship but also in his pastoral skills and administrative wisdom. Theodore had arrived in England just five years after the Synod of Whitby.[N] These were not easy years. Politics and personalities were causing division and wrangling within the church, while outbreaks of the deadly seventh-century plague were decimating the ranks of the clergy. It is a measure of Theodore's optimism that he imagined church councils could be held twice a year and it is a testament to his legacy that, even if there were missed years, synods nonetheless remained reasonably frequent occasions (cf. Brixworth[M]).

Canterbury is not, however, Kent's only episcopal see. Close by is Rochester.

ROCHESTER · Kent

[Rochester] is about twenty-four miles west of Canterbury and in it King Aethelbert built the church of the apostle St Andrew.

[II, 3]

Visitors to Rochester today are assailed by its associations with Charles Dickens. Indeed, Dickens for a time lived nearby and set many of his novels within the city. *Edwin Drood*, for instance, features a barely disguised Rochester:

> For sufficient reasons which this narrative will itself unfold as it advances, a fictitious name must be bestowed upon the old Cathedral town. Let it stand in these pages as Cloisterham. It was once possibly known to the Druids by another name, and certainly to the Romans by another, and to the Saxons by another, and to the Normans by another... A monotonous, silent city, deriving an earthy flavour throughout, from its Cathedral crypt, and so abounding in vestiges of monastic graves, that the Cloisterham children grow small salad in the dust of abbots and abbesses, and make dirt-pies of nuns and friars.

The reader should not be deceived: Dickens felt sufficient affection for the cathedral at Rochester to want to be buried there and he will have known that its past at least was neither monotonous nor silent. Nonetheless, very little archaeological evidence for post-Roman Rochester has survived, though if we follow Bede we learn that an English chief by the name of Hrof held such power there that the place became known as Hrofaescaestrae. (Bede enjoyed the etymology of names, but it is not always wise to place too much faith in his explanations.) But given that, by Bede's own reckoning, Rochester lies just some twenty-four miles away from Canterbury, how was it that it merited its own bishopric?

The most likely explanation is that Kent was originally made up of two kingdoms, the eastern lands centring on Canterbury, the western on Rochester. But King Aethelbert was clearly powerful enough to have gained control over both regions and it was he who founded Rochester Cathedral and continued to support it, giving it 'many gifts' as well as 'lands and possessions for the maintenance of the bishops' retinues'. Rochester, like Canterbury, was a walled city, situated in a key position on the Roman Watling Street; in addition, it had the advantage of providing the lowest bridging place on the river Medway.

Christian missionaries had costly needs (candles, wine, incense and much more besides), so it was vital for their new communities to have access to major routes, whether roads or rivers or both, and no bridge in Kent was more important than Rochester's. Remarkable archaeological and documentary evidence has survived that gives precise information about this bridge and its upkeep throughout the Middle Ages and beyond (right up until 1911, when a new system was finally introduced), so that it is possible to work out exactly how much both the archbishops of Canterbury and the bishops of Rochester were expected to contribute to keep the bridge in good repair.

Rochester's first bishop was Justus, a missionary who had come to England in 601 as part of the reinforcement party sent by Pope Gregory to help Augustine with his now-flourishing mission. He was consecrated in 604 to his new see (in the same year that Mellitus became the first bishop of London). Nothing remains of Justus's cathedral, but excavations in the nineteenth century suggest that it was similar in design to the other early churches of Canterbury, in which case it too will have had an apse and a Roman-style reddish floor made of crushed terracotta. The location of this supposed apse is marked out on the floor of the present cathedral. Justus dedicated the cathedral to St Andrew, a much-venerated missionary as well as the patron saint of Pope Gregory's own monastery in Rome. But despite the splendours of his church and his hopes for a 'Rome in Rochester', Justus's episcopacy was troubled and, but for a brief interlude, the subsequent history of the see makes for dismal reading.

For a start, the pagan reaction that set in after the death of his patron, King Aethelbert, forced both Justus and his fellow bishop of London, Mellitus, to flee to Gaul until the tide in Kent turned once more in favour of the new religion. Thereafter, bishop succeeded bishop: in 619 Mellitus became bishop of Canterbury, followed by Justus in 624; Rochester, meanwhile, went in 633–34 to Paulinus, formerly bishop of York, guardian of the Kentish-born Northumbrian Queen Aethelburh, who, together with Eanflaed, had abandoned York[N] following a pagan coup in Northumbria. When Paulinus died in 644, he was buried within the cathedral at Rochester.

Ithamar, who succeeded him, was the first of the non-Italian bishops of the see, being (according to Bede) 'a man of Kentish extraction, but the equal of his predecessors in learning and in holiness of life' [III, 14]. Of great interest here is the possibility that Ithamar was in fact a British Christian, since the custom of taking an Old Testament name (such as Ithamar) upon consecration is otherwise only found in churches within those strongholds of British Christianity such as Wales and Cornwall. Ithamar's promotion thus provides a precious hint of the survival in Kent of British Christians and of their integration into the Augustinian mission. A South Saxon, Damian, followed Ithamar, but thereafter Rochester fell on troubled times. Bede describes, with outrage, how in 676, Aethelred, king of the Mercians, launched a vicious attack on Kent (its ports were a constant source of envy to the land-locked Mercians) in which he sacked monasteries and churches and 'in the general devastation he also destroyed Rochester' [IV, 12].

Rochester's bishop at the time of this raid was Damian's successor, Putta, a man for whom Bede seems to have felt an exasperated respect. Putta was, Bede tells us, no administrator. His chief love was music, and he was 'especially skilled in liturgical chanting after the Roman manner, which he had learned from the disciples of the blessed Pope Gregory' [IV, 2]. Faced with the destruction of his cathedral, as well as the theft of all its contents, Putta appealed to the bishop of those responsible, Seaxwulf of the Mercians. Seaxwulf responded by giving Putta a church and a small estate where (according to Bede) 'he ended his life in peace, making no attempt whatever to re-establish his bishopric; for... he was more concerned with ecclesiastical than with worldly affairs. So he served God in this church and went round wherever he was invited, teaching church music' [IV, 12]. (Compare the story of James the Deacon in Bede [II, 20] who had stayed in York[N] after the death of Edwin and who continued to teach chanting once peace was restored in Northumbria.)

Whether or not Bede is giving us Putta's full story (*see* Hereford[M]), the results, for Rochester, were certainly not good and Archbishop Theodore found it hard to find a bishop prepared to accept office in so impoverished a see as Rochester had become; Putta's immediate successor, Cwichelm, did not stay long, resigning, according to Bede, 'for lack of means' [IV, 12]. Thereafter, however, the situation at Rochester seems to have improved. For much of Bede's adult life, the bishop was Tobias, a former pupil of both Theodore and Hadrian to whom Bede gave the warmest seal of approval. Tobias was, he said, 'a most learned man', who had learnt Greek and Latin 'so thoroughly that they were as well known and familiar as if they were his native tongue'. Tobias must also have found the resources to enlarge or at the least embellish his cathedral since Bede described him as being buried 'in the chapel of St Paul the Apostle which he had built within the church of St Andrew as his own burial place' [V, 23].

Rochester suffered further attacks in the ninth century from the Vikings, but after the Norman Conquest, when the cathedral was rebuilt, its Anglo-Saxon past was not forgotten. In the twelfth century new shrines were created for the relics of both Paulinus and Ithamar while the west façade displayed (as it does today) statues of King Aethelbert and Bishop Mellitus flanking the tympanum of Christ in Majesty. Last, but by no means least, mention should be made of the Rochester text of the twelfth century (*Textus Roffensis*), a manuscript of enormous importance for the history of English law since it contains our one record of the law code King Aethelbert is said to have drawn up soon after his conversion. These laws, Bede tells us, were written 'after the Roman manner', but they were written in English and in Bede's day still 'kept and observed' [11, 5]. Although the laws crucially bear witness to the implications of the new faith and the technology of writing it brought, they are not in fact much concerned with the church, beyond extending protection to its property. It is only in the decrees of Wihtred of Kent that Christianity is taken to be the established religion, providing social norms. These, drawn up in the presence of Archbishop Berhtwald of Canterbury and Bishop Gefmund of Rochester, demanded Christian marriage; no work on Sundays; no pagan sacrifice; observance of Christian fasts and prayers for the king.

FOLKESTONE · Kent

The children of Eadbald and the Frankish princess Ymme were Eormenred, Eorcenberht and Eanswith, who rests at the monastery of Folkestone which she founded.

(D. W. ROLLASON, The Mildrith Legend:
a study in early Medieval Hagiography in England,
LEICESTER UNIVERSITY PRESS, 1982, P. 77)

In the north wall of the chancel of the church of St Mary and St Eanswythe at Folkestone is kept a casket thought to contain the bones of St Eanswith, by tradition the first nun England ever had. There is no actual evidence as to whose relics the casket might really contain nor even about the claim that Eanswith was Folkestone's founder, nor that it housed Kent's first community for women. There can, however, be no doubt that there was at Folkestone a flourishing minster in the pre-Viking period and no reason to be over-sceptical about its founder, given the predilection of the women of the Kentish royal house for establishing minsters.

Eadbald had succeeded King Aethelbert in 616. Originally a pagan, he had accepted the new faith not long after his accession, at which point it is highly probable he also found himself his second wife, the Frankish Ymme mentioned in the Mildrith Legend (having broken off, according to Bede, his former liaison with his stepmother).

LYMINGE · Kent

*As the affairs of Northumbria had been thrown into confusion...
and as there seemed no safety except in flight, Paulinus took with
him Queen Aethelburh, whom he had previously brought thither,
and returned by boat to Kent... [II, 20]*

Lyminge is an ancient settlement that took its name from the river Limen, a derivation, perhaps, from the British word for elm. Today, the river is called the Rother and elms are rare, but Lyminge Forest is still one the largest of Kent's woodlands. Meanwhile Lyminge itself has recently been the object of much archaeological scrutiny and excitement. Nineteenth-century excavations of the churchyard led to the speculation that there might once have been a Roman basilica on the site. Historians and archaeologists today are still searching for evidence of this supposed Roman past, but what they already have is remarkable evidence of its importance as an early Saxon settlement and burial ground. A sixth-century cemetery containing high-status grave goods was excavated in the 1950s; more recent work has uncovered evidence of sixth-century pagan rites (in the shape of a horse burial) and of the prestige held by women (in the shape of a rich gold bracteate: a thin ornamental disc).

In 2012–13, excavations discovered a great hall whose dimensions and supposed grandeur put it easily on a par with the long-celebrated Northumbrian hall at Yeavering.[N] The possibility that this was a hall frequented by King Aethelbert is high; at the time of writing, excavations are continuing, but it seems clear that the advent of Christianity coincided with, in the first instance, the building of a splendid new hall, and thereafter with the establishment, on a new site on higher ground, of a minster. A precise date for the founding of this community has not yet been ascertained, but certainly by the eighth century the minster was flourishing, its prosperity (and its supplies of fish) assured by its ownership of the trading centre of Sandtun, in the Romney Marshes.

It was at Lyminge that the first Middle Saxon window glass from Kent was discovered. Glass windows were one of the many wonders the new Christian culture brought in its wake, as Bede himself noted in his *Abbots of Wearmouth and Jarrow*.

After the Norman Conquest, Lyminge acquired a rich legendary history, according to which the minster had been founded by Aethelburh of Kent, daughter of King Aethelbert, Kent's first Christian king. Bede, however, never mentions Lyminge, though he does record how Aethelburh was forced to return to her natal home after her Northumbrian husband, Edwin, had been killed in battle by the pagan Penda.

Bede's account gives a graphic picture of the danger in which the widowed Aethelburh found herself. She was saved by the efforts of Bishop Paulinus, who brought her back home by boat, together with a certain Bass, described by Bede (in loose translation) as 'a very brave chap'. The boat was laden with treasure that had formerly belonged to King Edwin which the canny Paulinus had managed to stow away: 'a great golden cross and a golden chalice', still to be seen in Bede's day 'in the church of the Kentish people' [11, 20] – probably a reference to Canterbury Cathedral. Royal children came too – a son and daughter of Edwin and Aethelburh's and a son of Edwin's from an earlier marriage. The boys were sent off to Gaul to King Dagobert, described by Bede as Aethelburh's friend (though probably he was a relative) because Aethelburh, at least in Bede's mind, seems to have feared a treacherously murderous alliance between Eadbald, king of Kent, and the new ruler of Northumbria, Oswald.

The two princes died before reaching adulthood; the princess of the party, Eanflaed, would in time return to Northumbria, first as a queen to King Oswiu and later as abbess of Whitby.[N] Aethelburh's own fate is mysterious, though it is reasonable to assume that Paulinus (now bishop of Rochester, *see* pages 18–23) continued to care for her and it is not impossible that Lyminge could have been where she was buried. However, the suggestion that she actually founded Lyminge is now considered unlikely, the date of her return to Kent in 633 being an exceptionally early date for such a venture and out of step with what we now know of other minster foundations of the seventh century. Moreover, Lyminge's chief saint seems to have been Eadburh, an eighth-century abbess of Minster-in-Thanet,[K] whom Lyminge had adopted when the two communities joined together under the leadership of the Abbess Selethryth in the early ninth century. But in the reorganisation of cults and saints that followed the Norman Conquest of 1066, the claim was certainly put forward that the bodies of both Eadburh and Aethelburh had been interred at Lyminge, whence they were taken by the new archbishop, Lanfranc, to add glory and a sense of history to his own foundation of the priory of St Gregory's at Canterbury.

MINSTER-IN-SHEPPEY · Kent

At that time, because there were not yet many monasteries founded in England, numbers of people from Britain used to enter the monasteries of the Franks or Gauls to practise the monastic life; they also sent their daughters to be taught in them and to be wedded to the heavenly bridegroom. [III, 8]

Until the founding of minsters in England, it was not unusual for aristocratic daughters to be sent abroad to suitable establishments in Gaul. This was how the community at Faremoutiers, near Meaux (founded *c.*620), recruited Eorcengota, a daughter of Queen Seaxburh and King Eorcenberht of Kent, where two of Eorcengota's aunts were already living. But Bede never lets us forget Eorcengota's Kentish origins. He reports her vivid premonition of her own impending death: she sees a crowd of men, all in white, who tell her they have been sent 'to take back with them the golden coin which had been brought thither from Kent' [III, 8]. Anglo-Saxon coinage was not introduced until the seventh century but it does at first include a number of gold coins, some of them struck in Kent, so the metaphor of Eorcengota as a 'golden coin' has particular resonance. (Examples of such coins can be found among the Crondall Hoard in the Ashmolean Museum, Oxford, or in London at the British Museum.)

In 664, Eorcengota's mother, Seaxburh, was widowed – her husband, King Eorcenbert, had died that year in one of the outbreaks of plague that hit England in the seventh century. At such a juncture Seaxburh might herself have been expected to go to Gaul, but she chose otherwise, perhaps because she was needed in Kent as regent to the new king, her son Egbert, who was not yet of age. So Seaxburh instead founded a community at Milton (about which we know nothing beyond the name), which she later transferred to her newer foundation of Minster-in-Sheppey. Seaxburh's foundations can thus claim to be among the first communities for women to be established in Kent (though cf. Folkestone[K]).

Seaxburh's abbey at Minster-in-Sheppey is today overshadowed by the adjacent parish church, but enough of it survives to make it possible to gain some sense of its size and to detect traces of Roman-style work in the north wall. The monastery's imposing position on a high point on the Isle of Sheppey and the clear views it commands over both Essex and Kent made it a highly desirable target for ninth-century Vikings. An eleventh-century legend recalls how Seaxburh herself had been warned by an angel of this impending fate.

Some years after the foundation of Minster-in-Sheppey, Seaxburh's sister, Aethelthryth, abbess of Ely[EA] (and former queen of Northumbria), died, whereupon Seaxburh entrusted Minster-in-Sheppey to one of her daughters and returned to her natal East Anglia. Seaxburh succeeded Aethelthryth as Ely's abbess and oversaw her sister's canonisation; when Seaxburh died, she too was buried in Ely.

Seaxburh's story has already taken us across the Channel and the length of England – from Northumbria, via East Anglia, to

Kent. But if her genealogy can be trusted (and it is not utterly implausible), her connections spread even further: indeed, to nearly every corner of the country. Thus a daughter, Eormenhild, married Wulfhere of Mercia; their child, Werburgh, became the chief saint of Chester;[M] Seaxburh's sister-in-law became abbess of Folkestone;[K] her brother-in-law had a daughter, Eafe, who married Merewalh of the Magonsaetan (*see* Mercia); and Eafe's own children included an abbess of Thanet[K] and an abbess of Wenlock.[M]

In exactly which ways their communities helped to consolidate both the newly emergent kingdoms and the new faith may even now not be fully understood, but it is abundantly clear that the contribution of royal women, both as abbesses and as mothers – and often as both – was crucial.

MINSTER-IN-THANET · Kent

Domne Eafe asked the king for land on the island of Thanet
where she could build a monastery in memory of her brothers.
He asked her how much land she wanted and she said as much
as her hind could cover in one circuit.

(FROM GOSCELIN OF CANTERBURY'S 'LIFE OF
MILDRITH' IN D. ROLLASON (ED.), *The Mildrith Legend:*
A Study in Early Medieval Hagiography in England,
LEICESTER UNIVERSITY PRESS, 1982, p.118
(Author's translation)

Anglo-Saxon Minster-in-Thanet has vanished, but the legends surrounding its foundation (albeit not recorded by Bede) are sufficiently remarkable to put it on the map. The story begins when

King Egbert, king of Kent (664–73), aided and abetted by his evil counsellor Thunor, arranges for the death of two young cousins whom he regards as a threat to his reign. The deed done, the king suffers terrible pangs of conscience. In remorse he offers compensation to Aebbe (also known as Domne Eafe) his victims' sister. Aebbe is wily, asking for as much of the Isle of Thanet as her tame hind can encircle. Once it becomes clear that this is no ordinary hind, wicked Thunor tries to persuade the king to break off the bargain, whereupon the ground opens up and swallows him. The hind meanwhile runs on. In this way Aebbe secures for herself a substantial piece of land on which to build the monastery of Minster-in-Thanet, where she becomes abbess until 694, when her daughter Mildrith succeeds her. (Aebbe's sister, on the other hand, at least in death, shunned this new minster, preferring to be buried in a barrow, a mile or so to the east of the new minster.)

Mildrith's own story, meanwhile, surpassed her mother's for drama. Entrusted originally to the monastery of Chelles, in Gaul, Mildrith was imprisoned in an oven in an attempt to get her to marry one of the abbesses' relatives; she escaped and made it back home across the Channel. Thereafter, the rock in Thanet where she landed displayed her footprints, which then proved to have miraculous healing powers.

These legends from Minster-in-Thanet were told and retold in both Anglo-Saxon and Norman England. Various reasons have been suggested for their popularity, but foremost among them must be the cleansing of Thanet, the very place where St Augustine had landed but which formerly had been home to the god Thor. An important part of the story, then, is the miraculous disappearance of the wicked Thunor, a representative of the old order, while the subsequent founding of Aebbe's monastery provided an exemplary Christian alternative to pagan strategies of feud and revenge (as similarly would Gilling[N] in Northumbria).

It would, however, be a mistake to regard the stories about Aebbe and Mildrith as 'merely' legendary. The history of the community can be reliably traced in a series of charters which make it clear, firstly, that Aebbe was indeed given a sizeable grant of land for her community and that thereafter both Mildrith and her successor, Abbess Eadburh, received from successive kings of Kent further land and trading privileges. Up until the Viking invasions in the ninth century, Minster-in-Thanet clearly remained a rich and powerful community, closely involved with trade between England and the Continent, though the community suffered severely during the Viking period, retreating for a time to Lyminge,[K] a religious house with which it had long been associated but which in time was also to fall victim to Viking attacks.

Abbess Eadburh has sometimes been identified with one of the correspondents of St Boniface of Crediton. It is now thought more likely that this was a different Eadburh. Eadburh of Minster-in-Thanet was undoubtedly an influential abbess. Some time between the death of Mildrith (c.735) and 748 she built a new church dedicated to St Peter and St Paul, to which the body of Mildrith was transferred. And with or without the connection to Boniface, it remains possible that Minster-in-Thanet may well have had a scriptorium; it could even be that this is the scriptorium where the manuscript known as the Stockholm Codex Aureus was made. The grandeur of this codex made it irresistible to Vikings, but it survived intact because a wealthy Kentish couple bought it back and presented it to Canterbury, writing inside why they did so: 'I Alfred... and my wife bought this book from the heathen army with our own money: that purchase was made with pure gold. And we did that for the love of God and for the benefit of our souls.'

Despite the probability that Boniface's Eadburh should be associated with Wessex rather than with Kent (*see* Wimborne[W]), it remains the case that Boniface would seem to have had at least two Kentish women among his correspondents: Abbess Eangyth and her daughter Bugga. It is not certain to which community they belonged, but since they were related to King Aethelbert II of Kent it is reasonable to assume that it was somewhere within his kingdom. The women were not happy and felt unsupported in their vocation – there had probably been a change of dynasty, hence their lament: 'the king has a great hatred for our line...', but the letters suggest that Boniface can provide them with solace. Thus Bugga regrets that she has not been able to find the book which Boniface wanted (a martyrology), but she sends some money and an altar frontal and promises that the martyrology will follow just as soon as she is able to get a copy. In return, she asks Boniface to say masses for her – and for extracts from Scripture: 'Comfort my lowliness,' she writes, 'by sending me some select passages as you had promised in your sweet letter.' In a later letter, Boniface accepts that Bugga might be well advised to go to Rome, where she may be able to find the peace she desires; Boniface has a friend in Rome – Wilthburga – who would be able to make the necessary arrangements, but he counsels Bugga to wait until she has heard from Wilthburga herself: it was not a good moment to travel because Rome was not very safe right now.

RECULVER · Kent

In the name of our Lord and Saviour Jesus Christ, I, Hlothere,
king of the people of Kent, grant for the relief of my soul land
in Thanet which is called Westan ae to you, Brihtwold,
and to your monastery [that is, Reculver], with everything
belonging to it, fields, pastures, marshes, small woods, springs,
fisheries, with everything, as has been said, belonging to that
land... May whoever attempts to contravene this donation
be cut off from all Christendom, and debarred from the body
and blood of our Lord Jesus Christ.

(English Historical Documents: VOL. I, NO. 56)

The Canterbury tourist website describes Reculver as a 'small, tranquil beach' while pointing out that it was once used as a testing site for the Second World War bouncing bombs. Its history certainly possesses a degree of drama. Its church of St Mary's claims to have been founded in 669 by King Egbert of Kent and given to his priest, Bassa. Bassa then built a minster within the walls of a third-century Roman coastal fort in a favoured position on the edge of the Wantsum Channel. The channel, navigable at the time of the foundation, ran between the Isle of Thanet (where St Augustine had originally landed) and mainland Kent. Over the centuries, the channel silted up, the coastline was eroded and in 1805 the inhabitants of Reculver were persuaded by their vicar (spurred on by his mother) to vote for the building of a new church further inland and to support the demolition of St Mary's. Only the twin towers, a twelfth-century addition, were left standing; they dominate the landscape still. (St Mary's fate was described by the architectural historians Harold and Joan

Taylor as 'an act of vandalism for which there can be few parallels even in the blackest records of the nineteenth century'.) Local farmers sold much of the original stonework to the Margate Pier Company but enough was left behind to make possible some sense of the original shape of Reculver and of its similarities to other early Kentish churches built under royal patronage, among them Rochester.

Thus, like Rochester, Reculver was built on a symmetrical plan with north, south and west doors; it too had an apse and north and south chapels or 'portici'. Similarly Reculver was not large – about 20 metres (66 ft) in length – but it was not in any sense a modest building. The remains of two elaborate columns, preserved now in the crypt of Canterbury Cathedral, provide a hint of the grandeur of the original Reculver and possibly of the influence of Ravenna. These columns most likely created a triple arcade designed to separate the apse from the nave; moreover, fragments of a cross-shaft, also kept in the Canterbury crypt, may well be all that is now left of the magnificent and 'most ancient cross' which so deeply impressed the antiquarian John Leland during his travels on behalf of Henry VIII. The fragments are certainly Anglo-Saxon, possibly of an early enough date to belong to Bassa's minster, though it may also be that the cross was carved in the early ninth century under Mercian influence, in the decades after King Offa had seized control of Kent.

Ten years after its foundation, in 679, Egbert's successor, his brother Hlothere, issued the charter (quoted above) conferring further lands on Abbot Berhtwald (Berhtwald later succeeded Theodore as archbishop of Canterbury) from 'the city of Reculver'. The charter is the earliest Anglo-Saxon charter extant in its original form. Its description of Reculver as a 'city' suggests that Bassa's church had very quickly become a place of considerable importance, its prosperity assured by its position on the trading routes between Francia and England. A grant of the early 760s by King Eadberht of a share in the profits of Fordwich (to be precise: exemption from the toll and tribute due on one ship) provides a glimpse of the minster's involvement with the trading world of the eighth century. The ship would have been Reculver's own to use, both for ferrying pilgrims and clergy, and for the trading of produce from monastic estates in return for luxury, albeit essential items such as wine, wax and oil. Similarly prosperous was nearby Lyminge.[K]

NORTHUMBRIA

At this time the Northumbrian race, that is the English race
which dwelt north of the Humber, together with their king
Edwin, also accepted the word of faith through the preaching
of Paulinus already mentioned. The king's earthly power had
increased as an augury that he was to become a believer and
have a share in the heavenly kingdom. [Book II, Chapter 9]

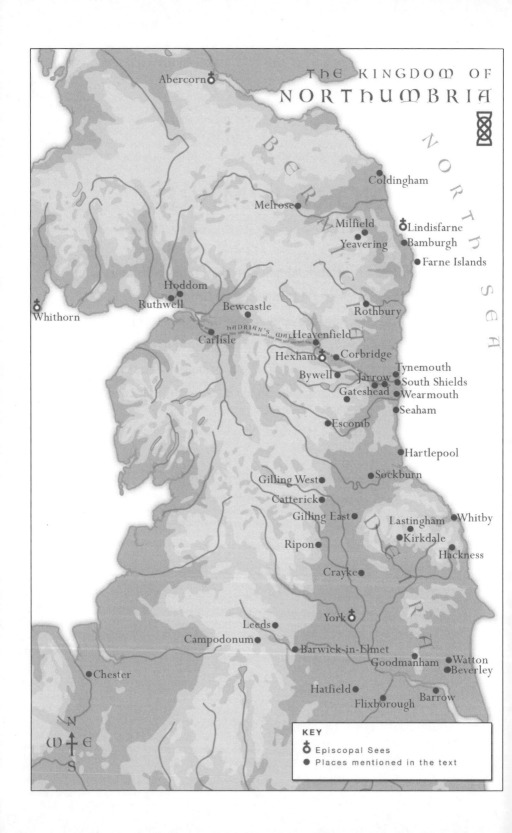

THE KINGDOM OF NORTHUMBRIA

Abercorn

Coldingham

Melrose

Milfield
Yeavering
Lindisfarne
Bamburgh
Farne Islands

Hoddom
Ruthwell
Whithorn
Bewcastle
Rothbury

HADRIAN'S WALL
Carlisle
Heavenfield
Hexham
Corbridge
Bywell
Jarrow
South Shields
Gateshead
Wearmouth
Seaham

Escomb

Hartlepool

Gilling West
Sockburn
Catterick
Gilling East
Lastingham
Whitby
Kirkdale
Ripon
Hackness

Crayke

York

Leeds
Campodonum
Barwick-in-Elmet
Goodmanham
Watton
Beverley

Chester

Hatfield
Barrow
Flixborough

NORTH SEA

KEY

⚲ Episcopal Sees

● Places mentioned in the text

Of all the kingdoms of Anglo-Saxon England, the one closest to Bede's heart was Northumbria. A good half of the History focuses on Northumbria; the dedicatee is King Ceolwulf (who had read the book in draft form) and it is Bede's explicit hope that the work will help the prosperity of the kingdom: 'In your zeal for the spiritual well-being of us all,' he writes to Ceolwulf in his Preface, 'you wish to see my History more widely known, for the instruction of yourself and those over whom divine authority has appointed you to rule.' Bede's concern for the future of the kingdom, his hope that his history would provide examples of good men to follow as well as dire warnings of what happened to the wicked, was timely and apposite. If King Ceolwulf's own reign (729–37) was far from smooth, much worse was to come: three of his eighth-century successors were murdered and two others exiled.

Northumbria's power was under constant attack from Mercia, while within the kingdom itself regnal instability sprang from the uneasy union into the one kingdom of its two peoples, the Deirans and the Bernicians, each of whom occupied territories with fluctuating boundaries. The Deirans claimed the south, an area stretching in Bede's day to the mouth of the Humber. Although no boundaries were ever fixed, it is likely that as a general rule it was the river Tees that separated Deirans from Bernicians. Bernicia's acquisitive zeal was seemingly limitless;

having successfully swallowed up the territory of the Deirans,
the Bernician kings set about conquering vast tracts of what is
now Scotland. (It is worth remembering that it is only in the
fifteenth century that the modern boundary between England
and Scotland finally takes shape.) At the height of its power,
Northumbrian rule thus extended at least as far north as the Firth
of Forth and as far west as the Solway Firth. Territorial ambitions directed towards the Pictish kingdoms further north were
curtailed by the crushing defeat inflicted on King Ecgfrith and
his army in 685 at the battle of Nechtanesmere. With this defeat
came a terrible warning to kings of the folly of not listening to
the advice of the holy men of their court. According to Bede,
Cuthbert, bishop of Lindisfarne (*see* page 43), had most urgently
counselled the king against the expedition. The failure to heed
this advice cost the king his life.

Bede's monasteries of Wearmouth and Jarrow,[N] were both
Bernician foundations, and among the kings of Northumbria
Bede's heroes were, on the whole, Bernicians. The kingdom's
founding father, for Bede, is the Bernician King Aethelfrith,
who in 604 had first united Deira and Bernicia. Aethelfrith's rule
(593–616) predates the arrival of Christianity in Northumbria,
and Bede presents him as having the stature of an Old Testament
king, comparing him with Saul, 'once king of Israel'.

In Bede's eyes, a great achievement of Aethelfrith's was his
success at 'ethnic cleansing': 'No ruler or king had subjected
more land to the English race or settled it, having first either
exterminated or conquered the natives' [1, 34] – 'natives' here
are the indigenous British, and whatever allowances one might
wish to make for exaggeration in Bede's testimony, it remains
remarkable that there is only one (unnamed) character actually

described as being 'of the British nation' to have even a walk-on part in Bede's history. The British urge for survival may well have been far stronger than Bede wished to suggest, and aggressive reticence would seem to lie behind his chosen title. His is a history of the 'English church'; Britons are not welcome. Northumbria is at the forefront, very specifically, of an English Christianity.

The story of how English Christianity first came to Northumbria, as Bede tells it, includes an epic tale [11, 12]: Edwin, of the house of Deira, in exile during the reign of the Bernician King Aethelfrith, wanders for years in secrecy 'through many places and kingdoms'. At last he comes to the court of King Raedwald of East Anglia. Raedwald takes him in; Aethelfrith is alerted; Raedwald, bribed by Aethelfrith, agrees to betray Edwin; Edwin is warned; he decides it would be dishonourable to flee; in fear of his life he sits 'sadly in front of the palace with his mind in a tumult, not knowing what to do or which way to turn'.

The drama quickens: while Raedwald's wife is attempting to persuade her husband it would be dishonourable to accept the bribe, Edwin (unaware of this possible reprieve) sits 'in silent anguish of spirit'. Suddenly he is approached by a mysterious stranger who asks him what he would do if his life were to be spared, and if, moreover, he were thereafter to become the most powerful king of the English there had yet been? Should all this happen, would he promise to follow the advice of whoever had foretold it? Edwin is certain that he would, whereupon the stranger 'immediately laid his right hand on Edwin's head and said, "When this sign shall come to you, remember this occasion and our conversation, and do not hesitate to fulfil what you are now promising."'

Soon after (in 616), Raedwald kills Aethelfrith in battle and Edwin does indeed become a 'most powerful king' of both Deira and Bernicia. He marries (c.624) Aethelburh, a Christian princess from Kent. Once again he is to be found in deep thought. At this moment, Paulinus, chaplain to Edwin's wife, approaches: 'placing his right hand on the king's head [he] asked him if he recognised this sign. The king began to tremble'. (In the Whitby *Life of Gregory*, the mysterious stranger at Raedwald's court is in fact already identified as Paulinus, but Bede's narrative prefers supernatural intervention.)

Edwin had already been under considerable pressure to convert: there had been letters from Pope Boniface, together with exotic gifts – a robe embroidered with gold for Edwin and a silver mirror and an ivory comb for Aethelburh to encourage her to redouble her efforts to convert her husband. And there had been promising auguries. On Easter Sunday 626, Aethelburh had given birth to a daughter after an easy labour; that very same evening Edwin escaped an assassination attempt, spearheaded from Wessex. At Pentecost, Edwin duly allowed the newborn daughter, Eanflaed, to be baptised: the first Northumbrian to be given this sacrament. Paulinus officiated and eleven of Edwin's courtiers were converted. But Edwin himself now made further conditions. First, he said, he must lead a punitive expedition against Wessex; then, before he finally accepted the Christian faith – or so he told Paulinus – he needed to consult his chief men in the hope that all might be baptised together. Exactly where Edwin held this council is uncertain, but for its dramatic outcome we must visit Goodmanham.[N]

LINDISFARNE • Northumberland

Oswald, as soon as he had come to the throne, was anxious
that the whole race under his rule should be filled with the
grace of the Christian faith of which he had had so wonderful
an experience in overcoming the barbarians. So he sent to the
Irish[†] elders among whom he and his thegns had received the
sacrament of baptism when he was an exile. He requested them
to send a bishop... On the bishop's arrival, the king gave him
a place for his episcopal see on the island of Lindisfarne, in
accordance with his wishes. [III, 3]

At low tide Lindisfarne can be reached by a causeway, but at high
tide it becomes an island. The unwary tourist should beware, but
for Aidan, sent from the island of Iona c.635 to King Oswald to
be his bishop, the ebb and flow of the tides was precisely the
attraction of Lindisfarne. In conformity with the customs of
Iona, Aidan was first a monk and only then became a bishop,
and the island nature of Lindisfarne provided him with at least
some sense of the monastic solitude he had lost on leaving Iona.
But in his role as bishop, Aidan was, as Bede describes him,
an exemplary missionary who worked tirelessly to convert the
Northumbrians to the new faith. His one failing in Bede's eyes
was his adherence to the method of calculating the date of Easter
in use at Iona, which differed from any Northumbrian system.

---

† Much ink has been spilt and much confusion created by the terminology surrounding the different missionary efforts in Northumbria. In what follows, the
term 'Irish' is used in the broadest possible sense. It is not to be confused with
either a precise geographical location, nor with any fundamental differences of
doctrine. It refers simply to certain regional variations in both religious practice
and artistic styles.

The discrepancy was troubling: it was, to say the least, disturbing to find some Christians fasting (as was enjoined during Lent) while others were already enjoying Easter feasts, and some years after Aidan's death, the issue came to a head. It was settled in 664, at the Synod of Whitby,[N] in favour of the method by then in use at Rome, and Lindisfarne's status undoubtedly suffered as a result. Colman, bishop of Lindisfarne at the time of the synod, was both hurt and angry. Seeing (in Bede's words) that 'his teachings were rejected and his principles despised' [III, 26], Colman went back to Lindisfarne, gathered together all like-minded monks and returned to Iona, taking with him as precious relics some of Aidan's bones.

Despite Bede's abhorrence of the Ionan method of calculating the date of Easter, his respect for Colman in all other ways knew no bounds and he paints a glowing picture of Lindisfarne under his rule, taking it as emblematic of all that once was right and good in the Northumbrian church. In those days, he wrote, monks lived frugally: 'They had no money, only cattle' [III, 26]. Any money they received was promptly passed on to the poor. The rich and the great came to Lindisfarne, but for prayer, not for entertainment. The king himself would come whenever he could, but should he chance to stay for a meal after his prayers he was content with the common fare. Bede's eulogy here follows on immediately after his account of the Synod of Whitby[N] and of Colman's departure; it makes it an especially striking, even poignant, indictment of his own day. 'At that time,' he writes:

> the religious habit was held in great respect... so that
> whenever a cleric or a monk went anywhere he was gladly
> received by all as God's servant. If they chanced to meet

him by the roadside, they ran towards him and, bowing
their heads, were eager either to be signed with the cross
by his hand or to receive a blessing from his lips. Great
attention was also paid to his exhortations, and on Sundays
the people flocked eagerly to the church or the monastery,
not to get food for the body but to hear the word of God. If
by chance a priest came to a village, the villagers crowded
together, eager to hear from him the word of life; for the
priests and the clerics visited the villages for no other
reason than to preach, to baptize, and to visit the sick,
in brief to care for their souls. They were so free from
all taint of avarice that none of them would accept lands
or possessions to build monasteries, unless compelled
to by the secular authorities. This practice was observed
universally among the Northumbrian churches for some
time afterwards. [III, 26]

Bede was also very careful to praise Eata of Melrose,[N] who had
had the difficult task of succeeding Colman. Colman had evidently made a point of asking Oswiu if Eata could be appointed
as abbot over all those who wanted to stay at Lindisfarne – since
Eata had been one of twelve English boys whom Aidan had
trained for ministry when he had first arrived as bishop. Oswiu
had agreed because, despite the wounds of Whitby, the king,
according to Bede, 'greatly loved Bishop Colman on account of
his innate prudence' [III, 26].

Colman's departure after the Synod of Whitby temporarily
ended Lindisfarne's status as an episcopal see. The subsequent
plan was for Wilfrid to become Northumbria's bishop but with
his see at York[N] (as in the days of Paulinus), and despite various

delays and complications, Wilfrid was indeed recognised as Northumbria's bishop in 669. However, in 678, after Wilfrid and King Ecgfrith of Northumbria quarrelled violently, Wilfrid left the country, whereupon Archbishop Theodore divided the Northumbrian see so that in future Lindisfarne, Hexham and York[N] would each have their own bishop. In 685 Cuthbert was recalled from the Farne Islands,[N] to which he had retreated, and elected in 685 as the new bishop of Hexham (though in fact he persuaded Eata to accept this see while he went instead to Lindisfarne).

It had taken time for Lindisfarne to recover from the ordeal and aftermath of the Synod of Whitby in 664, but after the death of Cuthbert (not long after he had become bishop) and his speedy canonisation, its reputation was secured for good; when Ceolwulf, the Northumbrian king addressed by Bede in the Preface to his *Ecclesiastical History*, abdicated to become a monk, Lindisfarne was where he chose to go. (Tradition has it that as a result of his intervention the monks were henceforth allowed to drink beer and wine.)

Lindisfarne is now one of Northumbria's most frequented tourist sites. This may seem ironic since Aidan had chosen it for the relative isolation the tides guaranteed. But Cuthbert himself is said to have foreseen that were he to be buried on Lindisfarne (rather than on the Farne Islands where he died), then it would lose its tranquillity, so celebrated would the island become.

In 793, when it was first attacked by Vikings, the raid prompted a remarkable outpouring of grief – 'The most venerable place in all England is given as prey to pagan peoples,' lamented Alcuin, former master of the school at York. The further attacks that followed finally forced the monks to abandon Lindisfarne and to endure an unsettled period of itinerancy, always taking with them the body of their saint, together with the other relics they held most dear. The final resting place for Cuthbert was Durham Cathedral (where his tomb still is), but crowds continue to flock to Holy Island, as Lindisfarne has long been known.

Lindisfarne's first monastery seems to have been situated in the southwest edge of the island but it is difficult now to get any certain idea of its size or layout, all the more since the Norman priory was built on the same site. The likelihood is that it was enclosed by at least one earthen bank – possibly two, as at Iona – and that it had two or more churches, built of wood; Bede does not describe Aidan's church but he does tell us that his successor, Finan, 'constructed a church on the island... suitable for an episcopal see, building it after the Irish manner, not of stone but of hewn oak, thatching it with reeds' [III, 25].

Along the southern tip of the island, the Heugh, there may have been a series of further buildings, including perhaps the watchtower manned by those monks waiting for the prearranged signal from the Farne Islands that would have announced to them that Cuthbert, known to be extremely weak and beyond recovery, had indeed died. It seems there was also some stonework at Lindisfarne; a number of eighth- and ninth-century carved stones have survived, including the stone often taken as depicting Viking marauders (but more probably a pointer to the Day of Judgement) and the grave-marker for a certain Osgyth, evidence of the presence of women in the Lindisfarne community. (For grave-markers, *see* Whitby.[N])

Cuthbert's burial and reburial (known as a 'translation') established a tomb cult such as England had never known before. Except for the case of Aethelthryth of Ely[EA] there is little evidence of cultic activity centring around the tombs of any of the first generation of Christian notables, despite the evident care taken (as at Canterbury, *see* pages 7–18) to provide suitable mausolea for the holy dead.

The bodies of both Aethelthryth and Cuthbert aroused special interest since on exhumation neither were found to have decayed (and hence they were declared 'incorrupt'), but this was a bonus rather than a necessary proof of their sanctity. Proof came in the shape of the miracles performed at their tombs, while the splendour of such tombs both proclaimed and advertised the power of this miracle-working holiness. In Cuthbert's case, eleven years after his death he was taken from his original stone coffin, clad in a new shroud, and then placed in a coffin of oak, decorated with carvings of the Virgin and Child, angels and the symbols of the evangelists. The remains of this new coffin can be seen today in the treasury at Durham Cathedral, along with a number of the further treasures found within the coffin in which, in 1104, Cuthbert was once more reburied.

The opulence of these treasures stands in stark contrast to the sense of austerity given in the description of Cuthbert's life on the Farne Islands, but the paradox here runs throughout early Christianity – and indeed, beyond. An ascetic lifestyle did not preclude lavish cultic display and it is possible to imagine many of the coffin's treasures in regular liturgical use. Cuthbert's pectoral cross has twelve inlays of garnets set in gold in each of its arms; gold, for Bede, was a symbol of God, and the garnets a probable reminder of the twelve apostles. The paten and chalice and the travelling altar suggest items that Cuthbert might have used as he travelled across the Northumbrian countryside administering the sacraments in remote places, as Bede tells us he did.

The tiny copy of the Gospel of St John, bound in red goatskin and encased in a satchel, (a book for long in the possession of the monks of Stonyhurst Abbey but acquired recently by the British Library) is now thought to have been added to his tomb at the time of his translation, rather than being his own personal copy. (But for an instance of Cuthbert's reading of St John's Gospel, *see* Melrose.[N])

And what, then, of the Lindisfarne Gospels? Was this sumptuously illustrated book, long in the possession of the British Library, indeed made at Lindisfarne, and was it made in honour of Cuthbert? This was the claim made in the tenth century by Aldred, provost of Chester-le-Street, who added a number of glosses, in English, to the Latin text of the original. Aldred names Eadfrith, Cuthbert's successor as bishop, as scribe of the book; a further bishop, Aethilwald, as its binder; and finally an anchorite, Billfrith, as the maker of the bejewelled cover or box that would have protected the work.

Aldred's attributions cannot be conclusively proved, but neither can they be disproved. It is, moreover, possible to demonstrate that, unusually, the writing and the illuminations are indeed the work of just one scribe, while the condition of the manuscript makes it clear that this was a book kept only for special occasions. Its long association with Cuthbert was celebrated initially in 1987 during the 1300th anniversary of his death, when the manuscript, escorted from London to Durham Cathedral by four members of the British Library staff, was placed for a time on Cuthbert's tomb and more recently held in the exhibition in Durham in 2013 of the Gospels alongside a rich collection of Anglo-Saxon treasures.

The birds that richly adorn the Lindisfarne Gospels have been studied with great intensity in an attempt to prove – or disprove – the idea that their depiction owes something to Eadfrith's observation of actual Northumbrian birds. 'Look,' says the one camp, 'at the realistic plumage given to St John's eagle.' 'Ah,' says the other camp, 'just consider how many cormorant-like birds there are which don't have the requisite webbed feet.' This is not a controversy easily settled, nor will it ever be determined exactly when the book was made. Tempting though it is to imagine that it was commissioned for the occasion of Cuthbert's translation, this is an idea which should be resisted. It is far more likely that it was only after the discovery of Cuthbert's incorrupt body and after the death of Wilfrid of Ripon[N] in 710 that this further proclamation of Cuthbert's supreme holiness and superior sanctity was given shape through the pages of the Lindisfarne Gospels.

The debt St Cuthbert's cult owes to Bede himself was immense: not only did Bede dedicate several chapters of his *History* to him; in about 705 he also wrote a metrical life of Cuthbert, and then some fifteen years later updated the original Lindisfarne life that Eadfrith had commissioned in 698. The homage paid to Cuthbert, both as bishop and as hermit of Farne, was thus in all respects lavish; and it was also long-lasting. Throughout the Middle Ages and beyond Cuthbert showed himself to be a saint to be reckoned with – William the Conqueror fled from him in terror; he survived the Reformation; and allegedly he saved Durham Cathedral from bombing in the Second World War.

ABERCORN · West Lothian

*Many of the English were either slain by the sword or enslaved
or escaped by flight from Pictish territory; among these latter
was Trumwine, a reverend man of God who had been made
bishop over them and who retired with his companions from
the monastery of Abercorn, which was in English territory but
close to the firth which divides the lands of the English from
that of the Picts. [IV, 26]*

At the time of Bede's birth (*c.*673), Northumbrian power was
at its height: King Ecgfrith had recently defeated the Picts and
could claim dominion over lands as far as the Firth of Forth. In
680 it seemed that the time had come to establish a diocese on
the Pictish/Northumbrian border, close by the Antonine wall,
and Trumwine was duly appointed its bishop. However, Ecgfrith
had yet further plans, and either because of his mistrust of his
half-brother, Aldfrith, or because of the Ui Neill of Ireland (or
both: they may have been in alliance), he decided on further campaigning. In 684 he sent an army to Ireland and the next year
took the fatal decision to attack the Picts (against the explicit
advice, according to Bede, of St Cuthbert: *see* Carlisle[N]).

Disaster followed. At the battle of Nechtanesmere (fought in
the Highlands, either at Dunnichen or at Dunachton), Ecgfrith,
together with the greater part of his army, was trapped and
slain: 'From this time,' as Bede famously lamented (in Virgilian
terms), 'the hopes and strength of the English kingdom began
to "ebb and fall away"' [IV, 26]. Trumwine, meanwhile, beat a
retreat, abandoning his see; his community he housed in whichever monasteries would take them, while he himself retired to

Whitby. There he spent his last years, enjoying, according to Bede, a fruitful relationship with Abbess Aelfflaed.

The museum at Abercorn, on the southern shore of the Firth of Forth, houses a cross shaft that may date to the seventh century, while in Northumberland the National Trust at Wallington boasts a fine picture by William Bell Scott of the occasion, in 684, when King Ecgfrith and Trumwine persuaded Cuthbert to become a bishop (cf. iv, 28).

BAMBURGH · Northumberland

... [King Oswald's hand and arm] have remained uncorrupt until the present time; they are in fact preserved in a silver shrine in St Peter's church, in the royal city, which is called after Queen Bebba, and are venerated with fitting respect by all. [iii, 6]

Various legends surround the founding of Bamburgh, but as far as Bede is concerned the city took its name from Bebba, first wife of King Aethelfrith of Northumbria (d. c.616). Aethelfrith was one of Bede's pre-Christian heroes because he had managed to establish his rule over both Deira and Bernicia, those kingdoms whose rivalries regularly threatened to destablilise and weaken Northumbrian power. At heart Bede was himself a Bernician and one of the attractions of Bamburgh as a 'royal city' for Bede was that it was Bernician. Added to this was its closeness to the episcopal centre of Lindisfarne (*see* page 43) and to the Farne Islands[N] – that chosen place of retreat for men on the path to sanctity.

After his victory over Caedwalla at the battle of Heavenfield[N] in 635, the new king, Oswald, anxious to renew the Christian mission in Northumbria, turned for help to Iona, where he had lived while in exile. Of the missionaries who came, the first had to be sent back because he was too rigorous in his approach, but the next, Aidan, was by all accounts the perfect choice.

As a monk, Aidan lived on Lindisfarne but his work as a missionary necessarily involved close cooperation with the king (all the more so at the start as his English was poor and the king had to act as his interpreter). Meetings between king and bishop would often have been at Bamburgh – but even if he was elsewhere Aidan seemingly kept a watchful eye on the royal city; Bede relates how once when Aidan was on the Farne Islands[N] he noticed smoke and flames coming from the direction of Bamburgh. Recognising at once that the city was under attack from King Oswald's great enemy, Penda of Mercia, Aidan began to pray. The direction of the wind changed; the city was saved.

The closeness of the partnership between king and bishop is a constant theme in Bede's accounts of Aidan. On one memorable Easter Sunday, king and bishop were dining together. In came a silver dish laden with delicacies, but even before it could be blessed, in too came a palace official with the news that a great crowd of the poor was clamouring outside in the courtyard. The king did not hesitate – immediately he ordered not only that the food be taken out to the poor, but even that the silver dish should be broken up and similarly distributed. So struck was Aidan by this generosity on the part of the king that he blessed Oswald's right hand, saying, 'May this hand never decay' [III, 6].

Years later, in 642, at the battle of Maserfelth (possibly Oswestry) in which the pagan King Penda of Mercia finally defeated and slew Oswald, Penda hacked off Oswald's head and arms and stuck them on stakes as victory trophies. But the hand

and arm that Aidan had blessed were rescued from the battle-field and taken back to the palace at Bamburgh. There they were enshrined in a silver reliquary, where allegedly they remained incorrupt. In the later Middle Ages, reliquaries of body parts, shaped to match, and made with no expense spared, were to be found at major shrines throughout Europe. But in the seventh century this practice was not yet customary. Pope Gregory the Great was known to deplore the habit of dividing bodies and he had tried hard, if ultimately unsuccessfully, to resist the spread of this practice. But Oswald in any case was different: here was a body already in bits, with a prophecy attached, and Oswiu, his brother and successor as king of Bernicia, made the most of it.

Bede tells us that at Bamburgh Oswald's reliquary was housed in a church dedicated to St Peter, whereas later traditions mention Bamburgh churches dedicated only to Oswald himself and to Aidan. One solution to the discrepancy is to suppose that the fame of the relics led to the name of the church changing over time. If so, then following Bede, we can imagine St Peter's/St Oswald's church to be in the heart of Bamburgh, probably on the same site where later the castle chapel was built. Aidan's own church and residence will have been part of the same royal estate but in a village a little way beyond the castle perimeter; this would fit with Bede's description of the church and cell 'not far from the city' (of Bamburgh) which Aidan used as a centre of his preaching activities. During Aidan's final illness, a tent was set up for him, attached to the west wall of this church. Here it was that Aidan died, evidently leaning against a buttress. This we know because, according to Bede, in death as in life, Aidan had power over fire.

Although Penda had been repulsed once before from Bamburgh, after Aidan's death he returned to the attack. This time he burnt down the village where Aidan had built his church, but even though the church itself, which seemingly was built of wood burnt down, the buttress did not: 'The miracle was such that, though the flames had entered the very nail holes by which it was attached to the building, yet they could not injure the buttress itself' (III, 17). Once more the church was rebuilt, but this time, so as to commemorate the miracle, the buttress was placed inside the church. Here people would kneel to ask for God's mercy and in cases of sickness they would take splinters from the buttress and as a cure put them in water.

Throughout the Middle Ages Bamburgh remained an important castle. Nothing has been left standing of the pre-conquest building, but recent archaeological work has uncovered remains of the seventh-century crypt where Oswald's reliquary was perhaps housed. And the castle ramparts, of course, still provide stunning views across the sea in the direction of Lindisfarne.

BEVERLEY · East Riding of Yorkshire

Many miracles were told [about John] by those who knew
him well and especially by the most reverend and truthful
Berhthun, once his deacon but now abbot of the monastery
called Inderauuda. [v, 2]

Beverley Minster dates from the thirteenth century but it owes its fame to its association with Bede's friend and mentor St John of Beverley, for it was John who, c.692, ordained Bede first as deacon, and then some ten years later as priest. John had been one of the five prize pupils of Whitby[N] who had gone on to become a bishop – in John's case twice over, since he was Bishop of Hexham[N] before becoming Bishop of York.[N] On retiring from York, John spent the rest of his days at a monastery called Inderauuda, which Bede tell us meant 'in the wood of the men of Deira'. Tradition has long identified Inderauuda with Beverley, and as the supposed burial place of John (d. 721) it was a major place of pilgrimage throughout the Middle Ages.

Bede attributes a number of miracles to John which between them highlight the pastoral concerns as well as the practical good sense Bede admired in a bishop. Bede tells us, for example, how when he was bishop of Hexham, John used to have a place of retreat on a promontory – probably to be identified with the village of Warden – between two branches of the river Tyne. Here, in an oratory dedicated to St Michael (for which Bede himself may have written a dedicatory epigram), John would spend Lent, taking with him some needy down-and-out. One year, the chosen beneficiary was a particularly unattractive young man, who was dumb as well as having a skin condition that had left him bald. John taught him how to speak and found for him a doctor who cured him so effectively that he grew a fine head of curly hair.

Another miracle, given Yorkshire's continued fame in horse-racing circles, has a topographical setting: it relates how one day when John and his entourage were making a journey by horse they came across a road that seemed to call out for a competitive gallop. John was against the idea, but most of the company were laymen and in the end John gave way, though he specifically told Herebald, one of his clergy, not to join in. However, Herebald was overcome by, in his own words, 'a sense of wantonness', and he was soon galloping off. Disaster followed: Herebald's horse threw him and Herebald suffered a fractured skull and a broken thumb. Throughout the following night John kept vigil; when morning came he went to Herebald's bedside, called him by name and asked him if he could recognise him. Assured of his immediate safety, John then took the further precaution of calling for a doctor to set Herebald's skull, at the same time checking whether Herebald had been properly baptised; unskilled priests performing this sacrament were a constant source of anxiety to the early church.

Further miracles of John's, described by Bede, reveal a nunnery at Watton, to the north of Beverley, and two churches dedicated on private (but unidentified) estates (cf. Escomb[N] and Seaham[N]). Passing references to places not otherwise documented serve as useful reminders of how patchy is our knowledge of the ecclesiastical geography of Bede's day.

BEWCASTLE · Cumberland

Hwaetred... Alcfrith (?)... Kyneburg...

(BEWCASTLE INSCRIPTIONS)

Bewcastle, to the north of Hadrian's Wall, was an ancient Bronze Age settlement, reused by the Romans who established on its hilltop a sizeable outpost fort. At what point all the Roman troops finally struck camp cannot be determined, nor indeed the identity of those who subsequently occupied the site. The mystery is compounded by the appearance in (probably) the early eighth century of an enormous stone monument. This has remained where it was first erected, but there is still some debate

is as to whether it was always, as it appears today, just a column
– a Roman-style obelisk – or whether it was once surmounted by
a cross. Whichever it was, the monument is generally referred
to as a cross and is now thought to be slightly older than the
cross at Ruthwell.[N] (The interlace on one of its panels closely
resembles the eighth-century Durham manuscript that contains
Cassiodorus's sixth-century treatise on the Psalms.) If it was in
fact a cross, then it has a claim to be one of the earliest examples
of a Northumbrian free-standing carved cross, quite possibly
designed to claim for the new faith a site long sacred to the worship of Jupiter.

As at Ruthwell, a panel of the Bewcastle cross shows John the
Baptist holding a lamb (a symbol of the eucharist), while on the
panel below (as also at Ruthwell) Christ is depicted acclaimed by
two animals. The striking similarity between the two crosses is
offset, however, by equally striking differences. The Bewcastle
cross has weather-worn runic (but no Latin) inscriptions; these
runes inform us that it was erected by a certain Hwaetred and two
others in commemoration of a name that most probably should
be interpreted as Alcfrith. On the north side is carved the name of
a woman: Kyneburg. The identity of any of these people is probably irrecoverable (though it has been suggested that Alcfrith and
Kyneburg could be the son-in-law and daughter of King Penda of
Mercia: *see* Castor[M]) and arguably it is less important to attempt
to do so than it is to register the witness the cross bears to the
value placed by an early Christian community on the practice of
praying for their dead. All but the east side of the cross has names
and room for more names. On the west side, below the heavily
inscribed panel of runes, is the figure of a man with a bird. Who
is he? He has long been assumed to be of some ecclesiastical

significance – perhaps St John together with his eagle, his symbol as an evangelist? But it has been suggested more recently that he is a layman, a falconer, complete with hawk and perch, and that probably he was the monument's chief beneficiary. This, then, is the man for whom, above all, we are to pray.

On the south face of the Bewcastle cross is a sundial (with twelve divisions). It is one of the earliest known in England, though both Kirkdale[N] and Escomb[N] provide other Anglo-Saxon examples.

CARLISLE · Cumberland

Now when King Ecgfrith, rashly daring, had taken an army against the Picts... Cuthbert... came to the town of Carlisle [Lugubalia]... to speak to the queen who had arranged to await the issue of the war there in her sister's monastery. On the next day, while the citizens were conducting him to see the walls of the city and a marvellously constructed fountain of Roman workmanship, he was suddenly troubled in spirit...

(BEDE, *Life of Cuthbert*, CHAPTER XXVII)

Carlisle had once been a rich and substantial Roman fort; over the fourth and fifth centuries it was gradually deserted. In the sixth century it may have been little more than a ghost town, but by the seventh century it had become an important outpost of Northumbrian power west of the Pennines. It was also a place of some wonder, well worth a sightseeing tour, and it is highly likely that the surviving Roman statuary in the city contributed in some measure to the development of sculpture within Northumbria (*cf.* Bewcastle[N]).

Where the fountain that Bede alludes to above actually stood is not known, though excavations have revealed sophisticated Roman plumbing. The monastery (in the quotation) may have already been founded during the reign of King Oswald, who reputedly had established links with Urien, the British ruler of Rheged. It was probably built close to the present cathedral.

According to Bede, Cuthbert had set out for Carlisle from Hexham,[N] a journey of about 40 miles (64 km). Halfway there, Cuthbert stopped to offer confirmation to the crowd of people who had gathered together 'from the mountains' to meet him. Once in Carlisle, Cuthbert had further pastoral work: a nearby church to dedicate and a sermon to deliver to the monks.

But Cuthbert's visit to Carlisle seems to have been prompted by Ecgfrith of Northumbria's ill-conceived campaign against the Picts, culminating in the battle of Nechtanesmere in 685. While the expedition was underway, Ecgfrith's queen, Iurminburg, had gone to stay with her sister in her monastery at Carlisle and it seems as if Cuthbert wanted to be on hand. And, indeed, a sudden premonition of the disastrous outcome of this battle makes it possible for Cuthbert to warn Iurminburg even before the news is confirmed. Shortly afterwards, Cuthbert 'confers upon the queen the garb of consecrated life': the implication must be that the now-widowed queen had decided to join her sister's monastery.

Hearing that he was in Carlisle, Cuthbert's hermit friend Hereberht left his hermitage to come and see Cuthbert – as, according to Bede, he did every year. On this occasion Cuthbert confided to him his sense that he would soon die. At the news, Hereberht became extremely upset, begging Cuthbert to ask God to allow them to die on the same day. In the light of other deathbed scenes, it is not hard to guess what lay behind Hereberht's anxieties: might not some demon successfully intercept his soul on its journey to heaven and claim it? Hereberht's merits were in no way commensurate with Cuthbert's, but Bede thought that the long illness he had to endure compensated for this and he was able to report a satisfactory ending: Cuthbert and Hereberht did indeed die at the same time and 'the ministry of angels' took them both straight to heaven.

The terrors of that final journey were very real. To have made it in the company of a saint would have provided immeasurable solace.

COLDINGHAM · Berwickshire

About this time, the monastery of virgins at Coldingham… was burned down through carelessness. However, all who knew the truth were easily able to judge that it happened because of the wickedness of those who dwelt there and especially of those who were supposed to be its leaders. [IV, 25]

Coldingham (at St Abb's Head in Berwickshire) is the only double minster mentioned by Bede as having ever occasioned scandal, but the fact that it burnt to the ground was in his eyes a suitable punishment for the 'wickedness' of those who had been living there, and the story of the disaster was a cautionary tale that deserved publicity. It was told to him by a former priest of the Coldingham community, Eadgils, who had taken refuge at Jarrow[N] after the fire had rendered Coldingham uninhabitable. The abbess in charge at Coldingham shortly before this – to Bede – shocking but salutary event was Aebbe (d. 683), sister of kings

Oswald and Oswiu. The fact that Bede includes this story is perhaps intended (as has been suggested recently) as a rebuke to the
generation of his own day, about whom we know (from his *Letter
to Egbert*) he had severe reservations.

Aebbe herself was not held directly responsible by Bede for the
fire since it broke out only after her death and the worst that Bede
reports of her is that she had failed to notice what was going on
around her and that no one had dared tell her in time to avert the
disaster. The warning came only when one of the community,
an Irishman named Adamnan, had a vision in which he foresaw
how the buildings would soon be consumed by fire. When ques-
tioned by Aebbe, Adamnan recounted how during his night-time
prayers he had suddenly become aware of a man standing next to
him. The man told him not to be afraid, before going on to reveal
that he had just made an inspection tour of the minster: 'I have
just visited every part of this monastery in turn,' he announced. 'I
have examined their cells and their beds and I have found no one
except you concerned with his soul's welfare; but all of them,
men and women alike, are slunk in slothful slumbers or else they
remain awake for the purposes of sin. And the cells that were
built for praying and for reading have become haunts of feasting,
drinking, gossip and other delights; even the virgins... put aside
all respect for their profession and... spend their time weaving
elaborate garments with which to adorn themselves as if they
were brides... or else to make friends with strange men' [IV, 25].

Accusations such as Adamnan's are commonplace in the
writing of the sixth-century Gregory of Tours, whose *Histories*
are full of racy scandals. Whether life at Coldingham deserved
such aspersions, we will of course never know. It has been suggested that it may be significant that Bede's Coldingham chapter

follows straight on from his account of Caedmon (*see* Whitby[N]); thus the virtue of the simple cowherd is juxtaposed with the dissolute behaviour of aristocratic women.

Whether this is so or not, it was certainly the case that the behaviour of the nuns of Coldingham, as Bede had reported it, was used in the later Middle Ages as a justification for the alleged misogyny of St Cuthbert. In the twelfth century, when the reputed body of Aebbe was discovered at St Abb's Head by a shepherd, a *Life* was written to promote her cult by Durham hagiographer Reginald. Reginald quotes extensively from Bede's account of Adamnan's vision, but he then concludes how when St Cuthbert heard of the goings-on at Coldingham, 'he enacted the famous decree... to be observed as a perpetual law by his servants, according to which not only was the company of women forbidden to them wherever his holy body was present but even the entry, access and sight of women was prohibited'. That this was indeed the case at Durham throughout the Middle Ages is well attested; but equally well documented are Cuthbert's friendships with women during his lifetime.

One of the best-loved stories to have been preserved about Cuthbert is located in Coldingham: both the *Anonymous Life* and Bede's *Life* give this story (for the two *Lives*, *see* Lindisfarne, page 43). The *Anonymous Life* lingers on the details: Aebbe had apparently invited Cuthbert to her community and, while there, he used to go out to the shore at night-time; this aroused the curiosity of one of the monks who followed him to see exactly where he went. The monk found Cuthbert 'going into the deep water until the swelling waves rose as far as his neck and arms and here he spent the dark hours of the night watching and singing praises to the sound of the waves'. At dawn, Cuthbert emerged from the

sea and then knelt on the shore to pray. As he did so, out of the
sea came 'two four-footed creatures which are commonly called
otters. These, prostrate before him on the sand, began to warm
his feet with their breath and when they had finished their min-
istrations they received his blessing and slipped away into their
native waters.' The monk was now mortified at having spied on
Cuthbert in this way, but Cuthbert needed no telling what he had
been up to and forgave him so long as he promised to tell no one
until after his death.

Aebbe's friendship with Cuthbert is notable since she was
also on good terms with Bishop Wilfrid of Ripon.[N] Aebbe had
given support and shelter to Queen Aethelthryth when, with
Wilfrid's encouragement, Aethelthryth had left King Ecgfrith
in favour of the monastic life and had spent her first year away
from court at Coldingham before returning to her native East
Anglia, where she founded a community at Ely.[EA] In the light
of this connection it was to be expected that a visit from King
Ecgfrith to Coldingham with his new queen, Iurminburg, might
be fraught, and so indeed it was, according to Stephen of Ripon's
Life of Wilfrid. During the night Iurminburg was afflicted with
such dreadful nightmares that by morning she seemed close to
death. It was Aebbe who saved her life, but on condition that
Wilfrid either be restored to the see of Ripon or at least that he
be released from prison and given the freedom to go where he
chose. And in addition Iurminburg was to return to Wilfrid the
relics the bishop had been in the custom of wearing around his
neck and which the queen now paraded in a box.

Excavations at St Abb's Head have identified the possible site
of Aebbe's community at Kirk Hill, together with evidence of a
seventh-century fire. A twelfth-century priory, belonging to the

monks of Durham, was built some two miles away, but the main
focus of Aebbe's cult was an oratory on the head, built also in
the twelfth century by a local devotee in response to visionary
commands.

CRAYKE • North Riding of Yorkshire

I, Ecgberht, [bishop of Lindisfarne, 803–21] urge all men
to give eloquent praise in plenty to the thunderer on high,
and with their hands stretched towards the stars let them give
thanks to the Lord, who sends winged birds to the prayers of the
pious, and these flood to the confines of the places of worship
and fly to the stars taking many prayers.

(AETHELWULF, *De Abbatibus* [THE SONG OF THE ABBOTS]
ED. A. CAMPBELL, CLARENDON PRESS, 1967, p. 16)

Crayke belongs to that cluster of eighth-century minsters established in or near the Vale of Pickering. Nothing of the Anglo-Saxon
foundation remains today, though excavations have located its
cemetery underneath the bailey of the medieval castle. The minster belonged to Lindisfarne, though the claim that the location
was specially chosen to provide Cuthbert, when he was bishop
of Lindisfarne, with a convenient place to stay whenever he
was visiting York depends on a forged document. Nonetheless,
Crayke's situation, just 12 miles (19 km) out of York, would have
made it an ideal stopping point on the last stage of any journey
from Lindisfarne.

   In the ninth century, Crayke served first as the headquarters of
Aelle, king of Northumbria, in his ultimately unsuccessful strug-
gles against the Vikings, and next, during the years 875–882, as

one of the places to which Cuthbert's body was carried both for safe-keeping and as a way of marking Lindisfarne's claim to the site. Crayke may also be the monastery central to the early ninth-century poem *De abbatibus* ('The Song of the Abbots'), and Crayke certainly figures in Alcuin's poem on York as the home of Echa, a hermit who was allegedly able to 'predict much of the future as if he were a prophet'. The date of Echa's death, at Crayke, is recorded in northern annals under the year 767.

The minster of 'The Song of the Abbots' seems to have been founded some time earlier, during the reign of King Osred (c.707–16). Whether it is or is not Crayke, 'The Song' remains an important poem for our understanding of an early Anglo-Saxon minster and its ambience. Notable is the emphasis, as in Aldhelm's poem for Bugga, on gold and silver, gems and light – thus gold flashes; silver shines; gems sparkle and bright lights burn. Through windows of glass, the sun 'diffuses soft light to the bright church' while 'beneath the roof of the church hanging torches dangle their tremulous flames in a number of rows'. The minster, moreover, bustles – men 'hasten from outside to the summons of ringing, and sing songs, which answer one another to their king'. An outstanding scribe 'ornaments books with fair marking'; a brother who knows how to 'control and shape metals of iron variety' wields his hammer. All this is witnessed by 'saints who haunt the midmost floor of the church, mustering in countless troops'. And over it all presides 'God the thunderer'.

Particularly notable in 'The Song' is the part played by birds. Birds 'flood to places of worship'; there they pick up prayers of the pious and with these they 'fly to the stars' carrying the prayers to God. On one occasion, when the time had come to translate the body of a beloved scribe of the monastery, two birds make a sudden appearance. The scribe's bones have just been washed and taken out to dry in the sunshine, when in fly two birds. They are colourful, glistening creatures who spread their wings over the skull of the holy man and then begin to sing. They sing all day until the bones are dry and the time has come to take them into the church, whereupon 'the musical birds mingled with the lofty clouds and kept out of men's sight for evermore'.

'The Song' is not, however, always mellifluous. It also contains an alarming vision of the afterlife. This was experienced by a certain Merhtheof. He seemingly dies and gets taken to a dark and terrifying region, at which point his dead children (possibly all plague victims) appear before him and lead him to face his former wife who, to put it mildly, is livid that Merhtheof has dared to remarry. Dressed in gold-embroidered robes, she threatens Merhtheof with pits of flames, gnashing of teeth and unending weeping, and it is only the intercession of the children that persuades her to be merciful and allow Merhtheof a second chance. Archbishop Theodore would not have minded Merhtheof's new wife, but rigorist views were not unknown in the early church and the story is a sobering reminder of the demands Christianity could make on private lives as well as on public worship.

'The Song' may, it should be stressed, have nothing at all to do with Crayke. An argument has been made that the poem was instead written at Bywell (not far from Hexham[N]) where the unusually large size of the parish suggests there was once an important monastic settlement.

ELMET · West Riding of Yorkshire

... in Campodonum... [Paulinus] built a church which was
afterwards burnt down... by the heathen who slew King
Edwin... The altar escaped from the fire because it was of stone,
and is still preserved in the monastery of the most reverend
abbot and priest Thrythwulf, which is in the forest of Elmet.
[II, 14]

Campodonum was a former Roman settlement near Dewsbury; Elmet was not just a forest, as Bede might seem to suggest, but rather a kingdom. A seventh-century reference to 'Elmet dwellers' points to a recognisably distinct region in West Yorkshire, somewhere between the rivers Don and Wharfe, known as Elmet, and preserved today in place names such as Sherburn-in-Elmet and Barwick-in-Elmet. The likelihood is that Elmet was an independent British kingdom that had managed to survive several centuries of conflict before finally falling into the hands of Edwin of Deira.

Thus we know that it was to the court of King Cerdic of Elmet that Hereric, father of St Hilda of Whitby, had fled, presumably on the accession to power in Northumbria of Aethelfrith of Bernicia – when it was no longer safe for Deiran royals such as Hereric or indeed Edwin to stay within easy assassination distance. However, whereas Edwin prospered in exile and went on to become king of Northumbria after Aethelfrith's death, Hereric met with treachery and died from poison. Edwin's attack on Elmet c.616 and his defeat of King Cerdic shortly after he had become king was perhaps a speedy act of retribution, but one that, in turn, would later be avenged, with the death of Edwin at the hands of British king Caedwalla (in alliance with Penda) at the battle of Hatfield Chase.[N]

Were the inhabitants of British Elmet Christian even before Paulinus began his mission? Given Bede's hostility to British Christians, his History is not going to provide us with any clues here. But place-name evidence does suggest that Ecclesfield, Exley and Exley Head may well have been Christian centres – their names deriving from the Latin for church, *ecclesia* – but there is as yet insufficient archaeological evidence to support any theory of the extensive survival of British Christianity. Meanwhile, Ted Hughes' poem 'Remains of Elmet' paints a very different picture of a powerful pagan past destroyed by Northumbrian might, but while his poem (accompanied by photographs by Fay Godwin) is deeply evocative and suggestive, it is, of course, no more help than is Bede in revealing the actual beliefs of Elmet-dwellers.

Thrythwulf is as mysterious a figure as Elmet is as a place. He occurs nowhere else in Bede's History and there are no other recorded Thrythwulfs in Anglo-Saxon history. But the marvel of an altar that withstands fire, not because of some miracle, but just because it is made of stone, is a reminder of the value now placed on stone (as opposed to wood) for sacred purposes.

ESCOMB · County Durham

Edwin... promised... he would allow her [Aethelburh] and
all who came with her, men and women, priests or retainers,
to follow the faith and worship of their religion after the
Christian manner. [II, 9]

The church of St John at Escomb is not mentioned by Bede, but it is a rare survival of a barely altered Saxon church. It is a small, carefully proportioned building, situated in a circular graveyard, with a chancel that is just over 1 square metre (10 sq ft) and a nave three times longer than its width. On stylistic grounds the church is of an early Saxon date, perhaps predating Bede's own house at Jarrow[N] (founded in 674).

There is no evidence that any community was ever attached to Escomb and it must be considered a possibility that it was one of those rare private churches that noblemen established on their estates (cf. Seaham[N]). It may be that the founder hoped to be buried in the northern porch, now no longer visible, though archaeological traces remain; perhaps he belonged to the circle of Queen Aethelburh, who had come from Kent to marry King Edwin in 625. Whoever he was, he made significant use of Roman stones taken most probably from the ruins of the nearby fort of Innovia; particularly spectacular is the Roman arch separating the chancel from the nave. Such reuse of Roman *spolia* was not – or not primarily – a cost-cutting exercise, but rather a display of the ways in which Christianity reconnected the Saxons with the Roman civilisation which, paradoxically, they had first helped to destroy and then come to admire. It is equally notable at Jarrow and at Hexham – and indeed anywhere where Roman stone was available.

On the south wall at Escomb, between two of the windows, is a sundial. Three lines, still just visible, divide the day into four. There is no other known sundial of so early a date still to be found in its original setting.

FARNE ISLANDS • Northumberland

Now this place was utterly lacking in water, corn and trees; and as it was frequented by evil spirits, it was ill-suited for human habitation; but it became in all respects habitable as the man of God wished, since at his coming the evil spirits departed. [IV, 28]

It requires determination to get to the Farne Islands. The seas may be too rough, the boats too crowded, the weather too unpleasant. Fish and chips may help stiffen a traveller's resolve, but then come the gulls – it was ever thus.

No one, least of all St Cuthbert, Bishop of Lindisfarne (*see* page 43), ever imagined the islands were hospitable. They were not. Inner Farne (the island on which Cuthbert chose to live) was already inhabited by devils (so Bede tells us in his *Life of Cuthbert*), but Cuthbert was brave enough to take them on. He routed them and built his hermitage. Bede gives us details. The hermitage consisted of two buildings, one for living and one for prayer, both made of stone and peat with roofs of wood and straw, the whole being enclosed by a rampart of stones and compacted earth. By the landing stage was a guesthouse, but as time went on Cuthbert began to be reluctant to see anyone and kept his window shut, opening it only for special reasons rather than for the random pleasure of seeing visiting monks. He took to growing his own food and, since the islands are now a bird sanctuary, it seems appropriate to recall the trouble Cuthbert himself had with ravens who ate his barley (but who, at his rebuke, desisted). Luckily Cuthbert had green fingers: even when he planted barley long after the proper time, he still got, Bede tells us, 'an abundant crop'.

Cuthbert's first sojourn on Farne (possibly for as long as nine years) came after he had been prior at Lindisfarne, a post he relinquished most likely in 676. But in 684 or 685 he returned to Lindisfarne, this time as bishop. This was not, according to Bede, an appointment he readily accepted. The election was made at a council held near the river Aln, presided over by Archbishop Theodore, but Cuthbert succeeded in ignoring all the relevant messages and letters so that eventually the Northumbrian king himself, together with a suitable delegation, had to make the journey to Farne to persuade Cuthbert to accept a see (but at Lindisfarne rather than Hexham).

Two years later, Cuthbert was to be found back at Farne and it was there, early in 687, that he spent his last months. Monks from Lindisfarne were due to visit him during his final illness, but they were hit by the customary bad weather. For five days a storm delayed them. When they arrived Cuthbert was in severe distress, both physical and emotional. He had dragged himself down to the shore where the monks would immediately find him on their arrival, and there he had stayed, with nothing to eat but a few onions. He was in great physical pain from an ulcerated foot and in a state of mental anguish worse than anything he had ever known before. The monks stayed with him in these last tormented hours. On his death (on 20 March 687) they lit a candle that could be seen as far away as Lindisfarne, a prearranged signal to the rest of the community that their bishop was now dead.

What impulses had driven Cuthbert to set up a hermitage on such an inhospitable island? Seemingly many western ascetics, living thousands of miles from the Egyptian desert beloved by early Christian monks, opted instead for the solitude and discomfort an island could provide. Here, mortification of the kind

Christ himself had suffered during his forty-day retreat (now known as Lent) could be practised and here, away from the ecclesiastical politicking and jostlings of the court, a life of prayer could be cultivated.

Lindisfarne, especially to any monks coming from Iona, was something of a compromise, but the Farne Islands offered true solitude. Another possible retreat might have been Hobthrush, an island cut off from Lindisfarne at high tide, where Cuthbert had stayed before he went to Inner Farne and where, Bede tells us, Cuthbert's successor, Bishop Eadberht, used to spend every Advent and Lent 'in deep devotion, abstinence and prayer'.

It may indeed have been common practice to arrange for heirs to take over particular hermitages. After Cuthbert's death, his hermitage on Inner Farne was inherited by a monk from Ripon, Oethwelwald, who by all accounts continued the tradition of offering help to the Lindisfarne community, notably by making sure his monastic visitors did not get shipwrecked on their way home.

There can be little doubt that in writing his *Life of Cuthbert* (apart from his own verse *Life*; there was already a prose *Life* in existence), Bede hoped to promote Cuthbert's cult over and above Wilfrid's as Northumbria's patron saint. The contrast between the two men is so often accentuated that it is hard to remember that they belonged to the same world, but it is worth noting how, for all their pathos, Cuthbert's last days on the Farne Islands carry with them a hint that Cuthbert, like Wilfrid, perfectly understood the world of gift exchange, where presents mattered. Cuthbert was discreet in such matters whereas Wilfrid was flagrant, but, as Cuthbert lay dying, one of his last concerns was that he might not die with debts outstanding. So he purposefully asked the monk Beda to be with him because Beda had acted as his secretary and 'knew all about the gifts he had given and the presents he had received'. Such presents included the cloth made by an abbess in which he asked for his body to be wrapped before being placed in the sarcophagus which also was a gift.

Bede, too, on his deathbed, was worried about his possessions, though in his case his anxiety was about sharing out with his brethren before he died his pepper, incense and his handkerchiefs.

GILLING EAST and WEST • North Riding of Yorkshire

[Oswine] went with one faithful thegn named Tondhere and hid
in the home of... Hunwold, whom he believed to be his friend.
But alas, it was quite otherwise. [III, 14]

In 1976, a nine-year-old boy found a two-edged Anglo-Saxon sword by the edge of the stream that runs through Gilling West. The sword (now in the Yorkshire Museum) has been dated to the ninth century. This makes it too late to belong to the age of Bede, but it nonetheless evokes a dramatic episode related by Bede which has long been associated with one or other of the Gillings, either East or West.

The story is this: in 642, on the death of King Oswald, old loyalties and ambitions had resurfaced in Northumbria, which again split into two, with the Bernicians of the north coming under the rule of Oswald's brother, Oswiu, while Oswine, through his kinship with King Edwin, claimed the southern kingdom of Deira. Oswiu was the more powerful of the two rulers, and when war finally erupted, Oswine chose to avoid open conflict. He took refuge instead at a place Bede names as Gilling (*In Getlingum*) in the home of Hunwold, supposedly his loyal retainer. There, on 20 August 651, he was betrayed and murdered.

Foul and shocking though Oswine's murder seemed to Bede, he nonetheless offered by way of consolation a prophecy that Bishop Aidan of Lindisfarne (*see* page 43) had uttered concerning Oswine's death. The king had given Aidan a horse to use, should an emergency arise or supposing he had a river to cross. Aidan, used to going about his business on foot (as other monks from Lindisfarne, who had been trained in Irish customs, would have done), promptly gave the horse, together with its trappings, to the first beggar he met. Oswine was not best pleased. Why, the king wanted to know – they happened to meet on their way to dinner – had Aidan given away the very horse the king had singled out for him? Surely there were less good mounts that would have done for the beggar? Aidan felt no remorse: 'O king,' he said, 'what are you saying? Surely this son of a mare is not dearer to you than that son of God?' Silence. The king went to the fire to warm himself (he had just come in from hunting). After some moments of reflection, Oswine, taking off his sword, went to where Aidan was now sitting, threw himself before him and asked for his pardon. This Aidan readily gave, but as the evening went on he became more and more depressed. When asked what the matter was, he replied: 'I know that the king will not live long; for I never before saw a humble king. Therefore I think that he will very soon be snatched from this life; for this nation does not deserve to have such a ruler' [III, 14].

Little good did Oswine's murder do Oswiu. Power in Deira passed to Oswiu's nephew Oethelwald, while Oswine was honoured as a saint whom Oswiu himself felt compelled to venerate. At the instigation of his wife, Eanflaed (herself a daughter of King Edwin and thus a relative of Oswine), Oswiu gave Trumhere (another relative) land at Gilling on which to build a monastery where prayers could be said in expiation of the crime. It is, however, noteworthy that Oswine was probably not buried at Gilling; Gilling, in other words, may have been given as blood money, but it was not intended that it become a shrine. (It is still not entirely clear where Oswine was buried: cf. Tynemouth.[N])

But where exactly was Gilling? Was it Gilling East or Gilling West? The sword and the ninth-century fragments of sculpture, displayed now in the church at Gilling West, provide evidence of an Anglo-Saxon settlement but do nothing to disprove the counter-claims of Gilling East, in the Vale of Pickering, to be the site of the murder. Gilling East, too, has appropriate fragments of sculpture; moreover the Vale of Pickering was undoubtedly a centre of Deiran power and it is this which would seem to tip the balance in its favour, all the more given Ceolfrith's attachment to it.

Ceolfrith, later to be Bede's abbot at Jarrow,[N] had become a monk at Gilling in c.660; his brother Cynefrid had been abbot there before retiring to Ireland 'in his zeal for the study of scripture' (according to the anonymous *Life of Ceolfrith*), and it was now a further kinsman, Tunbert (later Bishop of Hexham[N]), who was abbot. It seems probable, then, that it was Ceolfrith who told Bede the story of the monastery's foundation, though it does not seem as if Ceolfrith was at Gilling for very long. Gilling was badly hit by an outbreak of plague, and Ceolfrith, together with Tunbert and a number of other monks, took refuge with Wilfrid at Ripon.[N]

Here, Ceolfrith became a priest; next he went on a tour of minsters in both Kent and Suffolk (*see* Icanhoe[EA]) before returning finally to Northumbria to join the monastery at Wearmouth-Jarrow[N]. But the likelihood is that he did forget Gelling, and that it was his wish to visit it one last time, which explains his itinerary when he decided to leave Wearmouth-Jarrow in order to end his days in Rome. Ceolfrith had made an emotional departure from Wearmouth-Jarrow by boat, but then, having crossed the Tyne, he made an inland journey to Rome before finally setting sail from the Humber. Gilling East could have been on his way.

GOODMANHAM · East Riding of Yorkshire

The place where the idols once stood is still shown, not far from York, to the east, over the river Derwent. Today it is called Goodmanham, the place where the high priest, through the inspiration of the true God, profaned and destroyed the altars which he himself had consecrated. [II, 13]

Goodmanham lies in the heart of the Yorkshire wolds. The site has long been hallowed; twenty-five round and two square barrows within the present parish testify to its importance even before the coming of the Romans. Here, beyond all reasonable doubt, was housed the major shrine of the Deiran royal house in the years before King Edwin's official acceptance of Christianity. This, then, is the place to which the chief priest Coifi rode after the great debate held nearby (possibly at York, more likely at the nearer royal villas of Londesborough or Market Weighton) in 627, when paganism was officially abandoned. Present on this occasion were, according to Bede, Paulinus, bishop of York and all of those in Edwin's close circle. Each was asked in turn to give his views on the proposed new faith. On this occasion, one of Edwin's councillors famously compared the life of man to the life of a sparrow:

> You are sitting feasting with your ealdormen and thegns in winter time; the fire is burning on the hearth in the middle of the hall and all inside is warm, while outside the wintry storms of rain and snow are raging; and a sparrow flies swiftly through the hall. It enters in at one door and quickly flies out through the other. For the few moments it is inside, the storm and wintry tempest cannot touch it, but after the briefest moment of calm, it flits from your sight, out of the wintry storm and into it again. So this life of man appears but for a moment; what follows or indeed what went before, we know not at all. If this new doctrine brings us more certain information, it seems right that we should accept it. [11,13]

More speeches were to follow; finally the time came for the Christian Paulinus and the pagan Coifi to bring the debate to a close. According to Bede, so persuasive was Paulinus that Coifi himself was won over, declaring that his paganism now seemed 'worthless' in comparison with a religion that could offer 'the gift of life, salvation and eternal happiness', whereupon Edwin publicly announced his acceptance of the new faith. (For Edwin's hesitations, *see* introduction to Northumbria, page 39; it should be noted, however, that a separate tradition suggests that Edwin had in fact been baptised once before while in exile, among British Christians during the reign of Aethelfrith (593–616).

Now Coifi volunteered 'to profane the altars and the shrines of the idols together with their precincts' [11, 13]. In flagrant defiance of pagan convention, which expected its priests to ride only mares and to be unarmed, Coifi asked Edwin to provide him with weapons and a stallion and off he set, duly girded with a sword and with a spear in his hand. To the amazement of the bystanders, who thought he had gone mad, Coifi rode up and cast the spear into the shrine; the shrine itself 'and all its enclosures' (most likely fences or hedges) he ordered his companions to destroy and burn.

Coifi's violation of the Goodmanham temple is unparalleled in the story of the conversion to Christianity in England and seemingly at odds with Pope Gregory's considered and explicit instruction to the missionaries not to destroy pagan shrines but only the idols within them: 'Take holy water,' he had written, 'and sprinkle it in these shrines, build altars and place relics in them... When this people see that their shrines are not destroyed they will be able to banish error from their hearts and be more ready to come to the places they are familiar with, but now recognising and worshipping the true God' [I, 30].

But Coifi was not, of course, in any ordinary sense of the word a Christian missionary: he was a pagan priest, even, it has been argued, a personification of Woden himself. His spear-hurling may itself have drawn on ancient pagan symbolical battle practice. As presented by Bede, here is the challenge of a defiant and embittered priest to the old gods whom, he claims, have done nothing much for him. Will they retaliate if he throws down the gauntlet? They do not. The conversion of Northumbria can now proceed apace.

Despite the destruction of the shrine, Bede makes it clear that Goodmanham itself continued to bear witness to the conversion story: 'the place where the idols once stood is still shown' [II,

13]. Today at Goodmanham a church dating from the eleventh century stands, prominently situated on what seems to be a man-made hillock. Excavation is necessarily precluded, but the likelihood must remain that this was a hillock of prehistoric significance, appropriated first by pagan worshippers and then by medieval Christians. And Coifi? Coifi has not been forgotten. A font in the church makes the apocryphal boast that it was from its waters that Coifi received baptism from Paulinus, bishop of York.

Coifi's font is unlikely to be earlier than the ninth century, but fonts were already in use in the time of Bede, the great men and women within any kingdom evidently not being expected to undergo the river ceremonies administered to the crowds of the newly faithful gathered by the river Glen (*see* Yeavering[N]), for the kingdom of Deira by the river Swale near Catterick, or for the women and men of Lindsey by the river Trent (*see* Lincoln[M]). After Goodmanham, Edwin's own baptism was staged at York[N] on Easter Day 627.

HACKNESS · North Riding of Yorkshire

On the same night it pleased Almighty God by a vision to reveal
[Hilda's] death in another monastery some distance away called
Hackness, which she had built that very year. [IV, 23]

Hackness was founded by St Hilda in 680, some 13 miles (21 km) away from the mother house of Whitby.[N] In that same year St Hilda died, an event witnessed by the communities of both Hackness and Whitby. At Hackness, a nun by the name of Begu had a vision in which she was awakened by the tolling of the abbey's bell, whereupon she saw Hilda's soul, guided by angels, being taken up to heaven in a great blaze of light. In terror, Begu ran from her dormitory to recount her vision to the acting abbess, Frigyth; Frigyth immediately called together the whole community and the rest of the night was spent in prayer and psalm-singing on behalf of Hilda.

Meanwhile, at Whitby, Hilda's soul was likewise seen ascending into heaven at precisely the moment those who were with Hilda later reported she had died. Thus both Hackness and Whitby fully shared in Hilda's death, in ways described by Bede as 'a beautiful harmony of events'.

The Hackness story provides the first reference to a church bell in England, but Bede does not describe its ringing as a novelty but rather as a familiar summons to prayer and the way any death would be announced to a community. The story also incidentally reveals that at Hackness the nuns slept in a dormitory, whereas at Whitby the archaeological evidence suggests that each nun had her own cell. The Whitby novices, however, had a separate building, some way away from the main monastic buildings.

The Hackness Cross, preserved in the parish church of Hackness, is incomplete: only the top and bottom of the shaft have survived, but these suggest a substantial piece of sculpture, in all some 4.5 metres (15 ft) high. Panels of interlace and vine scroll design, along with the feet of two facing beasts, give some indication of the original design. The cross dates probably from the eighth century and was erected to commemorate an abbess Aethelburga (or Oedilburga). This may be the Aethelburga who accompanied her kinswoman Aelfflaed, abbess of Whitby after Hilda, to the deathbed of Aelfflaed's half-brother King Aldfrith of Northumbria in 705, a further example of the monastic, familial and royal networks that are so striking a feature of the religious life of the period. The runic inscriptions on the cross have so far eluded any satisfactory interpretation. They may be in two different forms – English and Irish – but if we can judge by the Latin inscription, prayers are being asked for Aethelburga, 'a most loving mother'.

On the north impost of the chancel arch at Hackness cavort interlaced animals from the eighth century. While it is not impossible that this is evidence that the present church itself dates from the eighth century, it is rather more likely that the church is mainly of a later date and that the impost was simply saved from the original building as a 'souvenir' (as seems to have happened elsewhere, cf. Lastingham[N]).

HATFIELD CHASE • West Riding of Yorkshire

A fierce battle was fought on the plain called Haethfelth and Edwin was killed on 12th October in the year of our Lord 633
[11, 20]

Hatfield Chase, near Doncaster, is the traditional site for an epic battle in the history of Northumbria (but it is also possible that the battle took place further south, at Cuckney, where over 200 skeletons were discovered during work undertaken by the National Coal Board in 1951). But wherever the battle was fought, this was the occasion when Edwin, together with his sons, Osfrith and Eadfrith, faced Penda of Mercia in alliance with the British king Caedwalla. Edwin and Osfrith were both slain; Eadfrith, forced to defect (according to Bede), was killed later by Penda.

For an understanding of the battle it is important to note

that the neither Osfrith nor Eadfrith were Edwin's sons by his Kentish-born Queen Aethelburh (*see* Lyminge[K]). The sons who fought at Hatfield Chase had been born during Edwin's years of exile; their mother was the Mercian Princess Cwenburh, a daughter of King Ceorl (the king who at some point turns into the nursery rhyme figure, Old King Cole).

Impossible though it is to reconstruct all the tensions and rivalries that led to the battle, there can be little doubt that both the Mercians and the British felt not only anxiety about the growing power of Edwin (he had recently campaigned as far as Anglesey) but also a sense of betrayal. Had not the Mercians, and the British, too, sheltered him during his years of exile when Aelthelfrith of Bernicia was king and he had had to flee for his life? The savagery which Bede described as following on from the battle of Hatfield Chase when Caedwalla 'occupied the Northumbrian kingdoms for a whole year... tearing them to pieces with fearful bloodshed' [III, 1] would seem to make sense in the context of Edwin's supposed perfidy (even if Bede presents it somewhat differently).

Immediately after the battle, Edwin's remains were apparently neglected, but at some point, according to Bede, the king's head was rescued and taken to York[N] to the church that he had founded after his conversion by the missionary Paulinus. Here it was placed in a chapel dedicated to Pope Gregory (who had sent Paulinus to England). A further and separate tradition about Edwin's remains (which does not mention his head) comes from the Whitby[N] *Life of Gregory*. Here a priest named Trimma has a vision telling him that he must go to Hatfield Chase, recover the bones and take them to Whitby where Aelfflaed, Edwin's granddaughter, was now abbess. Three times the priest hears this vision before accepting that the message must be obeyed. He accordingly sets out, uncertain where to go, but with the knowledge that if he asks a local man named Teoful, he will show him the way. With Teoful's help, and after some careful digging, Trimma duly finds the bones and takes them to Whitby, where they are placed close to an altar dedicated to St Peter and to another dedicated to St Gregory.

The battlefield at Hatfield Chase never seems to have become a cult centre, though the Whitby *Life of Gregory* has a poignant passage of considerable interest, recalling how Trimma continued to visit the battlefield where 'he often saw the spirits of four of the slain, and certainly baptised, persons coming in splendour to visit their bodies'.

HEAVENFIELD · Northumberland

The place is still shown today and is held in great veneration where Oswald, when he was about to engage in battle, set up the sign of the holy cross and, on bended knees, prayed God to send heavenly aid to his worshippers in their dire need. [III, 2]

The battle of Heavenfield in 635 was for Bede a momentous event in Northumbria's history. Since the death of King Edwin in 633 at the battle of Hatfield Chase,[N] Northumbria had been in turmoil, a situation made worse by the alleged savagery of the British king, Caedwalla, whose ambition was such that he even hoped, claimed Bede, 'to wipe out the whole English nation from the land of Britain' [II,20]. But at the battle of Heavenfield, Caedwalla was killed and, as Bede saw it, Northumbria was restored to its rightful king, Oswald, grandson of the mighty

Aethelfrith. And how did Oswald achieve this great victory? The explanation was simple: before the battle the king had erected a wooden cross at which he and his whole army had prayed for victory. At the time Bede was writing, the cross was still in place and still (he tells us) working miracles: a splinter of the wood put into water and drunk could restore the health of both sick people and of their beasts.

This story of Bede's requires not so much scepticism as careful interpretation. In writing his history, Bede had a number of models to hand: one was the Latin version of the *Ecclesiastical History*, originally written by Eusebius, Bishop of Caesarea (c.263–339), who had described how the emperor Constantine, on the eve of the battle of Milvian Bridge (312), had seen in the sky the image of a cross and a promise that the sign would bring him victory. Jarrow's[N] attachment to this story is confirmed by the deciphering of the 'Constantinian' inscription on the fragment of an excavated cross (on display today in the church at Jarrow), which reads: 'In this special sign life is restored to the world.' But what are we to make of Bede's version of the Heavenfield battle when it is compared with that told by Adamnan in his *Life of St Columba* (a text Bede almost certainly knew)? In this account there is no mention of a cross – rather it is St Columba of Iona (whose cult Oswald will have known well from his period of exile in northwest Scotland) who comes to Oswald in a dream, promising him victory. Here, clearly, are stories representing two different traditions. Bede attempts to reconcile them. He attaches Oswald firmly to a classical, imperial past – but the wooden cross he describes can be seen as distinctly 'Irish': Columba had what seems to have been a wooden cross on Iona; so, too, did Cuthbert on the Farne Islands.[N]

Bede's statement that until the erection of the Heavenfield cross by Oswald there was no 'symbol of the Christian faith, no church, no altar' in Bernicia is, however, likely to be an exaggeration, even if Yeavering[N] (where at the least an altar might have been expected – for use during Edwin's reign) had been abandoned by the time Bede was writing.

Heavenfield itself had by then become the centre of a vigorous cult: each year monks from Hexham,[N] some 4 miles (6 km) away, would keep vigil by the cross to commemorate the anniversary of Oswald's death and so popular was Heavenfield as a place of pilgrimage that a church had been erected on the spot. The present church dates only from the nineteenth century, but it has clearly been built on Anglo-Saxon foundations. Moreover, inside the church there is part of a cross shaft of uncertain date (but possibly seventh century) and, secondly, a cross base made out of a Roman altar. This, too, may date from the seventh century. The two pieces do not fit together, but the cross base might once have held a wooden cross.

It has sometimes been suggested that Oswald's cross creates a bridge linking the pagan worship of trees and the later stone crosses of Northumbria. Although there is little explicit evidence for tree worship in England, it is so well attested in mainland Europe that it would be surprising if it did not also feature in Anglo-Saxon paganism. It must also be highly significant that the Anglo-Saxons did not adapt the Latin word for cross (crux), but rather used rood, treow or beam. The most memorable of all Anglo-Saxon trees is of course the tree in the early vernacular poem The Dream of the Rood, in which the tree destined to be fashioned into the cross on which Christ must die laments its fate. (For the use of this poem on a stone cross, see Ruthwell.[N])

But where did the actual battle action of Heavenfield take place? A long-standing controversy as to whether the erection of the cross, the fighting of the battle and the slaying of Caedwalla all took place in the same location – or whether Caedwalla met his end some miles away from the main battlefield, by the Rowley Burn – would now seem to have been resolved. The most likely scenario is as follows: the probable erection of the cross at Heavenfield (which at the time would not of course had this name) and the prayers of the soldiers at its foot prepared the army for a march to the Rowley Burn, some 8 miles (13 km) south, where they took the British troops by surprise, routed their army and killed their king.

It might spoil the story, but all the same it needs to be pointed out that Caedwalla was not, in fact, a pagan. However, as far as Bede was concerned, Caedwalla had behaved tyrannically; now it was up to Oswald to restore peace and Christian kingship.

HEXHAM · Northumberland

Acca, Wilfrid's priest, became bishop of Hexham in Wilfrid's place. He was a man of great energy and noble in the sight of God and man. He enriched the fabric of his church, dedicated to the blessed apostle Andrew, with all kinds of decorations and works of art. He took great trouble, as he still does, to gather relics of the blessed apostles and martyrs of Christ from all parts and to put up altars for their veneration, establishing various chapels for this purpose within the walls of the church. [v, 20]

Hexham, even more than Ripon,[N] was Bishop Wilfrid's great showcase. The land for the foundation had been given to him by his patron, Queen Aethelthryth of Northumbria, c.672, seemingly at about the time that the queen was preparing to leave court in order to join the monastery of Coldingham[N] (before going on to found Ely[EA]). With the exception of the crypt, there are few traces now of Wilfrid's church, but William of Malmesbury's comment in the twelfth century – 'Those who have visited Italy allege that at Hexham they see the glories of Rome' – adds credibility to the praise lavished on the building by Wilfrid's biographer, Stephen of Ripon.

Stephen found the wonders of Hexham hard to describe. The crypts were 'of wonderfully dressed stone', while above ground there were 'various columns and many side-aisles'. The great walls were surrounded 'by various winding passages with spiral stairs leading up and down'. There was, concluded Stephen, nothing like it this side of the Alps.

Stephen's hyperbole may need some qualification. Wilfrid was indeed devoted to Rome, to which he had first travelled as a young man, when he spent many months in the city visiting shrines (including that of St Andrew, the saint to whom Hexham was dedicated) and collecting relics. It is, however, likely that Wilfred drew his inspiration for Hexham not only from his Roman visit but also from the monastic site of St Augustine's in Canterbury (see page 13), which he may well have wanted to emulate, if not surpass. A further source of inspiration is likely to have been Gaul, which Wilfrid knew well from his travels and was the place he had chosen to go for his episcopal consecration (after the Synod of Whitby[N]) because he was not satisfied with any of the arrangements possible at the time in England.

Back home, Hexham would ensure Wilfrid – and future bishops – at least some continental splendour; Hexham's so-called 'frithstool' may well have been Wilfrid's throne and of Merovingian design. It is likely to have been placed against the wall at the east end of the church. But whatever Hexham was modelled on, for those who watched Wilfrid's church being built, what must have been truly astonishing was the quantity of Roman stone being transported from the Roman fort of Corbridge for the new building. Huge blocks of stone (some as much as a yard long) were used for the crypt; meanwhile, acts of vandalism – by modern reckoning – truncated and reshaped Roman monuments for use throughout the church.

Acca succeeded Wilfred as bishop of Hexham in 709–10 and continued to beautify the church, enriching its altars with gold and silver ornaments and precious cloths. He also invited (from Kent) a famous singer called Maban to come and teach the kind of church music the Roman missionaries had introduced. Acca was himself, according to Bede, an accomplished musician; knowing how to chant properly was a skill Bede valued highly.

When Acca died, he is said to have been buried at the east end of the church. The tradition that his grave was marked by the cross, richly decorated with vine scroll, which stands inside the church should now be discounted, though details in the scroll-work suggest that a mid-eighth-century date is likely. The vine scrolls are distinctive in that they are not inhabited; the model may be Byzantine. The cross would originally have been painted to produce a dazzling effect (as the reconstruction of the Ruthwell[N] cross in the museum at Manchester shows so well).

Some four years before his death, Wilfrid had a stroke. At moments of death, or imminent death, angels regularly appear in Anglo-Saxon sources. In this case, the angel who visited

Wilfrid was none other than Archangel Michael himself and he
came with something of a rebuke: Wilfrid had built churches in
honour of St Peter and of St Andrew, but he had not similarly
honoured the Virgin. Now the Virgin was giving him four more
years to live, but he must in return build a church dedicated to
her. Wilfrid duly obeyed.

All that now remains of this church are some stones built in
the walls close by the Hexham marketplace.

JARROW, *see* WEARMOUTH & JARROW[N]

KIRKDALE • North Riding of Yorkshire

Orm, son of Gamal, bought St Gregory's church when it was
completely ruined and collapsed, and he had it constructed
recently from the ground up to Christ and to St Gregory, in
the days of King Edward and in the days of Earl Tosti. And
Haward made me and Brand the priest.

(KIRKDALE: SUNDIAL INSCRIPTION)

St Gregory's minster, a building dating from the eleventh century, is situated today in a singularly remote position, sheltered
by woods, but vulnerable to floods. In the seventh or eighth century, an earlier church stood on the site, linked in all probability
to the nearby monastery of Lastingham.[N] Nothing remains of the
fabric of this earlier church beyond an eighth-century tomb slab
used in the rebuilding which may originally have stood inside the
church: a sure sign that it commemorated a figure of some stature. A similar stone of a slightly later date has a pattern of tassels
around three sides, suggesting that it was originally designed

to stand against a wall. Perhaps it was Viking depredations of the late eighth and ninth centuries that caused the devastation of the church. The eleventh-century sundial, itself a reused slab from an Anglo-Saxon sarcophagus, set into the south side of the church, records how a certain Orm, the son of Gamal, acquired the church 'when it was completely ruined and collapsed' and how he had it built anew 'to Christ and to St Gregory'. The dedication to Gregory is a reminder of the continued affection that that particular pope engendered among the Northumbrians, as evidenced in the *Life of Gregory* written (perhaps in the seventh century) at the monastery of Whitby.[N]

Recent excavations have made it possible to recover more of Kirkdale's history. The Vale of Pickering in which it stands was already settled in the prehistoric era. Under the Romans its proximity to York made it a favoured area and at least seven villas have been found within 20 or so miles (32 km). At Kirkdale itself, excavations close to the church have revealed sandstone slabs thought to bear Roman tooling, while within the church there may also be some reused Roman stone. Further clues, in a cemetery beyond the church, include a lead plaque that seems to have belonged to a reliquary containing bones and a fragment of a filigree glass rod of a kind known to have been associated with altar lamps. The question now may not be when was Kirkdale's first minster built, but rather, was Kirkdale originally a Roman-British Christian site later developed by Anglo-Saxon missionaries?

LASTINGHAM · North Riding of Yorkshire

*... in accordance with the king's desire, Cedd chose himself a
site for the monastery amid some steep and remote hills, which
seemed better fitted for the haunts of robbers and the dens of
wild beasts than for human habitations...* [III, 23]

The monastery of Lastingham, in the Vale of Pickering, was
founded by Cedd (d. 664), one of that remarkable quartet of
brothers whom Bede describes as 'famous brothers of the Lord'.
Cedd, originally a monk of Lindisfarne (*see* page 43), had left his
native Northumbria to become bishop of the East Saxons (*see*
Bradwell-on-Sea[E]), but he was recalled to Northumbria to give
support to the son of King Oswald, Oethelwald, who, after the
murder of Oswine (*see* Gilling[N]), had been entrusted with the
sub-kingdom of Deira.

According to Bede, Oethwelwald was already on good terms
with Cedd's brother, Ceawlin, and it was he who effected the
introduction between bishop and king. Oethelwald duly gave
Cedd land on which to build a monastery, with the expectation
that it would become his burial place and in the hope that the
daily prayers of the monks would benefit his soul. Here, clearly,
was a dynastic centre in the making. But before Cedd began
building, Bede tells us he sanctified the place so as to 'cleanse the
site... from the stain of former sins... [following] the custom of
those from whom he had learned the discipline of a Rule, when
they had received a site for building a monastery or a church,
they should first consecrate it to the Lord with prayer and fasting'
[III, 23]. Cedd's purification consisted of living at Lastingham
throughout Lent, surviving each day 'on a little bread, one hen's

egg and a little milk mixed with water'. A summons to Cedd from the king (whether of the Northumbrians or of the East Saxons is not clear) before Lent was over resulted in Cedd handing over to another brother, Cynebill, the task of completing the final days of fasting.

The fourth of the brothers was Chad (*see* Lichfield[M]), and it was to him that Cedd entrusted the daily care of the new foundation. But Cedd continued to visit Lastingham, one visit fatally coinciding with an outbreak of the plague to which Cedd succumbed and died. He was buried originally outside the monastic walls but in the course of time, Bede tells us, a stone church was built within the monastery and there Cedd's body was taken and buried on the right side of the altar. (The reference to 'a stone church' makes it seem likely that the original building was of wood, as at Lindisfarne.)

When Cedd's community in Essex heard of his death, they were distraught and a group (of about thirty) left their monastery to come to live in Lastingham, so as to be near Cedd, wishing, as Bede explains, 'to live near the body of their father, or if the Lord so willed, to die and be buried there' [III, 23]. (Compare the devotion shown to Ceolfrith and expected from the followers of Wilfrid: here, too, was holy solidarity.) Tragically, Lastingham was hit by a further outbreak of plague and all but one small boy died (there are clear echoes here of the situation at Jarrow[N]). The small boy was spared, according to Bede, through the intercessions of Cedd himself and grew up to become a priest. It was especially important to Bede that the boy had not died during the outbreak of the plague because, as he later came to realise, the boy had not been baptised, so his salvation would have been in doubt. Whether Cedd ever felt obliged to intercede also for

Lastingham's royal founder, Oethelwald, is not, of course, something we will ever know, but Oethelwald's disappearance from history after the battle of the Winwaed (*see* Leeds[N]) in 655, when he treacherously took the side of Penda against his uncle, may prompt the thought that if anyone ever needed Cedd's prayers it would have been he.

The original monastery of Lastingham was probably destroyed by the Vikings in *c.*866–7, but it was later rebuilt. Its crypt dates from the late eleventh century and contains important fragments of Anglo-Saxon sculpture, including the head of a cross which it is estimated would have been spectacularly tall 7.3 metres (24 ft). Legend has it that this cross once stood on the moor on the spot where Ana's Cross now is to be found, some two miles (3 km) away from Lastingham. It is tempting to imagine that here was a site of special significance to which monks from Lastingham may have processed, just as monks from nearby Hexham[N] made annual pilgrimages to Heavenfield.[N]

LEEDS · West Riding of Yorkshire

The battle was joined and the heathen were put to flight or
destroyed... the battle was fought near the river Winwaed
which, owing to heavy rains, had overflowed its channels and
its banks to such an extent that many more were drowned in
flight than were destroyed by the sword in battle. [III, 24]

Nothing remains now of Anglo-Saxon Leeds, but it was a place of considerable significance for Bede as it was, he tells us, 'in the district of Leeds' that King Oswiu of Northumbria was finally able to vanquish the pagan King Penda of Mercia, at the battle of the Winwaed in 655. Much depended on this battle and Bede is very clear about its consequences, both for Northumbria and Mercia and for the cause of Christianity. After the battle, Mercia became a Christian kingdom with a bishopric at Lindsey, while Deira and Bernicia each received equal shares of land for the building of new minsters. Straightaway Oswiu entrusted to the monastery of Hartlepool his daughter, Aelfflaed, a future abbess of Whitby[N] but at the time of the battle no more than a baby, as the offering he had promised to God in return for his momentous victory.

But where exactly did the battle of the Winwaed take place? Bede's information here is not entirely clear, but he does give us a precise date – 15 November. It was late in the year for any medieval battle and it may be that Penda was by then on his way back home after a season of battering Oswiu with what Bede calls 'savage and insupportable attacks'.

Oswiu had apparently tried to buy peace by offering Penda 'an incalculable and incredible store of royal treasure' – which Penda had scorned – but it is not impossible that Penda had nonetheless received, or accumulated, plentiful treasure and that it was while he was making his way home, encumbered as well as enriched by this booty, that Oswiu attacked him.

Penda had an army thirty times the size of Oswiu's (so Bede claims), but Oswiu took advantage of the heavy rains which had caused the river Winwaed to break its banks so that even more men were drowned in flight than were killed in battle. Such a scenario makes it almost certain that the Winwaed is the modern river Went and that the battle took place not far from East Hardwick in West Yorkshire. Here, Penda's men seemingly found themselves trapped in front of the swollen river with no easy escape. Penda was himself killed, as were many of his chief supporters. And what of the putative treasure these men may have had with them? Could this be the Staffordshire hoard, that extraordinary collection of abandoned war gear, discovered by a metal detector in 2009? Just possibly, yes: but there are still too many unanswered questions about the hoard to be certain. What is incontrovertible is the quantity and quality of the gold it contained, along with silver and garnets, and the baffling way in which many of objects had been hacked about.

At least one Northumbrian king, Edwin, had a palace near Leeds, situated according to Bede, at the Roman site of Campodonum, possibly inherited by Edwin after his annexation of the kingdom of Elmet.[N] Bishop Paulinus added a church built of wood, but both palace and church were burnt down after Edwin's death.

MELROSE • Northumberland

[Cuthbert] first of all entered the monastery of Melrose which is on the banks of the Tweed and was then ruled over by the Abbot Eata, the gentlest and simplest of men, who… was afterwards made bishop of Hexham or rather of Lindisfarne. [IV, 27]

Melrose today houses the exceptionally fine ruins of a twelfth-century Cistercian abbey, but just over 2 miles (3 km) away, 'almost encircled by a bend in the river Tweed' [v,12], is the site of a much older monastic foundation. This is the monastery entered by Cuthbert of Lindisfarne in 651, the year when Bishop Aidan of Lindisfarne died. Cuthbert was reputedly minding sheep at the time, but as he looked up into the sky he is said to have seen

Aidan's soul ascending into heaven and it was this vision which prompted his decision to become a monk. Cuthbert's eventual fame was such that we have an anonymous *Life*, as well as a prose and a verse *Life*, both written by Bede, quite apart from the testimony Bede provided in the *Ecclesiastical History*.

Given his vision of Aidan, Cuthbert might have been expected to join the community at Lindisfarne, but, or so Bede tells us in his *Life of Cuthbert*, he instead chose Melrose because of the 'reputation for holiness of the prior, Boisil'. Some ten years later, Boisil was dead, a victim of the plague. He spent his last week with Cuthbert and together they read the Gospel of St John, chosen since as Boisil explained, 'I have a commentary in seven parts. With the help of God we can read one a day and perhaps discuss if we want.'[†]

Soon after Cuthbert had joined Melrose, an invitation came from King Aldfrith (son of King Oswiu, and ruler of Deira) to Eata, the abbot of Melrose, to found a minster at Ripon.[N] Eata took Cuthbert with him and appointed him guest-master of the new foundation. But both Eata and Cuthbert were subsequently ousted from Ripon: Aldfrith had joined forces with Wilfrid in an attempt (or so it would seem) to make political capital out of the controversy over the dating of Easter, and since the monks of Melrose followed the Irish system, their presence no longer suited Aldfrith's purposes (*see* Whitby[N] and Ripon[N]) and they were compelled to return to Melrose where Cuthbert, following the death of Boisil soon afterwards, became prior in his stead.

† For the copy of the Gospel of St John found in Cuthbert's tomb, *see* Lindisfarne (page 43); for Bede's translation of the opening chapters of this Gospel, as he lay dying, *see* the *Letter on the death of Bede* in *Bede's Ecclesiastical History of the English People*, ed. and trans. B. Colgrave and R. A. B. Mynors (Clarendon Press, 1969; rev. repr.1991), p. 583.

As prior, Cuthbert preached across the countryside, sometimes, according to Bede, riding, though more often going on
foot. The devastation caused by the plague had caused many to
desert the new faith but Cuthbert continued undeterred, sometimes spending weeks away because he went to villages Bede
described as situated 'on steep and rugged mountains' where
'the poverty as well as the ignorance of the villagers prevented
teachers from approaching them'. The many miracles Bede
relates include the curing of a reeve's wife from madness: the
story has several points of interest – could her body be buried
in consecrated ground? What was the difference between
demonic possession and 'ordinary infirmity'? And it also very
clearly gives the lie to the later stories that were circulated about
Cuthbert's misogyny.

In around 670 Cuthbert left Melrose for Lindisfarne where
Eata was now abbot; as one of the Irish who had accepted the
decisions of the Synod of Whitby,[N] Eata (like Cuthbert) was one
of Bede's heroes. His willingness to compromise for the sake
of peace was further demonstrated in 685 and 686 by the way
in which he allowed Cuthbert to become Bishop of Lindisfarne
while he moved to Hexham[N] (despite Cuthbert's initial election
to Hexham). Eata died shortly afterwards and was buried at
Hexham.

Melrose, meanwhile, continued to welcome visionaries.
Around 700, a Northumbrian Christian, Dryhthelm – 'the father
of a family who lived a religious life together with his household'
– was so ill it appeared that he was dying. Mourners were gather-
ing by his bedside when suddenly he sat up. The mourners fled,
all but his wife 'who loved him dearly and remained with him
though trembling with fear'. Dryhthelm explained to her the

vision he had had and that in consequence he must now give away all his possessions (one portion went to his wife; one to his sons; and one in alms) and live a quite different sort of life. Shortly afterwards he went to Melrose where he was tonsured and went to live in some 'secret retreat', but his vision became famous. Dryhthelm himself told it to a monk named Haemgisl who had once lived in a cell nearby (though – Bede tells us – he had subsequently gone to Ireland) and Haemgisl had written an account with which Bede was familiar. This, then, was the vision [V, 12].

Dryhthelm had been taken by an angel to a deep and broad valley. On one side, fire raged, while on the other, hail and icy snow blew about. Both sides were full of the souls of men who were being tossed from one side to the other. Dryhthem thought this might be hell, but his guide interrupted his thoughts: 'Do not believe it,' he said. 'This is not hell as you think.' So on the pair went. They came to a place of terrible darkness, illuminated only by balls of fire and the tips of flames and the flames were 'full of human souls which, like sparks flying upward with the smoke, were now tossed on high... and [then] sucked down into the depths'. The stench was terrible. After what seemed an age there came a hideous sound of jeering and a crowd of evil spirits came into view, bringing with them the souls of five captured humans (Dryhthelm could make out a man, a woman and one tonsured soul). For a terrible moment, it looked as if Dryhthelm himself might be dragged into the abyss, but then 'something like a bright star glimmering in the darkness' came towards him and he recognised it as his guide.

Now the angel took him on another tour. This time Dryhthelm was led to a long wall and from here he could see 'a very broad and pleasant plain, full of... a fragrance of growing flowers' with happy groups of people sitting around. Was this perhaps...? 'No,' said the guide, 'this is not the kingdom of heaven as you imagine.' On the two went until they could spy (but did not enter) a yet more beautiful place, brightly illuminated, from which emanated wonderful smells and the sweet sound of singing. But Dryhthelm was allowed to go no further. Now came the time for an explanation of each of the places – only heaven and hell are named but the two other regions are recognisable as purgatory and paradise. And while the bad news was that hell might await anyone – man, woman or priest – the good news was that even deathbed repentance could bring salvation: 'The prayers of those who are still alive, their alms and fastings and specially the celebration of masses, help many of them to get free even before the day of judgement'. Dryhthelm himself was assured his spot in paradise, provided in future he lived well. He took no chances: he would chastise his body by standing in freezing water and when asked how he could bear it, he would say: 'I have known it colder', and when asked how he could endure so harsh a life, he would reply, 'I have seen it harder.'

Dryhthelm's vision may have been known by the monk of Wenlock.[M] The similarities are indeed striking and the moral of both stories is unequivocal – for those who repent there is hope, but for the unrepentant it will indeed be hell.

RIPON • West Riding of Yorkshire

[Wilfrid] was a boy of good disposition and virtuous beyond his years. He behaved himself with such modesty and discretion in all things that he was deservedly loved, honoured, and cherished by his elders as though he were one of themselves.

After he had reached the age of fourteen, he chose the monastic rather than the secular life. [v, 19]

Ripon from its earliest days was involved in controversy. It owes its foundation to Aldfrith, son of King Oswiu. Aldfrith had initially given the site to monks from Melrose,[N] but then he transferred it to his protégé, Wilfrid. Wilfrid was newly back from Rome, an ambitious young man, eager to show that he was abreast of all that was new in the practice of Christianity, including the 'Roman' system for calculating the date of Easter, which was different from the method in use at Melrose, where dating followed the practice of Lindisfarne and Iona. Aldfrith, meanwhile, seems to have been equally ambitious and keen to establish a different identity from his father's.

In 664, at the Synod of Whitby[N] called by King Oswiu, the whole of Northumbria, in a decision few could have foreseen, adopted Wilfrid's method for calculating the dates of Easter. Wilfrid's triumph led to his election as bishop of Northumbria, with his base at York,[N] in place of the bishop of Lindisfarne,[N] Colman. Colman promptly, and bitterly, returned to Iona. No more is ever heard of Aldfrith (though *cf.* Castor[M]), but Wilfrid set off for Gaul, so as to be consecrated in great splendour by Agilbert, formerly bishop of Wessex but now bishop of Paris. However, Wilfrid stayed abroad for so long – lingering even after he had returned to England in Sussex – that his see was taken from him and given to Chad, abbot of Lastingham.[N] When finally he returned to Northumbria, Wilfrid had to be content with being abbot at Ripon and seemingly acting bishop for Mercia and Kent (where there were short-term vacancies; for his possible foundations at this period, *see* Oundle[M]).

At Ripon, Wilfrid had a star pupil in Willibrord, later archbishop of the Frisians. Willibrord's father had entrusted him to
the minster as an oblate before himself becoming a monk – and
thereafter a hermit of some repute, whose holiness was later venerated at Ripon. Willibrord himself stayed at Ripon until 678,
when he went to Ireland, spending twelve years there, before
joining the Anglo-Saxon mission in Frisia. His success in Frisia
was such that he became both archbishop of the Frisians and
abbot of Echternach. It was through Willibrord that the cult of
King Oswald reached as far as Germany.

Today, little remains of Wilfrid's church at Ripon beyond the
crypt. This is of similar design to the crypt at Hexham[N] but sim-
pler, having only two, rather than three, passages leading to it.
But in Wilfrid's own day Ripon was without doubt breathtak-
ingly magnificent and we have at least some idea of it from the
description given by Wilfrid's biographer, Stephen of Ripon:
the church was 'of dressed stone, supported by various columns
and side aisles'. When the work was finished, it was dedicated
to St Peter on an occasion made memorable on account of those
who attended – every kind of grandee – and because of the lavish
quality of the entertainment. The feasting lasted for three days.
The altar cloth was luxurious – 'purple woven with gold' – and
Wilfrid commissioned the four gospels to be 'written out in letters of gold on purpled parchment and illuminated... and a case
was made for the books, all made of gold and set with the most
precious gems'.

Less spectacular, but of lasting importance for the security of
the church, was Wilfrid's astute use of the occasion of Ripon's
consecration to read out to the assembled crowd a list of all
the lands Ripon had ever been given, as well as a list of all the

consecrated land abandoned by British clergy who had fled at the approach of Northumbria's armies. It cannot be a coincidence that in the next chapter Stephen recounts a miracle of Wilfrid's in which he restored to life a child brought to him for baptism, although he was in fact already dead. Wilfrid bargained with the mother: her child would be restored to life but she must surrender him to Wilfrid once he had reached the age of seven. The years passed; the mother broke her promise and hid the child among the Britons. Wilfrid dispatched his reeve, who found the boy and 'took him away by force' back to Ripon where he duly became a monk, dying years later of the plague. Although it can be no more than a conjecture, it is highly likely that such 'colonialism' also characterised many of the dealings between the Anglo-Saxons of Wessex and their British Christian neighbours (see Sherborne[W]).

By now Wilfrid's star was in the ascendancy. In 669 he was restored to York – Chad, meanwhile, became bishop of the Mercians – and he was able to extend his influence by building a minster at Hexham,[N] thanks to the generosity of Queen Aethelthryth (see Ely[EA]). But by 678 Wilfrid had fallen out of favour at court (the reasons are not entirely clear, though his support of Aethelthryth's vow of virginity may have had something to do with it) and he was forced to leave Northumbria.

The Northumbrian diocese was now divided, with new sees established at both Ripon and Hexham. Wilfrid, however, continued to battle for what he perceived as his rights, journeying to Rome in order to present his case to the pope. But the Northumbrian King Ecgfrith was not prepared to accept Rome's judgement, whereupon Wilfrid established himself in Sussex (see Selsey[S]). However, after the death of Ecgfrith and through the intervention of Archbishop Theodore in 686, Wilfrid was at last, in 686, restored both to the monasteries of Ripon and Hexham and to the diocese of York. The settlement was, however, based on compromises which soon caused friction and resentment, and by 692 a disgruntled Wilfrid, once more deprived of the see of York, was back again in Mercia. An attempt in 703 to limit his authority to Ripon galvanised Wilfrid into appealing again to Rome; papal support, but more tellingly a change of dynasty in Northumbria, worked to Wilfrid's advantage and he was able to die with his claims in large measure vindicated.

A stroke gave Wilfrid some premonition of his death, prompting him to set his affairs in order. According to Stephen, he called together a select group at Ripon. The Ripon treasurer was instructed to display 'all the gold, silver and precious stones' he had in his store and to divide them into four. The most valuable portion was to go to churches in Rome; of the other portions, one was to go to the poor; one to the abbots of Ripon and Hexham, lest they should ever need to give suitable presents to kings and bishops; and one portion was for those of Wilfrid's friends and allies who had been loyal to him during his years of exile from Northumbria but whom he had not otherwise been able to reward with lands or the wherewithal to keep themselves. As head of the monastery, he appointed his kinsman, Tatberht.

Wilfrid's death took place at Oundle[M] in April 710. His body was taken back to Ripon for burial. At a commemoration of his death, Stephen reports that in the evening, 'The abbots went out with the whole community to compline in the evening twilight. Suddenly they saw a wonderful sign in the sky, namely a white arc, surrounding the whole monastery, like a rainbow by day but without its various colours.' Recent work has established that

in 712 there was indeed a moonbow of exceptional brightness
that would have been visible on this particular anniversary of
Wilfrid's death.

Bede gives us the epitaph that was inscribed above Wilfrid's
tomb:

> Here lie great WILFRID's bones. In loving zeal
> He built this church, and gave it Peter's name,
> Who bears the keys by gift of Christ the King;
> Clothed it in gold and purple, and set high
> In gleaming ore the trophy of the Cross;
> Golden the Gospels four he made for it,
> Lodged in a shrine of gold, as is their due.
> To the high Paschal Feast its order just
> He gave, by doctrine true and catholic,
> As our forefathers held; drove error far,
> And showed his folk sound law and liturgy.
> Within these walls a swarm of monks he hived
> And in their statutes carefully laid down
> All that the Fathers by their rule command.
> At home, abroad, long time in tempests tossed,
> Thrice fifteen years he bare a bishop's charge,
> Passed to his rest, and gained the joys of Heaven.
> Grant, Lord, his flock may tread their shepherd's
> path! [v,19]

What Bede's feelings about Wilfrid really were has been a matter
of endless speculation among historians – it would be surprising
had they not been mixed.

RUTHWELL · Dumfriesshire

Almighty God stripped himself/when he wished to mount the
gallows/brave in the sight of all me. I dared now bow. /
I [raised aloft] a powerful king.
The Lord of Heaven / I dared not tilt. Men insulted the
pair of us together.
I was drenched with blood.

(NORTH SIDE OF THE CROSS)

Christ was on the cross. / But eager ones came hither from afar.
Noble ones came together. I beheld all that.
I was terribly afflicted with sorrows. / I bowed.
Wounded with arrows / they laid him down, limb-weary;
They stood at the shoulders of the corpse.
They looked upon the Lord.

(SOUTH SIDE OF THE CROSS)

Ruthwell, under the Romans, is likely to have been a place of importance because of its proximity to Hadrian's Wall and its use as an iron-smelting centre. As an early Christian settlement, at the extreme northwestern corner of Northumbria, what may have mattered most was its closeness to the sea, to the trading settlements around the Solway Firth and to the monastic community of Hoddom about 10 miles (16 km) away. Today, what makes Ruthwell remarkable is the preservation of its cross, an immense monument of red sandstone, over 5 metres (17 ft) tall. In the seventeenth century, the images on the cross caused it much suffering at the hands of iconoclasts; later restoration work compounded the challenge of decoding the meanings of the cross, and even now there is much about its symbolism that remains controversial. Nonetheless, some conclusions at least are possible.

The cross is one of the earliest examples we have of the new kind of decorated cross which the Northumbrians created. Each of the four sides of the cross is richly carved. The base and cross head of the two broad faces have four panels depicting Gospel and early Christian scenes, together with Latin inscriptions; the two narrower sides, adorned with vine scrolls, birds and animals, are inscribed with runes.

These runic inscriptions are recognised now as precursors of the Anglo-Saxon poem *The Dream of the Rood*, a poem which relates the crucifixion of Christ from the viewpoint of the tree cut down to fashion the cross on which Christ must die. Such use of vernacular poetry, together with the possible dating of the cross to the early eighth century, made irresistible the claim by earlier scholars that here was the work of Caedmon, Bede's cowherd hero, who at the prompting of Abbess Hilda of Whitby,[N] put into the vernacular the whole story of the creation. The rigorous scholarship of more recent years has made such a theory untenable, but the now-recognised anonymity of the poem does nothing to detract from its importance, nor deflect us from pondering its early appearance on the cross. Does this use of the vernacular suggest that this was a preaching cross, designed to make intelligible the central truths of Christianity to a newly converted people?

The possibility of preaching before the Ruthwell Cross cannot be ruled out, but Anglo-Saxon crosses would seem to have had multiple uses and diverse meanings. At Ruthwell, interpretation of the cross is bedevilled from the start by the uncertainty (thanks to the work of the iconoclasts) of where it originally stood. Can we even be sure which is its 'front' and which its 'back'? Does it matter (as the siting of cross at Bewcastle[N] would suggest) where the cross was positioned in relation to the rising and the setting of the sun? It would be hard to see how it could be otherwise, given the importance attached in early Christian calendrical calculations to the natural rhythms of the year. Thus Christ, born at the time of the winter solstice, was believed to have been both conceived and crucified during the spring equinox; the autumn equinox, meanwhile, was marked by the conception of John the Baptist; the summer solstice by his birth. It would therefore be fitting for the 'front' of the Ruthwell Cross to face, not eastwards as at present, but rather westwards; thus any putative Ruthwell monk, facing east (the traditional stance) to say his early morning prayers before the cross would have contemplated, as the sun rose, the panel of John the Baptist, depicted holding a lamb, symbol of the eucharist. (The translated runes quoted at the head of this entry follow what would seem to be the original sides.)

As for preaching, it is worth pointing out that the runes can never have been easy to read, while the panels require greater interpretive understanding than Bede, for one, would have expected any neophyte to need. Yet precisely what is striking about Christianity in Bede's time is, on the one hand, the challenge of providing basic catechetical instruction to new converts in inaccessible places and, on the other, the eagerness to grasp and interpret the latest doctrinal teaching emanating from Rome on topics such as the precise nature of Christ's human will. Despite their complexity, the carvings of the Ruthwell Cross, together with its poetry, can perhaps be imagined as tackling both these tasks.

The new convert, baptised very likely in the nearby Thwaite Burn, could not but be mesmerised by the spectacle of this mighty cross: stunning both in size, in craftsmanship and – most shocking of all for today's spectator – in its colour. The original cross did not enjoy 'natural' colouring. It was bright, even gaudy (there is a coloured reconstruction in the Manchester Museum) and its message was bold. Its runes proclaimed a man 'drenched in blood', who had 'willed to mount the gallows' but who yet was a 'lord of heaven' and a 'powerful king'. Its carved panels and Latin inscriptions meanwhile told of a God who could cure the blind, who forgave sinners and whom even beasts and dragons recognised as 'the saviour of the world'. (The panels on the west depict John the Baptist, Christ in Majesty adored by beasts, Paul and Anthony and the Flight to or from Egypt; and on the east, the Visitation, Mary Magdalene at Christ's feet, the healing of the blind man, and the Annunciation.)

It may be worth noting the likelihood that the Ruthwell Cross would have been further damaged by the iconoclasts had there not been a view that it represented the 'Celtic church', a body independent from and even antagonistic to the Church of Rome. Even allowing for those differences (see Whitby[N]) that did indeed exist between the practices of missionaries from Rome and those from Lindisfarne (see page 43), the idea that there was ever a separate Celtic church has long been discredited, and with it the idea that the beasts at Christ's feet (as found on both the Ruthwell and Bewcastle crosses) represented some particular Celtic fondness of animals. In fact, the iconography here depends upon a verse from the 'Canticle of Habakkuk' – 'between two living creatures you will become known' – a canticle long used in the Roman liturgy and about which Bede himself wrote a treatise – though this is not, of course, to dispute the special relationship St Cuthbert (*see* Coldingham[N]) may have had with otters...

SEAHAM · County Durham

Now, at that time, it happened that the man of God [John of Beverley] was called by [Puch] to dedicate a church, and after the dedication, the man invited the bishop to dine at his house. [v, 4]

St Mary's, a church situated in a striking position on cliffs by the edge of the town of Seaham, appears first in the historical record in 934, when King Athelstan visited Chester-le-Street, showering the community with many gifts, one of them being St Mary's Church, Seaham.

Architecturally, however, Seaham can claim to date from the seventh century, sharing as it does many features with Escomb.[N] It has similarly constructed windows, the same long nave, evidence of a western annexe and use of Roman stone. The question that remains is what kind of an establishment was Seaham? Historians have recently placed growing emphasis on the importance of monks and minsters as the providers of pastoral care in early Anglo-Saxon England, to the point at which there is now considerable scepticism as to whether small private churches (of the kind known to be plentiful on the Continent) played any role whatsoever in the conversion of England. Bertha's chapel of St Martin's in Canterbury (*see* page 11) would, however, seem to be one such example and, given the links between the royal houses of Northumbria and Kent, it is at least probable that there may have been Northumbrian aristocrats eager to build private chapels on the same model as Bertha's, both for use during their lifetimes and as a memorials to themselves and their families after their deaths. If so, then it is just possible that Seaham (and maybe Escomb[N] too) were such churches. A miracle performed by John of Beverley,[N] as recorded by Bede, lends substance to this idea: it took place in the house of a nobleman, Puch, who had asked the bishop to dedicate a church, and had then prevailed upon him to stay on for a meal. (As Bede tells the story, however, the point is not the dedication of the church or Puch's hospitality, but rather the cure of Puch's wife by John of a disease from which she had been suffering for several weeks.)

TYNEMOUTH · Northumberland

At the time he [Herebald] was one of the bishop's clergy, but is now ruling as abbot over the monastery which is at the mouth of the Tyne [Tynemouth]. [v, 6]

Tynemouth is mentioned only incidentally by Bede in one of the stories he has to tell about John of Beverley[N] when John was bishop of York. It was a prime target for the Vikings, and nothing remains now of Herebald's minster (though the ruins of the later castle and priory are justly famed and some fragments of Anglo-Saxon sculpture in the museum give a hint of its earlier glory).

In the late eleventh century, it claimed to be where King Oswine's body was taken after his murder at Gilling.[N] In 792 it had indeed been the chosen minster for the burial of King Osred, but whether this would suggest that Tynemouth had special claims to be a royal mausoleum or that the names 'Osred' and 'Oswine' got confused must remain an open question. What is clear, however, is the extent of Bernician royal and ecclesiastical power at the mouth of the Tyne and a reminder that Northumbria had minsters which barely surface in Bede's narrative.

WEARMOUTH & JARROW • County Durham

I, Bede, servant of Christ and priest of the monastery of St Peter and Paul, which is at Wearmouth and Jarrow, have, with the help of God and to the best of my ability, put together this account of the history of the Church of Britain and of the English people in particular, gleaned either from ancient documents, or from tradition or from my own knowledge. [v, 24]

It has long been customary to regard Wearmouth and Jarrow as sister foundations, united under the rule of one abbot. Such, indeed, is the impression Bede gives, notably in the *Abbots of Wearmouth and Jarrow*, written (probably) soon after the death of Abbot Ceolfrid in 716. Recently, however, the differences in the foundation stories between the two houses have come under close scrutiny and a rather different story is now emerging.

Wearmouth had been founded in 674 by the 'millionaire' monk, Benedict Biscop. Biscop was a Northumbrian nobleman who, at the age of twenty-five had left the court of King Oswiu to go to Rome. Rome captivated him. He became a monk in southern Gaul, though this did not interrupt his journeying. The spiritual and the aesthetic appeal of Rome never left him. In 668 he was back in Rome at just the moment when Theodore was chosen as the new archbishop of Canterbury (*see* pages 10–11) and it became Biscop's task to escort Theodore to England and to help him in his earliest years at Canterbury.

When Biscop conceived the idea of establishing his own foundation is not clear, but Northumbria was not his first choice: his intention was to found a community in Wessex and but for the death of his friend, the king of Wesssex, in 672, he might never have returned to his native Northumbria. But return he did, to be given land by King Ecgfrith for the foundation of the community at Wearmouth (named after the river Wear), over which he presided as abbot until his death in 689 or 690 (albeit often as an absentee for his journeys abroad continued).

King Ecgfrith, meanwhile, had plans for a community of his own, for a specifically royal foundation to be built near the mouth of the Tyne at Jarrow. Ecgfrith was an empire-builder: what could better glorify his achievements than a royal monastery? It can be no accident that Jarrow was dedicated on the eve of the king's departure to Scotland in 685; the foundation stone set in the chancel arch of the present church provides an exact date: *23rd April in the 15th year of King Ecgfrith and in the 4th year of Abbot Ceolfrith, founder by the guidance of God, of the same church.* The likelihood is that Ecgfrith thereafter mustered his ships at the Jarrow harbour. It was his death just a month later, on 20 May 685, at the battle of Nechtanesmere, that obliterated the chance of any triumphant return.

Ecgfrith's successor, Aldfrith, had no such particular use for the new foundation. Five or so years later came a solution: by now both abbots of Wearmouth – Biscop and his deputy, Sicgfrith – were ill: 'They were put together in the same place by their servants, with both their heads on the same pillow.' (*Abbots of Wearmouth and Jarrow*, page 13) They talked; they summoned Ceolfrith, abbot of Jarrow, and reached a conclusion. The houses should henceforth be joined, coming under the leadership of

Ceolfrith himself, a man for whom Bede himself felt deep affection; when in 716 Ceolfrith abdicated to go to Rome, his departure upset Bede to such an extent that it interrupted his *Commentary on the Book of Samuel*. (In the early days of Jarrow, when plague had incapacitated the community, it was only Ceolfrith and one small boy, thought by some to be Bede himself, who had maintained the singing of the offices.)

Today, only the west wall of Anglo-Saxon Wearmouth and the two lower storeys of the west tower still stand, but even they provide some sense of the grandeur and dazzling novelty of Biscop's foundation. Strange carved creatures – half fish, half bird – adorn the western archway; above, it's possible to make out a frieze of animals, above that again a haloed figure, perhaps of St Peter. Except perhaps at Hexham,[N] nothing like this had been attempted in England before; Biscop's vision was based on what he had seen in Italy and Gaul and until his commission there was no English exemplar. The building of it surpassed the skill of local craftsmen so that Biscop had to send for stonemasons and glaziers from Gaul. Such a church also of course needed furnishings, and here, too, what was at hand was inadequate.

Biscop therefore set off again to search 'in the area around Rome [for] attractive and useful items for his church which could not even be found in Gaul'. He returned with a 'countless number' of books and relics and also with many paintings: 'His aim was that all who came into the church, even those who did not know how to read, should always gaze on the lovely sight of Christ and his saints wherever they looked' (*Abbots of Wearmouth and Jarrow*, page 35).

Right next to this main church, at its east end, was a chapel dedicated to the Virgin, where Biscop himself was later buried.

At both of these churches, archaeological research has revealed a grand roofed walkway, complete with coloured glass windows, which led southwards to a number of buildings before it reached the boundary wall. To the west was a cemetery, seemingly used by the laity.

Biscop apart, Wearmouth had other special dead: in the nineteenth century, under the tower, a stone sarcophagus was discovered buried under a number of slabs that had in it the bones of about twelve people. Tempting though it is to imagine these belonged to Wearmouth's earliest community, we cannot for certain tell. In the chapter house an impressive stone grave-marker of yellow sandstone commemorates a certain priest, Herebericht, perhaps a contemporary of Bede's.

And what, then, of Jarrow? In design, Jarrow seems to have been not dissimilar from Wearmouth – it will always have seemed, like Wearmouth, startlingly and strikingly Mediterranean. Little of the original building except for the chancel and lower end of the tower has survived, though displayed in the church are some important fragments of stained glass and of Anglo-Saxon sculpture, notably the wall slab of Roman stone, possibly added a few decades after the dedication of the church, on which there is a cross surrounded by the words IN HOC SINGULARI SIGNO VITA REDDITUR MUNDO ('In this unique sign life was restored to the world'). Across the road, in the visitor centre, further treasures are on display, together with a model of Jarrow in the time of Bede, a reconstruction made possible thanks to the extensive archaeological work on the site over many decades. Here can be seen the layout of the whole site: the church together with its separate funerary chapel, the refectory, two dormitories, guest house and workshops.

Today, outside the visitor centre, in the surrounding fields, appropriate breeds of animals and selected crops recall the description Bede gives of one caretaker abbot of Wearmouth, Eosterwine, who used to make a point of showing his humility by taking his turn at farm chores. Once past the particularly fine pigs, visitors may be tempted to climb the incline pointing the way towards a modern replica of a Northumbrian cross. Then comes a shock – below, dominating the landscape, stretches a vast Nissan car plant. Yet this may not be as inappropriate as it immediately seems; Jarrow was once a centre of industry. The glaziers who worked here came from overseas, as did much else besides; olive oil and pepper had to be imported, likewise luxury materials such as gold, silver and ivory. And of course, there were books.

Both Wearmouth and Jarrow had quite exceptional libraries, made remarkable both because of the books which Biscop and then Ceolfrith had acquired for them, and without which much of Bede's scholarly work would have been impossible, and because of the books made in their own scriptorium. A magnificent example of the scriptorium's workmanship is the massive illustrated copy of the Bible known as the *Codex Amiatinus*, the oldest complete copy of the Vulgate to have survived. When Ceolfrith set sail in 716, this was the Bible he was taking with him as a present for the pope. Two further copies had also been made – one each for Wearmouth and Jarrow. Since Ceolfrith died before reaching Rome, he was never able to present the Pope with his copy. Years later, this same book found a safe haven in a monastery in northern Italy, and so closely did it resemble its Mediterranean exemplars that it was not until the nineteenth century that its Anglo-Saxon provenance was recognised. Only by chance have fragments of the other Wearmouth and Jarrow copies survived, but the *Codex Amiatinus* amply demonstrates the sumptuous quality of the books that Ceolfrith's scriptorium produced and to which Bede himself may have contributed his own scribal skills.

To make enough vellum for these three bibles, it has been calculated it would have been necessary first to slaughter 1,550 calves. Better not tell that to the animals peacefully grazing next to the Jarrow Visitor Centre.

WHITBY • North Riding of Yorkshire

All who knew Hild[a], the handmaiden of Christ and abbess,
used to call her mother because of her outstanding devotion
and grace. She was not only an example of holy life to all who
were in the monastery but she also provided an opportunity for
salvation and repentance to many who lived far away and who
heard the happy story of her industry and virtue. [IV, 23]

Whitby today is probably best known for its association with Dracula. That evocative sunset of 'flame, purple, pink, green and violet and all tints of gold' of Bram Stoker's novel, combined with the absolute blackness he described as descending on the harbour as Dracula draws near in the shape of a huge dog, has captured the imagination in a way a community of seventh-century holy women and men might not seem able to do. But the community at Whitby does have its own gripping tales to tell.

Hilda, the first abbess of Whitby, was a great-niece of King Edwin of Northumbria. When she was baptised alongside the king at York[N] in 627, she would have been of marriageable age, perhaps with a husband already in the wings, but her fortunes changed dramatically after the death of Edwin at the battle of Hatfield Chase[N] (near Doncaster) in 633.

In the brutal year that followed, Hilda's father was poisoned and Hilda herself temporarily disappears from the historical record. She re-emerges, in Bede's pages, only in 647, on the point of departure for Gaul to join the monastic community where her sister, mother of King Eadwulf of East Anglia, was already established. But Aidan, bishop of Lindisfarne (*see* page 43), stopped her in her tracks and recalled her to Northumbria where she began her monastic life; within the year she was in charge of the monastery of Hartlepool.

Some ten years later, she was given the task of organising a new community comprising both men and women at a place Bede calls 'Streanaeshlach', on the land provided by King Oswiu not long after his victory at the battle of the Winwaed (*see* Leeds[N]) at which his arch-rival, King Penda of Mercia, had met his death.

A long-running controversy as to whether Streanaeshlach was in fact Whitby, rather than Strensall near York, has been settled to the satisfaction of most historians by the richness and complexity of the archaeological record at Whitby. Although the abbey ruins as seen today date only from the thirteenth century, extensive excavations have shown plentiful evidence of a seventh-century monastic settlement established there around the estuary of the river Esk. (Estuaries were much-favoured sites for early monastic houses, since they both needed and generated trade.) The early minster seems to have included forty to fifty stone cells, most likely intended for one or two nuns each, a number of wooden buildings and a significant cluster of workshops. Whitby was thus equipped to produce sculpture, fine metalwork, ceramics and books – *styli* (writing implements) have been found on the site.

Hilda was herself seemingly literate (we know of an angry letter of hers to the pope complaining about Wilfrid; *see* Ripon[N]), but the authority she exercised as abbess derived in the first place from her royal blood. Oswiu would have chosen Whitby for his new monastery, and Hilda as its abbess, as one of the ways of strengthening his position in the southern part of his kingdom, formerly the power-base of Hilda's great-uncle, King Edwin.

Deeply intertwined political and ecclesiastical rivalries in Northumbria continued, nonetheless, to erupt throughout King Oswiu's reign, and Whitby became a place both of reconciliation and of bitter controversies. Long-standing questions as to the correct shape of the tonsure and how to calculate the date of Easter (there was a so-called Irish and a so-called Roman method of doing this, each involving complicated lunar tables) were finally settled at Whitby, at a synod called in 664, but the rulings also split the Christian community (*see* Lindisfarne, page 43).

Hilda herself famously built an enormously successful bridge between Northumbria's Latin and vernacular cultures. As many as five future bishops were educated at Whitby under Hilda's aegis, but it was also during her term of office that Caedmon the cowherd (as Bede describes him) was given the gift of translating scripture into vernacular poetry and received encouragement and permission from Hilda to do so. Although it is no longer possible to attribute to Caedmon more than (at most) a few lines from the *corpus* once thought to be his, there is no gainsaying the importance attached to the use of the vernacular in spreading the new faith among the Anglo-Saxons (*cf.* Ruthwell[N]).

Hilda, Bede tells us, was much loved by all who knew her and deeply mourned when she died, both at Whitby and at the sister house at Hackness.[N] As he considers the influence of her life, Bede includes a telling story: when Hilda was no more than a baby, her mother, Breguswith, had a dream in which she was looking for her husband. She failed to find him, but while she was looking she discovered under her garment 'a most precious necklace, and as she gazed closely at it, it seemed to spread such a blaze of light that it filled all Britain with its gracious splendour' [IV, 23]. Necklaces of extraordinary quality and beauty have been found in many graves of the sixth and early seventh centuries. Christian women – notably Aethelthryth of Ely[EA] – were bothered by the vanity such jewellery encouraged, but new meanings as well as new uses for jewels did not prove hard to find.

At Whitby, no memorial has been found to Hilda, despite the impressively large number of seventh-century commemorative stones discovered there during the excavations. These stones have no decoration beyond a simple border and, in some cases, a plainly inscribed name. Are these, perhaps, skeuomorphs: stone versions, that is, of the type of wooden cross erected by King Oswald at Heavenfield?[N] If this is so, then these crosses may represent an important transitional stage in the development of the Northumbrian decorated cross. It has also been suggested recently that at least some of these stones (together with those of a similar shape at Lindisfarne; *see* page 43) were designed in part to help identify the dead at the time of the final resurrection; this would explain why they are often very small (some are no more than 19 cm (7 inches) high) and are sometimes buried under the head of the dead. They are quite simply a form of name tape.

Hilda was succeeded as abbess at Whitby first by Eanflaed,

widow of King Oswiu, and then by Eanflaed's daughter, Aelfflaed. When Eanflaed died (sometime after 685), she was buried, as Oswiu had been, within the church at Whitby. Aelfflaed added to this royal mausoleum by recovering the remains of her maternal grandfather Edwin's body from Hatfield Chase,[N] where he had fallen in battle, and bringing them for reburial to Whitby. (His head had been rescued earlier and, according to Bede, taken to York.[N]) No significant cult developed around Edwin, as Aelfflaed perhaps had hoped, but his presence in her church, dedicated to St Peter, will have been a constant reminder to her community of the role of king and pope in the conversion of Northumbria. It is also possible that among those commemorated at Whitby was Edwin's sister, Acha; a cross-head preserved there, inscribed '+AHHAE+' is likely to be hers.

Aelfflaed had been a baby when she had been entrusted by her father to the care of Hilda (still then at Hartlepool) in fulfilment of the vow he had made on the eve of the battle of the Winwaed (*see* Leeds[N]). Her apprenticeship under Hilda thus began early and she became in every way a fitting heir to Hilda and her position in the kingdom. Just as Hilda had been consulted by 'kings and princes', according to Bede, so, too, did Aelfflaed play a leading part in the affairs of Northumbria. Notably, in 685, she summoned Cuthbert to Coquet Island (some 20 miles (32 km) south of the Farne Islands) to talk to him about the future of the kingdom – she had a pronounced sense of foreboding that her brother Ecgfrith, king of Deira and Bernicia, would be slain at the battle of Nechtanesmere within the year – and to find out whether Cuthbert would agree now to become a bishop, which he did. In 706 (according to Stephen's *Life of Wilfrid*), it was Aelfflaed – 'always the comforter and best counsellor of the kingdom' – who came to the Synod of Nidd to discuss with King Osred and the Archbishop of Canterbury the Wilfridian question (*see* Ripon[N]).

Aelfflaed appears in Bede's *Life of Cuthbert* as 'a wise woman and learned in Holy Scripture'. Further evidence is provided by a letter she wrote *c*.700 to an abbess of Trier, asking for her protection of an (unidentified) English abbess who was making her way on pilgrimage to Rome. It was also while Aelfflaed was abbess at Whitby, and possibly at her command, that the *Life of Pope Gregory* was written, a *Life* that can claim to be one of the earliest works of hagiography to have been written in England.

Visible from Whitby, on the next promontory, is Lythe, a place rich in fragments from a Viking-age cemetery. There are, however, two pieces – a door jamb and a finial – which date from an earlier period, giving rise to the suggestion that Lythe might once have been a cell belonging to the Whitby estate.

WHITHORN · Wigtownshire

> His [St Ninian's] episcopal see is celebrated for its church,
> dedicated to St Martin where his body rests, together with those of
> many other saints. The see is now under English rule. This place
> which is in the kingdom of Bernicia is commonly called Whithorn,
> the White House, because Ninian built a church of stone there,
> using a method unusual among the Britons. [III, 4]

St Ninian of Whithorn was an important figure for Bede, a Briton of unimpeachable orthodoxy who had been to Rome and who by his preaching had converted the southern Picts. But establishing who St Ninian was, even the century in which he lived (was it the fifth or the sixth century? Were there two St Ninians? Should the name be Finnian?) are questions which continue to elude definitive answers. But what is clear is that Whithorn was an early Romano-British Christian settlement, an important port for trade with Ireland and the Isle of Man. At some point in the late seventh or early eighth century, it fell to the Northumbrian advance, and a see was established with Pehthelm as its first bishop.

Pehthelm was no hedge-priest: he was a pupil of Aldhelm's (cf. Malmesbury[W]) and well enough regarded to be consulted by Boniface of Nursling[W] on a point of canon law. It was through him that Bede heard of the vision of the reprobate Mercian nobleman. This man was evidently an associate of King Cenred. Cenred (who in due course resigned his kingdom in 709 to go to Rome) had often warned his friend that he should make his confession, lest he die unshriven. But even when he was ill, the man refused, promising that he would do so when he had recovered; otherwise his friends would mock him for doing something 'for fear of death'. But die he did, and was presented in his last hours with an 'exceedingly small book' by an evil spirit, in which were written his good deeds and 'a volume of enormous size and almost unbearable weight', containing all his sins, written down 'in the most hideous handwriting'. Whereupon, 'two very wicked spirits who had daggers in their hands' struck the Mercian 'one on the head and one on the foot'; 'these daggers' (explained the man) 'are now creeping into the interior of my body with great torment and, as soon as they meet, I shall die and... be dragged down into the dungeons of hell' [v,13].

Although the Irish of Northumbria, whom Bede so deeply admired, built their first churches of wood, building in stone undoubtedly represented the advance of the Mediterranean-style Christianity that Bede was so anxious to promote. In one of the penultimate chapters of the *Ecclesiastical History*, Bede describes how Nechtan, king of the Picts, had become convinced of the need to adopt the Easter dates as calculated at Rome and agreed at Whitby.[N] At the same time he asked Abbot Ceolfrith 'for builders to be sent to build a church of stone in their country after the Roman fashion, promising that it should be dedicated in honour of the blessed chief of the apostles' [v,21]. The belief that Whithorn already had a stone church (together with its dedication to St Martin – *cf.* Canterbury, page 11) may have been seen as an indication that however 'British' the foundation, it was also in some particular way 'unusual'.

Today it remains a site particularly worth visiting, both because of the natural beauty of its position on the coast and because of the added attraction nearby of St Ninian's cave, a place of pilgrimage where seventh- and eighth-century hermits may well have lived.

YEAVERING · Northumberland

During these days, from morning till evening he [Paulinus] did nothing else but instruct the crowds who flocked to him from every village and district in the teaching of Christ. [11, 14]

Yeavering lies alongside a narrow stretch of road at the edge of the Cheviot Hills, close by the river Glen, in what was once the kingdom of Bernicia. But for a notice in the lay-by, it would be easy to drive past, noticing no more than a pleasant expanse of green fields beneath a looming hill, the Yeavering Bell, but it is now believed that this is the place Bede knew as Ad Gefrin, a British name meaning 'Hill of the Goats'. Aerial photography in the 1950s, followed by excavations, revealed a complex history for the site, with origins stretching back to an Iron Age hill fort, and long usage as a cultic centre.

Under the new Anglo-Saxon regimes of the sixth and seventh centuries, an ambitious building programme led to the erection of a series of halls, and most remarkably a wedge-shaped grandstand, akin to a Roman amphitheatre, but built of wood, designed to seat 150. It was enlarged thereafter to take twice as many, all of whom would have sat facing a tiny dais on which only a few notables could have stood. It is impossible to date any of the buildings with precision, but one or two general conclusions based on the archaeological evidence can still be drawn.

Up until Edwin's public acceptance of Christianity, Yeavering was the site of a pagan temple; inside the east door was a pit, brimming with skulls of oxen, recalling the Anglo-Saxon custom (as related by Pope Gregory) of the sacrifice 'of many oxen to devils'. But after Edwin's baptism at York,[N] Yeavering seemed to have been adapted to make it suitable for Christian worship. Wooden post-holds, of no structural significance, perhaps erected for pagan idol worship, could now be seen as symbols of the Christian cross. In this way, Yeavering may have been given a new lease of life as a place where (in accordance with Gregory's instructions) the people 'might make themselves huts from the branches of trees around the churches which have been converted out of shrines' [1, 30]. Thus it could have become, in line with papal thinking, a reasonable venue for further feasts. Such close adherence to Gregory's instructions is not implausible given that Northumbria's first missionary was Paulinus,

one of the monks sent by Pope Gregory himself in 601 to further
the Christian cause. Paulinus, according to Bede, at some point
spent thirty-six days at Yeavering with King Edwin and Queen
Aethelburh, catechising and baptising converts in the waters of
the nearby river Glen. (Bede is not explicit on this point, but it is
likely the thirty-six days represent a season of Lent as calculated
by Gregory the Great – that is, forty-two days minus six Sundays,
to be followed by mass baptisms at Easter.)

Paulinus's marathon missionary efforts raise a number of
questions. Clearly he preached to his neophytes; but could any
of them have been British Christians (*see* Elmet[N])? Did Paulinus
perhaps use the Yeavering grandstand? Was it his idea that it
should be built? (And is it therefore a later addition to the site?)
It resembles nothing in England at the time, bar the Roman theatre in Canterbury, which Paulinus will of course have known
well, so this would seem a possibility. But where did Paulinus
and the court party stay? Did Yeavering's halls have separate
sleeping quarters? There are no sure answers here, but the quality of the wood used in the buildings, together with the height
of walls and roofs, suggests these halls possessed considerable
grandeur. (The most magnificent measured approximately 25 x
12 metres (82 x 39 ft) with walls made of planks some 14 cm (5 ½
inches) thick.)

Undoubtedly these were places (*cf.* now Lyminge[K]) that provided the comfort, warmth and security to which the tale of the
sparrow flying through the hall in wintertime (as recounted near
Goodmanham[N]) so vividly testifies.

Yeavering, too, makes a plausible setting for a story preserved
in the Whitby[N] *Life of Gregory the Great*: here king and attendants
have gathered together 'for the catechising of those who hitherto

were in the bonds not only of heathendom, but of illegal wed-
lock also'. There's a sudden noise: it's a crow, 'croaking from
an unpropitious quarter of the sky'. Startled, the crowd, used to
taking such omens seriously, stood stock-still, whereupon the
bishop took action, ordering one of his servants to shoot the crow
and to bring him the arrow. Thereafter the bishop's catechising
continued, ending with a flourish; the arrow was produced and
the bird (and by implication paganism) pronounced well and
truly dead.

At some point – Bede does not specify exactly when, but 'in the
time of the kings who followed Edwin' – Yeavering was deserted
in favour of a new palace, at Maelmin, identified now as Milfield,
near Wooler, so just 2 miles (3.2 km) away. Like Yeavering,
Maelmin was an ancient sacred site, home to a henge erected
c.2000 BC. As yet, no reason for the move has been suggested.

YORK • West Riding of Yorkshire

[Edwin] *was baptized at York on Easter Day, 12 April, in the*
church of St Peter the Apostle, which he had hastily built of
wood while he was a catechumen and under instruction before
he received baptism. [II, 14]

By 601, just four years after the arrival of the first missionaries
from Rome, Pope Gregory the Great already had plans for York:
'We wish,' he wrote to St Augustine, 'to send as bishop to the
city of York, one whom you yourself shall decide to consecrate'
[I, 29].

For a Roman such as Gregory, York was a city of great significance, for it was here, in 306, that Constantine the Great had

been hailed as emperor. Seven years later, on the eve of the battle of Milvian Bridge, Constantine is reported to have seen a cross in the sky with the caption *hoc signo victor eris* ('by this sign you will be victorious'). Victorious Constantine certainly was, and his acceptance of Christianity, however faltering, can be dated from this moment. Constantine's Christian credentials were further enhanced by the actions of his mother, Helena, for it was Helena, thought to be of British birth, who, while on pilgrimage to the Holy Land, allegedly discovered the cross on which Christ had been crucified, a discovery later celebrated in the ninth-century Anglo-Saxon poem, *Elene*. Gregory himself recalled both Constantine and Helena as role models for, respectively, Aethelbert of Kent and his queen, Bertha (*cf.* Heavenfield[N]).

Very little has survived from Anglo-Saxon York, but for a king such as Edwin who was notable for his imperial pretensions – Bede tells us, wherever he walked he had carried before him a standard which the Romans called a *tufa* – York was an obvious choice in which to display his newly adopted Christian faith, and it was to York that Edwin hastened after his very public conversion near Goodmanham.[N] Here he erected, with all speed, a wooden church in preparation for his baptism on Easter Day, 627 (Easter being the traditional date for this sacrament).

Thereafter, Bede tells us, Edwin 'set about building a greater and more magnificent church of stone, under the instruction of Paulinus, in the midst of which the chapel which he had first built was to be enclosed' [11, 14]. Some limestone grave-markers of a Merovingian design have survived from this church, but little else. The chosen site may have been in the southern courtyard of the Roman basilica, which in Edwin's day is likely to have still been standing.

But Edwin did not live to see his building completed; this task fell to King Oswald, though Oswald (as a Bernician) was more interested in the northern part of his kingdom and it was not until Wilfrid became its bishop, following the demise of Lindisfarne (*see* page 43) as Northumbria's episcopal see after the synod of Whitby[N] of 664, that York once again flourished. Paulinus's church was by then in serious disrepair – the roof was leaking and there were bird droppings everywhere – but Wilfrid (according to his biographer, Stephen) lovingly restored it, providing it with windows of glass and enriching it with both precious objects and land.

None of this, however, would be enough to protect Wilfrid from the wrath he was to incur in the late 670s from the king of Northumbria, Ecgfrith. In 678 Wilfrid was banished from Northumbria and York was given instead to Bosa, formerly of Whitby.[N] Years of wrangling followed, but when finally the dust had settled and peace was restored, the claims of York to be an archiepiscopal see could be revived. In 735, under Egbert (a former student of Bede's and a recipient of one of the few of Bede's surviving letters) these were made good.

To the new archbishop must be given the credit for the success of the school at York which by the close of the eighth century had become one of the foremost centres of learning throughout Europe. Egbert's successor, Archbishop Aelberht, further enriched and advanced the school as well as building a new basilica, grandiosely dedicated to Beneficient Wisdom, but he did not neglect Edwin's original church. In his poem on *The Bishops, Kings and Saints of York*, Alcuin, star pupil of the York school, has this to say:

> In the spot where Edwin, the warrior king, was baptised
> the bishop raised a great altar
> and covered it with gold, silver and jewels
>
> ...
>
> High above this altar he hung a chandelier,
> which held three great vessels, each with nine tiers.
> At the altar he erected the noble standard of the cross
> covering it entirely with most precious metals.
> It was all on a grand scale and built on a lovely design,
> Weighing many pounds in pure silver. (ll.1490–1500)

How dazzled the Vikings must have been when, in 866, they seized the city! Here, indeed, was booty. To gain any idea of its glory our best option now will be to look at the work of Anglo-Saxon craftsmen for patrons on the Continent, such as the Tassilo chalice and the Rupertus Cross – but both are housed in Austria. By way of consolation, the museum at York displays a magnificent late-eighth-century iron and copper alloy helmet, decorated with interlacing creatures on its nose-band. Across the crown runs a Latin inscription which, translated, reads: 'In the name of our Lord Jesus, the Holy Spirit, God and with all we pray. Amen. Oshere.' Who Oshere was we do not know; what we can say is that he was perhaps just the kind of warrior of whom Bede would have approved.

In a stern letter on the state of the church written to Egbert of York, his friend and colleague, Bede expresses his deep concern at the lack of fighting men ready to defend their homeland. Northumbria, he wrote, had urgent need of more bishops, priests and teachers, but it also needed men 'of the secular power' who could protect the kingdom from barbarians. Maybe Oshere was one such. His literacy we may doubt (the inscription was fixed on to the helmet in such a way that the letters are all back to front), but such a mishap will not have detracted from its power to protect a Christian warrior.

THE KINGDOM
OF THE
EAST ANGLES
or
EAST ANGLIA

So great was Edwin [of Northumbria's] devotion to the true worship, that he also persuaded Eorpwold, son of Raedwald and king of the East Angles, to abandon his idolatrous superstitions and, together with his kingdom, to accept the Christian faith and sacraments. [II, 15]

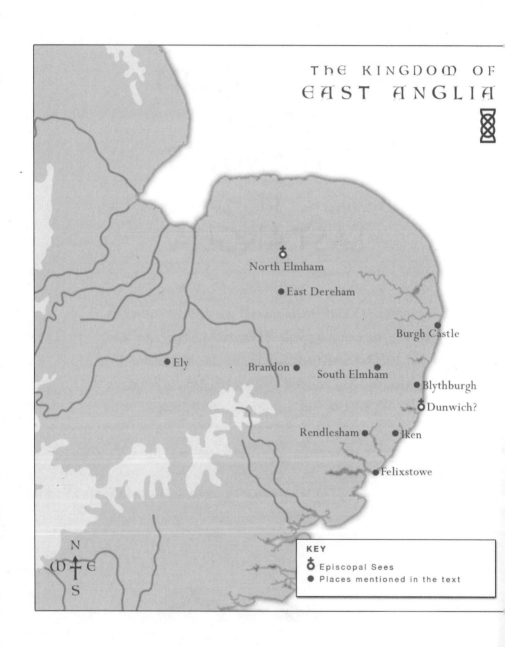

THє KINGDOM OF
EꓱST ꓱNGLIꓱ

North Elmham

East Dereham

Burgh Castle

Ely

Brandon

South Elmham

Blythburgh

Dunwich?

Rendlesham

Iken

Felixstowe

N
W E
S

KEY
Episcopal Sees
Places mentioned in the text

T he Viking raids of the ninth century caused such destruction to the monastic houses in East Anglia (and to their
archives) that information to supplement Bede's own
meagre account is difficult to find, even though in recent years
archaeology has added considerably to what was left of the written record. From the *Ecclesiastical History*, it would seem that Bede
himself believed that even within the lifetime of King Aethelbert
(c.560–616) the pre-eminence of Kent was being threatened by
the rise in power of King Raedwald of East Anglia (c.599–c.624).

Raedwald was thoroughly untrustworthy and susceptible
to the influence – for better and, ultimately in Bede's eyes, for
worse – of his wife. Bede's first story about Raedwald concerns
Edwin of Northumbria, in exile at the time from his own kingdom, to whom Raedwald had offered hospitality until, that is,
the moment when he was offered a big enough bribe to betray
Edwin and hand him over to the king of Northumbria, his
rival Aethelfrith. Raedwald was persuaded by his wife that to
accept such a bribe would be deeply dishonourable; and instead
Raedwald secured the throne of Northumbria for Edwin by win-
ning the battle fought on the Mercian border by the river Idle in
616, a battle in which Aethelfrith was slain, thus opening the way
for Edwin's own kingship of Northumbria.

Arguably it is that same sense of loyalty on the part of
Raedwald's wife that is at work in Bede's later story about her

when she prevents Raedwald from fully accepting Christianity. The suggestible Raedwald had evidently been converted to Christianity on a visit to King Aethelbert of Kent, but on returning home he was dissuaded by his wife from adhering strictly to his new faith. Instead, in the same temple, he kept one altar for pagan deities and another for the Christian God. Possibly this temple was at the East Anglian royal centre of Rendlesham.[EA]

Raedwald's syncretism has promoted endless speculation as to whether he could be the man, discovered in 1938, buried in lavish style within a ship at Sutton Hoo, by the river Deben, close to Woodbridge. Further excavations, completed only in 1997, have failed to establish whether the site was indeed the burial ground for the seventh-century kings of East Anglia and whether or not it was a defiant statement of paganism designed to defy East Anglia's Christian neighbours. But it is certainly clear that Raedwald would not have been alone in East Anglia in having doubts about the wisdom of conversion to the new faith: his successor, his son Eorpwold, persuaded by King Edwin of Northumbria to convert, was then killed by a pagan assassin – hardly an encouraging portent. Thereafter, as Bede tells the story, the kingdom retained its pagan beliefs for the next three years, until the accession of Sigeberht in c.630/31.

Sigeberht was Eorpwold's brother, but during Eorpwold's reign he had lived in exile in Francia, and while there he had become a Christian. On his return home he was supported in his efforts to convert his newly secured kingdom by Bishop Felix, a Burgundian bishop who, perhaps coincidentally, was at the time in search of a job in England. The archbishop of Canterbury assigned him East Anglia, giving him Dommoc as his see (often thought to be Dunwich[EA] – now under the sea – though

Blythburgh is another possibility, as is North Elmham). With the help of Kentish teachers procured by Felix, Sigeberht set about establishing schools for boys of the kind he had seen in Francia.

Seemingly less interested in being a king than a monk, Sigeberht in due course renounced his throne and entered a monastery, ceding power to his kinsman, Ecgric, who had already been ruling with him. Sigeberht seems, however, to have retained a strong degree of royal charisma, for when East Anglia was attacked some time later by Penda of Mercia, Sigeberht was literally dragged out of his monastery in the hope that his presence would give courage to the East Anglian army. The hope was in vain; Sigeberht adamantly refused to be armed and was killed, holding in his hand just a staff.

Penda's power continued to menace East Anglia throughout the reign of Sigeberht's (and Ecgric's) successor, King Anna. Burgh Castle[E] (Cnobheresburg) was apparently destroyed and Anna himself had to take refuge for a time amongst the Magonsaete (*see* introduction to Mercia, page 173). Anna nonetheless remained resolutely Christian, giving shelter at one point to Cenwalh of Wessex, whom he converted during his stay; as Bede explained, Anna 'was a good man and blessed with a saintly family'. Indeed, four of his daughters came to be venerated as saints (*see* Ely[EA]), though this did little immediate good to Anna. In 653/4, Penda again attacked East Anglia, this time killing Anna.

King Aethelhere, Anna's successor, seemingly decided on a new strategy: he would become Penda's ally, rather than remaining a target for his ambition. But the alliance proved fatal: both kings were killed fighting Oswiu of Northumbria at the battle of Winwaed in 655 (*see* Leeds[N]).

Thereafter East Anglia benefited from a period of remarkable peace and prosperity, in particular during the exceptionally long reigns assigned to kings Aldwulf (664–713) and Aelfwald (713–49), when East Anglia developed as a major trading centre. Of particular importance was Ipswich, but there were mints elsewhere: for example at Ely.[EA] The economic boom experienced at the time across the North Sea forms the backdrop to the missionary activities in northern Germany of Boniface of Nursling,[W] whom Bede so curiously omits from his History, alongside, it must be said, a number of East Anglia's early Christian heroes such as St Botulph of Icanhoe/Iken.[EA]

Had Bede been more forthcoming, or more knowledgeable about East Anglia, we might, for example, have been able to have put names to some of those who lived in Brandon in Suffolk, a recently excavated site that shows every sign of having once housed a monastic community. And, but for the fact that the local building stone is flint, we might have expected evidence of more sculptural work of the kind that has survived elsewhere from Anglo-Saxon England.

CNOBHERESBURG / BURGH CASTLE • Suffolk

Now [Fursa's] monastery was pleasantly situated close to the woods and the sea, in a Roman camp which is called in English Cnobheresburg, that is the city of Cnobhere. The king of that realm, Anna, and his nobles afterwards endowed it with still finer buildings and gifts. [III, 19]

According to Bede, Fursa, a freelance Irish missionary, together with his brother, Foillan, and a small band of like-minded countrymen, arrived in East Anglia during the reign of King Sigeberht, some time around 635. When he came to England, Fursa was already an experienced preacher whose reason for leaving his homeland was that he could no longer endure the 'noise of the crowds who thronged to him', but in making his decision to leave Ireland, Fursa was also following a distinctive Irish version of pilgrimage: voluntary exile from a much-loved homeland. King Sigeberht gave him Cnobheresburg, which may be (although this is by no means certain) the former Roman fort known now as Burgh Castle (cf. Reculver[K] and Bradwell[E]).

The success of Fursa's preaching in East Anglia, coupled with 'a vision of angels', prompted him to build the monastery on the site Sigeberht had provided for him and which, as Bede reports, King Anna further endowed. But even then Fursa proved restless. Leaving Foillan in charge of the monastery, he set off to live as a hermit with another brother, Ultan, for a year.

But then came threatening news of the approach of the pagan king of Mercia, Penda, and Fursa decided to seek refuge in Gaul; it was a prescient move, since during the ensuing conflicts in East Anglia Cnobheresburg was attacked and burnt. Fursa, meanwhile, built himself a monastery at Lagny-sur-Marne, a little way outside Paris. There he died and was buried, with great honour, some miles away at Péronne, and given a shrine Bede describes as very beautiful and befitting a body found to be incorrupt. All this Bede knew because he had before him a *Life* of Fursa; and this *Life*, possibly with just a few variations, we still have today.

The *Life* of Fursa was enormously influential throughout the Middle Ages, not primarily because of Fursa's missionary activities, or even because of his incorrupt body, but because of his visions. Of these the most important by far was the vision in which Fursa was taken by angels to the brink of heaven and hell, compelled to listen to diabolic accusations made against him, and to witness the four fires of hell. Throughout this ordeal, Fursa is protected by shining angels and granted the privilege of hearing their song, but nonetheless he did not come through unscathed: as punishment for having once received clothing from a dying man (described as a sinner), Fursa was burnt on his shoulder and on his jaw. Bede's source for his vision was not only the *Life* but also a Jarrow monk who knew a man who had himself met Fursa when he was in East Anglia and had heard of his visions from Fursa's own lips. And, added the informant, 'although it was during a time of severe winter weather and a hard frost and though Fursa sat wearing only a thin garment, yet as he told his story, he sweated as though it were in the middle of summer, either because of the terror or else the joy which his recollections aroused' [III,19].

To fully capture the intensity of Fursa's visions, it is worth reading not only Bede's summary but also his source, the *Life* of Fursa. In this work, the angels scintillate even more brightly than they do in Bede's *History* and the devils are even more alarming: 'filled with meagreness and filthiness and all horribleness; their heads did swell into the likeness of a casserole; but when they flew or did fight, Fursa could see no shape of their bodies but an horrible and flittering shadow… and he could never behold their faces because of the horror of darkness.' The stuff, indeed, of nightmares; no wonder Fursa sweated.

DOMMOC / DUNWICH · Suffolk

[Felix] received the seat of his bishopric in the city of Dommoc;
and when he had ruled over the kingdom as bishop for
seventeen years, he ended his life there in peace. [II, 15]

East Anglia's first see, Dommoc, may have been at Dunwich, but medieval Dunwich now lies under the sea. However, thanks to acoustic imaging and the work of researchers from Southampton University, far more can be said about it than might once have been thought possible.

Even so there is still much that remains uncertain and unknown; and other locations (such as the former Roman fort of Walton Castle, also engulfed by the sea) have been suggested as the site of Dommoc instead of Dunwich. Nonetheless, wherever Dommoc was we should imagine riches there and of precisely the kind that fascinated Bede. For in a tract written by Bede, probably for his friend, Nothhelm (in the years before Nothhelm became archbishop of Canterbury), he mentions having seen a richly illuminated book on the life of St Paul brought back from Rome by Cuthwine, bishop of the East Angles, whose see evidently was at Dommoc.

Soon after Bishop Felix's arrival in Essex, he and King Sigeberht set up a school for the education of boys on the model Sigeberht had witnessed in Gaul during his time in exile. Tradition holds that the school was at Soham (now in Cambridgeshire). William of Malmesbury believed that Felix had been buried at Soham before being 'appropriated' by the monks of Ramsey, some 20 miles (32 km) northwest of Soham, and there would seem no particular reason to doubt William's testimony.

ELY · Cambridgeshire

A year afterwards Aethelfryth was appointed abbess in the
district called Ely where she built a monastery. [IV, 19]

Nowhere outside Northumbria (with the exception of Canterbury) looms as large in Bede's *History* as does Ely. But there is
no mystery here: Ely had been founded by Queen Aethelthryth
of Northumbria after twelve years of unconsummated marriage
to King Ecgfrith. Released at last from her marriage vows, she
went first to Coldingham,[N] where Ecgfrith's aunt, Aebbe, was
abbess and where Bishop Wilfrid veiled her. (Ecgfrith had earlier
tried to bribe Wilfrid to persuade Aethelthryth to abandon her
vow of virginity.) Just one year later, in 673 – the date is provided
by the *Anglo-Saxon Chronicle* – Aethelthryth moved south to her
native kingdom of East Anglia, where she founded a community close to Ely, probably to the south of the present city on the
site of the future RAF Witchford of Second World War fame. In
679 (again, the *Chronicle* supplies the date) Aethelthryth died. She
was buried – and here the source is Bede – in a wooden coffin
which she instructed was not to be placed out of its due order; we
must imagine, then, that the dead were usually buried in rows,
and that as a mark of her humility Aethelthryth did not want special treatment.

Aethelthryth's life, in Bede's eyes, had been exemplary: not
only had she as queen preserved her virginity, despite the considerable pressures put upon her, she had also lived a life of admirable
asceticism as abbess. Bede supplies details: Aethelthryth wore
wool, rather than linen, and seldom took hot baths except
before the great feasts of Epiphany, Easter and Pentecost, when

it seems that everyone in the community washed as well. In his description of these occasions, Bede mentions Aethelthryth's 'attendants'. Even within monastic walls, aristocratic women such as Aethelthryth would have continued to live in some style, however austere their lives may have been compared to those who lived in royal palaces.

Sixteen years after Aethelthryth's death, her sister and successor as abbess of Ely, Seaxburh (widow of Eorcenberht, king of Kent, and abbess of Minster-in-Sheppey[K]), decided the time had come to give Aethelthryth a new tomb. It is possible that Seaxburh was inspired here by reports that her sister, Abbess Aethelburh of Faremoutiers-en-Brie in Gaul, had been discovered to be incorrupt on the occasion of her translation, for there seem as yet to be no English precedents. But whatever the motive or expectations, Aethelthryth's original coffin of wood was now considered insufficiently grand; the search was on for stone, a material in short supply in the marshy lands around Ely, but a posse of men from the community was sent out to try and find something suitable. The men got as far as Grantchester, some 17 miles (27 km) away, and there, near the walls of the deserted Roman fortress, they found the very thing: a coffin of white marble that even had a nicely fitting lid.

All was now ready for Aethelthryth's translation. A tent was erected around the original coffin. The community gathered to chant: men on one side, women on the other. The expectation was that Abbess Seaxburh would remove the skeleton so it could be washed before being placed in the newly acquired coffin, but to her astonishment, the abbess found her sister's body had not decayed. Particularly miraculous, according to Aethelthryth's former doctor, who was present at the translation, was the fact

that the incision he had made in order to drain a tumour on her
neck shortly before Aethelthryth died had now healed, leaving
only a tiny scar. (Aethelthryth is said to have considered the
tumour a just punishment for the necklaces of gold and pearls
she had worn in her youth.) The new coffin fitted the incorrupt
body perfectly; and the old coffin proved particularly efficacious
in curing eye diseases, while the original linen shroud with
which Aethelthryth's body had been clad proved also to have
healing qualities.

At this point in the narrative, Bede breaks into poetry, insert-
ing a hymn 'in elegiac metre' which he had composed in honour
of Aethelthryth's virginity. Bede also wrote in verse to honour
St Cuthbert of Lindisfarne (see page 43); it seems clear that he
composed far more poetry than has survived. In the list he gives
of his own writings, he mentions, for example, 'a book of hymns
in various metres and rhythms. A book of epigrams in heroic
and elegiac metre.' 'Holy Scripture', according to Bede, also
included songs; and his hymn to Aethelthryth thus followed biblical tradition.

What happened to Ely in the ninth century is uncertain.
Tradition has it that the Vikings sacked the monastery while
sparing the tomb of Aethelthryth, but it was the tenth-century
monastic reform movement that really secured the future of
Aethelthryth's cult. From then on and throughout the Middle
Ages, Aethelthryth in her marble tomb – seemingly the same tomb
Bede had described – continued to be venerated, as indeed was
her sister, Seaxburh. The twelfth-century History of Ely provides
graphic evidence of the affection felt throughout the neighbour-
hood for this particular 'lady' of their house. On one occasion,
a priest of a local parish failed to remind his congregation that

Seaxburh's feast day was forthcoming. His punishment for this oversight was an embarrassing attack of vomiting and diarrhoea as he tried to say Mass. So acute was the illness that the priest had to be led away and stripped of all his vestments. 'May God be praised,' concluded Ely's chronicler.

In the tenth century, yet a third sister was added to Ely's collection of saints. Her name was Wihtburg. Bede does not mention her, but her cult was originally based at East Dereham, a minster some 15 miles (24 km) east of Norwich. In 974, having been given Dereham, Abbot Byrhtnoth of Ely, 'a pirate in the cause of faith' (as the twelfth-century chronicler described him), stole Wihtburg's body (with particular happiness, once he had discovered it was incorrupt) and in the dead of night took her by land and by river to Ely where, it was said, Aethelthryth and Seaxburh joyfully welcomed her.

After the Norman Conquest of 1066, a major rebellion against William the Conqueror, c.1070, centred on the Isle of Ely, was led by the rebel Hereward the Wake and his ally, Earl Morcar. This was the rebels' stronghold and, as the twelfth-century history of the community records, it was on the incorrupt body of Aethelthryth that the rebels swore fidelity to their cause.

Both Aethelthryth's and Seaxburh's tombs were dismantled during the Reformation, but allegedly a hand of Aethelthryth's was rescued and is now located in the Church of St Etheldreda in London. Recently, moreover, excavations at Westfield Farm, Ely, have uncovered what may be the graves of a number of Aethelthryth's community. A cluster of graves (fifteen in all) of well-fed women, men and children (their teeth were in good condition and they had eaten more fish than would have been available to the population in general) dates from the later seventh century. The dead were arranged around one particular grave. This belonged to a young girl, who had been buried with a rich assemblage of jewels and two blue-green palm cups. Not all the graves, however, had grave goods; here, perhaps, is an example of a cemetery belonging to what has been called 'the final phase' of furnished burials. Whether it would have seemed disrespectful, or simply odd, to commit a body to the ground completely unadorned we will never know, but we can tell that it took time for old habits and practices surrounding funeral rites to be abandoned.

Yet more recently, in March 2012, a gold and garnet cross, slightly smaller but very similar to that worn by St Cuthbert of Lindisfarne, was found in a rare seventh-century boat burial of a young girl of about sixteen. Her grave was on the outskirts of modern-day Cambridge on land that perhaps belonged to the Ely minster.

ICANHOE / IKEN • Suffolk

In this year King Anna was slain, and Botwulf began to
build the minster at Icanho.

(Anglo-Saxon Chronicle, 654)

Bede's omission of St Botulph from his Ecclesiastical History is puzzling since it would seem impossible that he did not know about him: Bede's abbot, Ceolfrith, had himself visited Botulph while making his tour of minsters in order to learn more about their customs, and it is recorded in Ceolfrith's Life that Botulph was a man known to be 'of unparalleled life and learning, and full of the grace of the Holy Spirit'.

The Icanho of the *Anglo-Saxon Chronicle* is thought to be Iken, not least because of the discovery of a cross-shaft that had been built into the base of the church tower. It is now displayed inside the church. The shaft dates to the ninth century, but the nature of the site, on a 'ho' or spit of land (cf. Sutton Hoo in the introduction to the Kingdom of the East Angles, or East Anglia), close to the estuary of the river Alde (and on the opposite side from the sixth-century boat burial at Snape), would have made it a highly appropriate site for a seventh-century minster.

St Botulph came to be a popular saint – over sixty churches were dedicated to him and his relics were much sought after in the tenth century, though none seem to have been kept at Iken. The hand of Aethelwold, the tenth-century bishop of Winchester,[W] can be seen at work here: the relics were apparently divided by him into three, with the beneficiaries being Ely,[EA] Thorney and Westminster.[E] In the eleventh century, Folcard, abbot of Thorney, wrote St Botulph's *Life*.

Anna, the king referred to in the epigraph from the *Chronicle* above, was a king much admired by Bede. He met his death at the hands of Penda c.654. The tradition, for long disregarded, that he was buried not far from Iken at Blythburh has begun to seem distinctly more likely since the discovery there of an eighth-century leaf from a writing tablet, a luxury item that would suggest the existence of a high-status, literate settlement.

NORTH ELMHAM · Norfolk

When Boniface [bishop of the East Angles] died after being bishop for seventeen years Bisi was made bishop in his place and consecrated by Theodore. He was prevented from

> *administering his diocese by a serious illness so, while he*
> *was still alive, two bishops were chosen and consecrated in*
> *his place... and from then on until this day, the kingdom*
> *has had two bishops.* [IV, 5]

East Anglia's original see was at Dommoc, which, as we have seen, probably was Dunwich,[EA] though the Roman fort of Felixstowe also has its advocates, and it seems unlikely that the controversy will ever be resolved.

The new see created by Archbishop Theodore, which Bede mentions, presents a similar puzzle. Was it at North or at South Elmham? In Norfolk or in Suffolk? Both Elmhams have much to be said in their favour, not least the fact that both were close to former pagan burial sites which Christians might well have wanted to appropriate, and both have ruins. But even though there may never be consensus, there is now a majority view and it is in favour of North Elmham. The history of the see and its bishops remains, however, extraordinarily difficult to recover because of the disruptions caused by Viking conquests, followed by the absorption, until the mid-tenth century, of the see into the diocese of London. Thereafter, in 1075, the see was moved to Thetford, and finally, in the 1090s, to Norwich, the moves causing the lamentable loss of all of the see's episcopal archives.

RENDLESHAM · Suffolk

> *Swithhelm, the son of Seaxbald, was successor to Sigeberht. He*
> *was baptised by Cedd in East Anglia, in the royal village called*
> *Rendlesham, that is, the residence of Rendil.* [III, 22]

Rendlesham could be where King Raedwald of East Anglia had his temple, and where, shockingly (as reported by Bede), he had two altars, 'one for the Christian sacrifice and another small altar on which to offer victims to devils' [11, 15].

Even after the conversion of East Anglia, Raedwald's temple had clearly not been destroyed (perhaps in conscious obedience to Pope Gregory's injunction). Bede's information came from King Ealdwulf (d. 713) who 'used to declare that the temple lasted until his time and that he saw it when he was a boy' [11, 15]. Whether the temple was ever considered sufficiently Christianised to be used for Christian services is not known. A church would not, in fact, have been necessary for a baptism, though it would seem from Bede's accounts that river baptisms were reserved for peasants and that the nobility expected the more august ritual a building could provide.

Recent excavations at Rendlesham have shown how prosperous – and long-lived – a settlement it was; already being farmed in the late Iron Age, it became an important industrial centre in the early Anglo-Saxon period. Gold bullion and silver pennies dating from the late seventh century, together with the weights needed to guarantee fair transactions, suggest that until Ipswich challenged its position, Rendlesham was a major emporium. Even then, Rendlesham continued to thrive. Who Rendil was is not known.

THE KINGDOM
OF THE
EAST SAXONS
or
ESSEX

About this time the East Saxons, at the instance of King Oswiu, received the faith which they had once rejected when they expelled Bishop Mellitus. Now Sigeberht was king of this people, successor to Sigeberht the Small and friend of King Oswiu. The latter used to urge Sigeberht, on his frequent visits to the kingdom of Northumbria, to realise that objects made by the hands of men could not be gods... King Oswiu often put forward these and many other similar reasons to King Sigeberht in friendly and brotherly counsel until at last, supported by the consent of his friends, he believed. [III, 22]

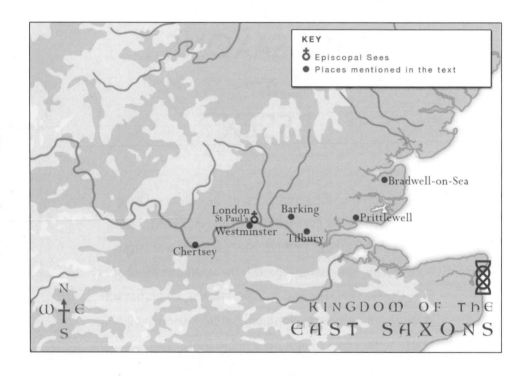

KEY
⚥ Episcopal Sees
● Places mentioned in the text

Bradwell-on-Sea

London
St Paul's
Barking
Prittlewell
Westminster
Tilbury
Chertsey

N
W—E
S

KINGDOM OF THE
EAST SAXONS

The kings of the East Saxons are memorable because their names always begin with the letter 'S'; they also differ from the rulers of Bede's other kingdoms since at no time were they dominant over any of the others. Thus none of these East Saxon kings ever had any pretensions to be any kind of *bretwalda* and indeed more often than not they were usually someone else's client-king.

This may seem surprising given that London[E] lay in the heart of the East Saxon kingdom, a city which, even with its Roman magnificence in tatters, was to remain throughout the Anglo-Saxon period an important trading centre: a lead seal, found at Putney, inscribed with Greek letters and thought to be a baling seal, suggests that precious Byzantine cloth was coming up the Thames not much later than the mid-sixth century. In the early seventh century, London had a mint producing gold coins (known as *tremissis*); by the time of Bede, London was, he tells us, 'an emporium for many nations who come to it by land and sea', and very possibly, as a story of Bede's suggests, the centre of a brisk slave trade [IV, 22]. When the missionary saint Boniface of Nursling[W] made his first journey to Frisia in 716, it was from London that he set sail. 'Lundenwich', his biographer explained, was a place 'where there was a market for the buying and selling of merchandise'.

London, not Canterbury (*see* page 7), was where Gregory the

Great had expected the southern English archbishop to reside (with a northern counterpart installed in York). Fate, in the shape of King Aethelbert of Kent, had decided otherwise, but it is nonetheless striking how quickly St Augustine, together with Aethelbert, moved to appoint Mellitus in 604 – so just four years after Augustine's own arrival at Canterbury – as bishop of the East Saxons with his see in London. Bede makes it clear that the initiative here came from Kent: the East Saxon king, Saeberht, was Aethelbert's nephew, but it was Aethelbert himself, according to Bede, who built St Paul's Cathedral[E] for the bishop and endowed it with land.

The new faith, coupled with the implications it carried of dependence on Kent, was not fully welcomed by the East Saxons and when Saeberht died (c.616] – buried, perhaps at Prittlewell[E] – there was serious trouble, indeed, in Bede's words, 'a tempest of troubles'. Saeberht had left three sons as his heirs but none of them had become Christians. Nonetheless, and despite their active worship of idols, they felt angered that Bishop Mellitus refused them communion: 'Why,' they asked, 'do you not offer us the white bread which you used to give our father Saba?' [II, 5]. Mellitus remained steadfast in his insistence that without baptism they could have no such thing. In mocking terms, the brothers chastised Mellitus for his obstinacy over so 'trifling a matter' and threw him out of the kingdom. God's revenge, as Bede saw it, was quick: an army from Wessex killed all three brothers. Yet it took a long time for the East Saxons to again accept Christianity. New missionaries were needed and a committed king. Such a one was Sigeberht II.

Sigeberht II was a Northumbrian protégé. The bitter rivalry between the pagan Penda of Mercia and the Christian Oswiu of

Northumbria dominated English politics in the mid-seventh century and each and every alliance makes sense in this context. Yet this does not mean that all conversions to Christianity can be understood only in political terms as the story of Sigeberht makes plain.

Sigeberht was persuaded by Oswiu of the futility of idol worship and was baptised in Northumbria by Finan, Bishop of Lindisfarne (*see* page 43), following the death of Bishop Aidan in 651. Oswiu thereupon recalled the priest Cedd, working at that time among the Middle Angles, and asked him to transfer his pastoral skills to the East Saxons. So successful was Cedd in this new role that Finan made him a bishop. Cedd's mission continued to prosper; crowds flocked; a minster was established at Bradwell-on-Sea,[E] and another at Tilbury. Then came a crisis.

Around 660, Sigeberht was murdered, apparently by two of his own kinsmen, because he had been too lenient – in other words, too 'Christian' – towards his enemies. At this point Bede's story takes an unexpected twist: Sigeberht's death had apparently been foretold by none other than Cedd himself on the occasion when the latter had discovered that Sigeberht had flouted his authority: rather than shunning the company of a man whom Cedd had excommunicated, Sigeberht had accepted his hospitality. But in Bede's eyes Sigeberht, by his death, atoned for this act of disobedience and ultimately acquired an aura of sanctity.

Despite Sigeberht's reputation, and despite all Cedd's efforts, Christianity among the East Saxons remained fragile and when, in c.664, plague struck the kingdom, paganism returned. There were at the time two kings of the East Saxons; one of whom, Sebbi, remained faithful to the tenets of the new faith (after thirty years of exemplary rule, he abdicated to become a monk;

see St Paul's, London^E), while the other, Sigehere, restored pagan worship in the hope of protecting himself and his people from the plague.

The Mercians saw this as an opportunity to intervene: Wulfhere of Mercia, now busily active as a Christian king, sent Bishop Jaruman to the East Saxons. Jaruman, according to Bede, acted 'with great discretion' and, by travelling and preaching 'far and wide', he persuaded the pagan party to abandon their temples and to reopen their churches. Their mission successfully completed, Jaruman and his helpers returned to Mercia. Nonetheless, politically the East Saxons remained vulnerable to outside help and pressure, not only from Mercia but also from both Kent and Wessex.

Throughout the 'Age of Bede', London would remain a magnet for political rivals. It has also been suggested that London's accessibility via major land routes, together with memories of its Roman grandeur, explain why ecclesiastical councils, such as those held at Hertford in 672 and at Hatfield (Haethfeld) in 679 – both summoned by Archbishop Theodore – were held within its diocese.

LONDON

St Paul's Cathedral

> Theodore then appointed Eorcenwold bishop in London...
> Both before and after his consecration Eorcenwold lived
> so holy a life that even now miracles bear witness to it.
> [IV, 6]

The Anglo-Saxon cathedral of St Paul's was built within the Roman walls, at Ludgate Hill, close to where the cathedral still stands. Archaeology has failed to find any trace of the Saxon church, but the importance of such a position within the walls, while at the same time close both to the gate and to the road which led out of the city to the port, is easily grasped.

Mellitus, its first bishop, belonged to the reinforcement party Pope Gregory had sent to help Augustine, following on from the early successes of the mission. Mellitus brought with him a further supply of vestments, relics and books, as well as the letter the pope had sent as an afterthought when Mellitus's party was already on its way, spelling out that, after careful consideration, the pope had decided that pagan temples in England should not be destroyed but instead put to use as Christian churches. Bede quotes this letter in full (as he often did with papal documents).

In 610 Mellitus went back to Rome where he attended a papal synod concerned with monastic practices and observances; he returned with further papal letters and most probably more ecclesiastical treasures and necessities. But these halcyon days were soon to end: on the deaths of their first Christian kings, both Essex and Kent reverted to paganism and their bishops felt unsafe. Mellitus took refuge for a while in Kent, but soon fled to Gaul, together with Justus, bishop of Rochester. Mellitus never went back to London as, on the death of Laurence (Augustine's successor), he was chosen as Canterbury's next archbishop.

There is no evidence of any cult of Mellitus at St Paul's, whereas Eorcenwold, appointed in 675 by Archbishop Theodore, made a lasting impression. Eorcenwold had already founded both Chertsey[E] and Barking[E] before becoming bishop and such was the power of his holiness, as Bede relates it, that he performed many miracles. When he was ill, he used to be carried in a horse-litter; in Bede's day this litter was still curing those placed in or near it and splinters were gathered from it to take to the sick. A twelfth-century *Life of Eorcenwold* recalls the litter, as well as noting the further miracles performed both before and after Eorcenwold's translation in 1140 from the crypt of St Paul's to a shrine behind the high altar. St Paul's, according to the *Life*, had not secured Eorcenwold's body without a tussle; Eorcenwold had died at Barking where the nuns naturally hoped to keep him; the monks of Chertsey, on the other hand, claimed that since Chertsey had been founded before Barking, they should have the body. With the help of a miracle, St Paul's trumped both communities on the grounds that his tomb should be in the city where he had been bishop.

The difficulty the bishops of London might find themselves in, given the precarious nature of kingship in Essex, is well illustrated by the letter of Waldhere, the bishop of London who succeeded Eorcenwold, addressed to Brihtwold, archbishop of Canterbury, c.704–5:

> ... now that a matter of necessity is threatening, I think it worth while to inquire with entreaty of your Grace's sagacity what ought to be done. Indeed, I do not think it can have been hidden from your notice how many and what sort of disputes and discords have arisen between the king of the West Saxons and rulers of our country, and, what is still more unfortunate, also the ecclesiastics on both sides who share the direction of the government under them, have willy-nilly been involved in this same dissension... But a few days ago they assented to this decision by common

consent, that all the kings of both parties, bishops, abbots and other councillors, should assemble on 15th October at a place which is called Brentford; and having summoned a council there, should determine the causes of all dissensions, and in as far as each shall have proved to have offended, he shall make amends to the other with legal compensation. It is fitting that I should be at this council... hence I implore your Holiness's authority... that you deign to inform me what I ought to do in this matter, because I can by no means reconcile them, and become as it were a hostage of peace, unless a very great amount of intercourse takes place between us and this I will not and dare not do unless you wish it and give permission.

(*English Historical Documents*, vol. 1, p. 792)

Waldhere did, however, have the satisfaction of securing a further saint for St Paul's. This was Sebbi, king of the East Saxons. Sebbi had long wanted to become a monk but could not do so until his wife agreed and she was reluctant to do so. But by the time Sebbi had been king for thirty years and had become ill, his wife relented and Sebbi went to see Waldhere. He took with him a substantial sum of money to be given to the poor, and asked Waldhere to clothe him as a monk. But as his illness progressed, Sebbi began to worry about how he might deport himself in his last hours. In Bede's words, 'his disposition being such as befitted a king, he feared that if he felt great pain in the hour of death, he might by his words or his gestures act in a way unworthy of his character'[IV, 11]. So he asked Waldhere if just he and two of his servants could be with him when the moment came. Waldhere gladly agreed and Sebbi then had the further comfort of a vision in which he was assured that his death would come soon (within three days) and that it would be painless. And so it was.

But there was now the problem of finding a suitable coffin. A stone sarcophagus had already been found (cf. Ely[EA]), but for a dreadful moment it seemed as if it might be too small and that Sebbi's knees might have to be bent to make him fit, but miraculously all was well and the assembled crowd (including the dead king's sons, Sigeheard and Swaefred, now joint rulers) shared the relief of seeing the body comfortably fit into the sarcophagus, even with the addition of a pillow. The sarcophagus was then buried in St Paul's.

Westminster

> At the time of which I speak, Mellitus, with the help of
> God and the support of Aethelberht, showed his quality by
> spreading Christianity in the province. He was prompted
> to do this, it is said, by a message from the apostle
> himself. Peter appeared in person to dedicate the newly
> built church, and by the hands of a countryman sent the
> bishop a most acceptable present in the form of a fish.
>
> (WILLIAM OF MALMESBURY, *The History of*
> *the English Bishops*, BOOK II, CHAPTER 73)

The Bayeux Tapestry, together with many accounts of Westminster Abbey, gives the impression that the abbey was founded by Edward the Confessor. In fact, what Edward did was to rebuild it and it remains difficult, if not impossible, to know even the approximate date when the minster was first established. Its situation on Thorney Island, to the west of the City, would have presented an advantageous position when trade began to revive in London in the seventh century, but it is hard to know whether the tradition that Bishop Mellitus grasped this opportunity is anything but legendary.

Bede is no help here and the later stories are designed to inspire faith rather than confidence in their historical veracity. William of Malmesbury and the Anglo-Norman *Life* of Edward the Confessor both report how St Peter himself ordered Mellitus to build the minster and how he even came to the abbey to perform its consecration himself: he came in the dead of night, but the evidence of the candles, the holy water and oil, were plain for all to see, as was a great fish caught as a present for Mellitus to mark the occasion.

Given Mellitus's stormy episcopacy (he fled from a pagan reaction: *see* St Paul's, page 157), it is quite likely that Westminster was not in fact founded until some time later, possibly not until the reign of Offa when he was attempting to gain control of London, but the evidence remains unreliable.

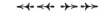

BARKING · Essex

Before he [Eorcenwold] was made bishop, he founded two famous monasteries, one for himself and the other for his sister Aethelburh, and established an excellent form of monastic Rule and discipline in both. His own was in the kingdom of Surrey near the river Thames at a place called Chertsey... His sister's monastery he established at a place called Barking in the kingdom of the East Saxons where she was to live as mother and nurse of a company of women devoted to God. [IV, 6]

Take the Hammersmith and City Line on the London Under-
ground, go as far east as you can, and you will arrive at Barking.
In the year 2000, the district was classified as one of the most
deprived areas in England; in the late eighth century it was one
of the wealthiest, its prosperity both signalled and supported by
its abbey.

Nothing of this Anglo-Saxon abbey now survives, though
excavations have confirmed its grandeur and importance.
According to Bede, the house was founded as a community for
men and women by the abbot of Chertsey, Eorcenwold, before
his appointment in 675/6 to the see of London. As bishop,
Eorcenwold secured further land for the foundation. The first
abbess was Eorcenwold's sister, Aethelburh; the chances of this
pair having royal blood seem high, either through connections
with the ruling families of Kent or the East Saxons (or both).

The women of Barking were themselves of aristocratic birth,
some almost certainly royal. Fragments of gold thread and the
elegant pins discovered during the excavations at Barking suggest greater luxury than Aldhelm, a great scholar and ecclesiastic
(*see* Malmesbury[W] and Sherborne[W]) – who had a relative, possibly a sister, in the community – considered appropriate. But as
Aldhelm knew, aristocratic accoutrements did not necessarily
imply a dissolute life, and among the luxury items were also
styli (writing instruments), evidence of the nuns' literacy (such
styli were also found at Whitby[N]). In his prose treatise on virginity, written for the nuns of Barking, Aldhelm is full of praise
for their learning and scholarship; he recognises their 'verbal
eloquence' and lavishly praises 'their mellifluous studies of the
Holy Scripture... [and]... the extremely subtle sequence of [their]
discourse'. Some time after the completion of the treatise,

Aldhelm produced a new version in hexameters, designed this time for the nuns to perform. It is a lengthy work, presupposing a high level of musical talent (perhaps Aldhelm even contemplated the idea that the nuns could use an organ as accompaniment).

Barking was sorely hit, as was Bede's own house of Jarrow, by one of the outbreaks of plague that intermittently hit England in the later seventh century. Bede's account of the Barking plague is based on a lost *Life* of Aethelburh (which in turn may be based on a Frankish saint's Life). Whatever the ultimate source, it remains a remarkably vivid account. First, plague struck the men's quarters; meanwhile a sense of their impending fate led the nuns to wonder where, when their turn came, they should be buried. A divine sign told them: one night, as they were chanting besides the graves of the deceased brethren, a brilliant light illuminated the south side of the monastery – and so their question was answered, though the toll exacted by the plague was so heavy, and the site so constricted, that Hildelith (Aethelburh's successor as abbess) felt the spot could no longer be spared for use as a graveyard. The bones were therefore dug up and reburied all in one place inside the church.

Bede recalls a number of exemplary Barking deaths. Particularly poignant is his tale of the death from plague of a little boy, no more than three years of age, who called out with his dying breath for 'Edith'; that same day, Edith, seemingly one of the nuns who had been caring for him, also died. Bede's other accounts of the deaths of severely disabled nuns creates a picture of Barking acting as a hospice, quite as much as a nursery or seminary. It may also have provided a refuge for Cuthburh when she decided to leave the Northumbrian court – where she had been married to King Aldfrith – and return to her native Wessex.

Here she founded Wimborne[W] (though the sojourn at Barking must remain speculative).

BRADWELL-ON-SEA · Essex

He [Cedd] established churches in various places and ordained priests and deacons to assist him in preaching the word of faith and in the administration of baptism, especially in the city Ythancaestir in the Saxon tongue and also in the place called Tilbury. [III, 22]

Ythancaestir or Bradwell-on-Sea, situated on the remote Dengie Peninsula, where the river Blackwater flows into the North Sea, was once a Roman fort. It was adapted for Christian use as a minster by Bishop Cedd under the patronage of King Sigeberht of Essex, shortly after Sigeberht's baptism in Northumbria in c.653.

Oswiu of Northumbria had long urged Sigeberht to convert to Christianity, pointing out to him, Bede tells us, that 'objects made by the hands of men could not be gods'. The Christian God, in contrast to any pagan deity, lived in heaven, 'not in base and perishable metal' [III, 22]. Oswiu's arguments finally prevailed. Sigeberht converted and took counsel with his friends, all of whom agreed to be baptised. The ceremony took place not far from Hadrian's Wall (possibly at Wallbottle).

Thereafter Sigeberht returned home, asking Oswiu to send him someone who could help to convert his people. Oswiu sent Cedd and one other priest. Cedd, the eldest of four brothers, all of whom had been at Lindisfarne in the time of Bishop Aidan, had already a year's experience as a missionary behind him, gained in Mercia where he had been sent following the marriage of Peada (son of the pagan Penda) to Oswiu's daughter, Alhflaed. The mission among the East Saxons was to prove sufficiently successful for Bishop Finan of Lindisfarne (*see* page 43) to consecrate him as their bishop.

The sea has by now eroded much of Cedd's building, but the nave of a seventh-century church (in use over many centuries as a barn) still stands. Excavations carried out in the nineteenth century have confirmed the existence of an apsidal chancel and of 'portici' on both north and south walls. The church was built throughout of reused Roman stone and brick, while the Roman walls of the fort provided a suitable enclosure for the whole site.

The early Christian appeal of islands is clearly evident (Lindisfarne may be the best-loved example, but islands of one kind or another appear throughout Bede's *History*), but for many monastic communities boundaries other than those afforded by water also had their attractions. Across Europe the walls of Roman forts were often used to create monastic enclosures; in England, Reculver[K] provides another example. But important though enclosure was for monastic communities, what seems to have mattered most was the designation and definition of sacred space rather than any absolute safeguarding of monastic seclusion: Anglo-Saxon monasteries were above all mission centres, so access was paradoxically as important as seclusion. Thus the Bradwell church, built on the fort's western wall, most probably acted as the gateway to a much larger minster complex which over centuries has been swept away by the sea. Among the minster's functions, then, conversion took pride of place.

As bishop, Cedd, according to Bede, built churches across the kingdom of the East Saxons, but it was at Bradwell-on-Sea (and at Tilbury on the north bank of the Thames, though no trace of his activities remain there) that he concentrated his preaching and the administration of baptism in the waters of the river Blackwater. Cedd, however, continued to visit Northumbria, where he remained an important figure in royal circles, and particularly Lastingham,[N] a community he had helped to establish (and of which he remained abbot) and where he was buried.

CHERTSEY · Surrey

Before he [Eorcenwold] was made bishop, he founded two famous monasteries, one for himself and the other for his sister...
His own was in the kingdom of Surrey near the river Thames at a place called Chertsey, that is the island of Ceorot. [IV,6]

Eorcenwold became celebrated as the bishop of London who, when ill, used to be carried around in a horse-litter which thereby acquired miraculous powers: even splinters from it cured the sick. Tales of such cures, as recounted by Bede, remained in circulation throughout the Middle Ages, but to the modern reader what may seem most remarkable about Eorcenwold is his political nous.

While the original endowment for Chertsey came from King Egbert of Kent, just a few years later, Chertsey's holdings were substantially increased by a grant from Frithuwold of Surrey, self-styled 'sub-king' of Wulfhere, king of the Mercians, who gave 290 hides of land along the Thames, together with a further ten hides situated by the 'port of London where ships come to land'. This is one of the earliest references we have to the revival of trade in London, though it is likely that by the 660s this may have been flourishing for some time, with boats drawing up along what is known now as the Strand, but which in the seventh century simply meant 'the shore'.

The Chertsey foundation charter is thus of considerable interest, not least because it highlights the contrast between a fast-changing political landscape and deep-rooted local boundaries. Who was king and of which territory might vary from one year to the next. What seems unchanging were those local boundaries. In Eorcenwold's case, the land Frithuwold gave him had evidently belonged at one point to a tribe led by a certain Fulla, about whom we know nothing beyond the charter. The land given is carefully described as running alongside the Thames:

> ... as far as the boundary which is called the ancient ditch,
> that is Fullingadic; again, in another part of the bank of
> the same river as far as the boundary of the next province,
> which is called Sonning. Of the same land, however, a
> separate part, of 10 hides, is by the port of London, where
> ships come to land, on the same river on the southern side
> by the public way. There are, however, diverse names for
> the above-mentioned lands, namely Chertsey, Thorpe,
> Egham, Chobham, Getinges, Molesley, Woodham and
> Hunewaldesham, as far as the above mentioned boundary.

From a charter such as this it becomes possible to see how monastic foundations helped the process of kingdom-formation in Anglo-Saxon England. Relatively small units of land could be amalgamated to form the landholdings of minsters and while such minsters depended on royal largesse for their survival, they in turn helped dynasties to survive and prosper, even sometimes to supplant each other. Thus Bishop Eorcenwold, having served

kings of Kent, Surrey and Mercia, ended his days in the entourage of Ine, King of Wessex, Ine at this point being a notably
powerful king in southern England.

PRITTLEWELL · Essex

... when [King Saeberht] departed to the eternal kingdom,
he left three sons as heirs to his temporal kingdom who had all
remained heathen. [11, 5]

In 2003, prior to road-widening works, excavations were undertaken at what had long been known to be an Anglo-Saxon
cemetery in Prittlewell. Revealed was a substantial burial chamber (about 4 metres square (43 sq ft) – bigger than the average
university student's room). In it the body of a man had been laid
out. He had been buried with great splendour, accompanied by
rich grave accoutrements, some time early in the seventh century.
He had seemingly been dressed in a tunic ornamented with gold
braid. Two tiny gold-foil crosses were found near where his head
would have lain. These suggest, though they do not prove, that
the dead man was a Christian, buried with pagan, or perhaps
mixed rites (Christians did not originally eschew grave goods).
Though it can only be a matter of conjecture, this could be the
burial place of King Saeberht, king of East Anglia (*see* introduction to The Kingdom of the East Saxons, page 154). It would
be a fitting grave for a Christian king buried by pagan sons.

Similarly conjectural, too, is the exact date of the church of
St Mary the Virgin at Prittlewell, but since the north door of the
chancel has been dated to the seventh century, it is not out of
the question that this was Saeberht's church.

MERCIA

Now King Penda (of Mercia) did not forbid the preaching of
the Word, even in his own Mercian kingdom, if any wished to
hear it. But he hated and despised those who, after they
had accepted the Christian faith, were clearly lacking in the
works of faith. [III, 21]

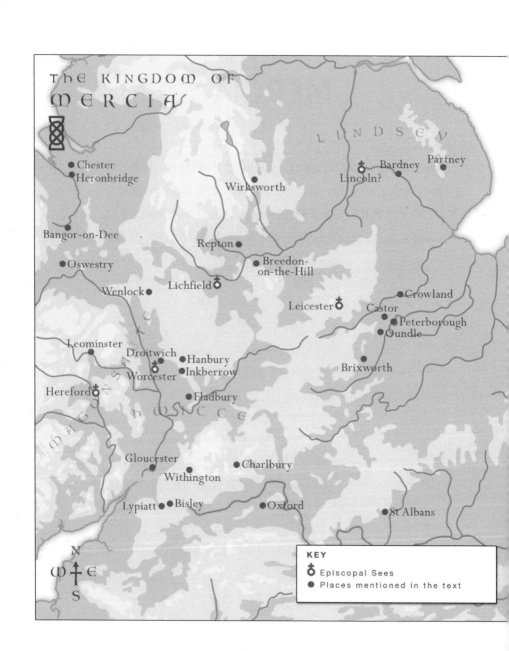

The name 'Mercia' denotes a people who lived close to a border. How it was that just these people came to dominate pre-Viking England remains something of a puzzle, but we can start with the two entries from the *Anglo-Saxon Chronicle* which for long were held to be key to the story:

577 In this year Cuthwine and Ceawlin fought against the Britons and killed three kings, Conmial, Condidan and Farinmail, at the place which is called Dyrham; and they captured three of their cities, Gloucester, Cirencester and Bath.

628 In this year Cynegils and Cwichelm fought against Penda at Cirencester and afterwards came to terms.

'Dyrham' is six miles north of Bath, along the A46. (A park and mansion now occupy the site; episodes of *Dr Who* were recently filmed here, though perhaps it is even better known as a location for the 1993 film, *The Remains of the Day*.) The 577 entry is, however, suspected of reflecting West Saxon claims to the cities mentioned rather than being a report of an actual battle. When the *Chronicle* was compiled it had come to seem important that these former Roman cities be captured at this particular juncture. But even supposing 577 to have been the year of an actual battle, success for the West Saxons proved short-lived: real power in the region was fast passing to the Mercians under their new leader, Penda. Thus in the battle of 628, these key lands (in effect what is now Gloucestershire) passed out of Wessex hands and, until the arrival of the Vikings, remained Mercian (even if for quite some time the Mercians were content to rule through the sub-kingdom of the Hwicce).

By the early seventh century, Mercia had become the kingdom from which not only Wessex but also Northumbria had the most to fear. After 628, Penda augmented his power by making alliances with British rulers and in 633 at the battle of Hatfield Chase,[N] together with Caedwalla of Gwynedd, he defeated and killed King Edwin of Northumbria. Nine years later he launched a further attack on Northumbria, this time killing King Oswald at a place known as Maserfelth (but probably to be identified with Oswestry). Penda again had British help and it may be that some Welsh elegiac poems, lamenting the loss of warriors, relate to the battle of Maserfelth.

But in 655 Penda's luck ran out; at the battle of the Winwaed, near Leeds,[N] the Northumbrians under King Oswiu finally defeated and killed him. After the battle, Penda's son, Peada, briefly ruled southern Mercia under Oswiu's overlordship before being murdered through the treachery (or so it was said) of his Northumbrian wife. Nonetheless, Mercia proved resilient and a younger son of Penda's, the protégé of certain Mercian noblemen, successfully fought off Northumbrian rule and, at the time Bede was writing, Mercia was a prosperous, influential and independent kingdom.

Bede himself admitted that Mercia's king, Aethelbald, held power over all the kingdoms south of the Humber and if he was uneasy as to where Aethelbald's ambitions would take him next, it would have been with good reason: only six years after the completion of the *Ecclesiastical History* in c.731, Aethelbald did indeed ravage Northumbria, returning three years later in an attempt to take advantage of the Northumbrian king's preoccupation at the time with the Picts on his northern borders.

The information Bede gives us on Mercia is grudging, but crucial. He tells us that after the battle of the Winwaed the kingdom fell into a northern and a southern part, divided by the river Trent. He estimates the size of both regions as amounting to 12,000 hides (a hide being considered adequate for the upkeep of a household), though calculations based on an eighth-century document (the Tribal Hidage) that may be as early as the *Ecclesiastical History* suggest a much bigger kingdom. The conclusion has to be that, bit by bit (and the chronology is likely to remain uncertain), Mercia had swallowed up smaller regions, amalgamating them into a kingdom which, by the end of the eighth century, would consider itself as grand as any within Europe. Such regions included as well the territory of the Hwicce, based around Worcester; the Middle Angles centred on Leicester; the Magonsaete of Herefordshire; and, in northern Lincolnshire, the kingdom of Lindsey.

If Mercia's political hegemony is hard to trace, so too is the story of the kingdom's conversion to Christianity. As Bede tells it, Christianity officially came to Mercia after the death of Penda at the battle of the Winwaed. However, even keeping to Bede's own narrative, it becomes apparent that other, peaceful strategies had also been attempted: only a few years before the battle of the Winwaed, Oswiu and Penda had agreed on marriages between Oswiu's son and a daughter of Penda's (see Castor[M]) and a symmetrical match of Oswiu's daughter to Peada, a son of Penda's, on the condition, in this last case, that missionaries be allowed into Peada's sub-kingdom of the Middle Angles. Peada himself had converted, evidently with his father's blessing (Penda's scorn being reserved, so Bede tells us, only for those who accepted Christianity but then 'clearly lacked the works of faith'), and four missionaries were sent to the Middle Angles – Cedd, Adda, Betti and Diuma (*see* Charlbury[M] and Wirksworth[M]).

After the battle of the Winwaed, Diuma became bishop both of the Middle Angles and of the Mercians. Three years later, another son of Penda's, Wulfhere, wrested Mercia back from Oswiu, but there seems to have been no suggestion of a return to paganism; on the contrary, Wulfhere was a busy patron of the new faith, seemingly maintaining his brother's predilection for Irish-trained priests. Thus by the time Bede was writing, Mercia had a number of bishoprics. A major see had been established at Lichfield,[M] close to the royal palace at Tamworth, but the former sub-kingdoms of Hwicce and Lindsey had their bishops too, as did those Mercians Bede described as living west of the Severn River (in other words, the Magonsaete; *see* Leominster[M] and Hereford[M]). However, Bede only tells us some of this, and what he either did not know or did not choose to report remains striking.

Particularly remarkable is Bede's silence about Mercian monasteries, even though other sources give an indication of just how many were already in existence well before he was writing. Hanbury,[M] Much Wenlock,[M] Leominster,[M] Tetbury, Gloucester,[M] Withington and Fladbury are just some of the communities for which we have evidence from relatively early dates. It is, then, hard to resist the conclusion that had Bede been more curious about Mercian Christianity, he could have discovered more. Very possibly, he was simply reluctant to admit the survival and influence in the region of British Christians. As far as Bede was concerned, these were people to airbrush out of his narrative. This much he signals in the very full account he gives of the encounter between St Augustine of Canterbury and British dignitaries somewhere along the borders of the Hwicce. The occasion was a disaster. Thereafter, as far as Bede was concerned, British Christians were 'a nation of heretics' who deserved the destruction Augustine allegedly prophesied they would suffer, and which indeed, as Bede tells the story, duly befell them when a large party of British monks, praying for victory before a battle against the Northumbrians, were summarily massacred near Chester.[M] Since at the time the Northumbrians were still pagan, the story serves well as a reminder of how partisan Bede was in his sympathies and how alert we need to be in our search for clues as to what he chooses not to divulge.

BARDNEY · Lincolnshire

There is a famous monastery in the kingdom of Lindsey
called Bardney... [III, 11]

Bardney in Lincolnshire lay at the heart of Anglo-Saxon Lindsey, that sizeable territory (possibly once a kingdom) which was coveted throughout the seventh century by both Northumbria and Mercia. For Mercia, possession of this region was especially valuable because it provided access to the North Sea and the prosperity offered by its trade.

In 679, at the battle of the Trent, Mercia, under its king, Aethelred, finally won Lindsey, but the enmity he incurred was such that it took the intervention of Archbishop Theodore to secure the peace. A brother of the Northumbrian king, Ecgfrith, had been killed in the battle, a death of particular significance since he was also brother to Osthryth, wife of King Aethelred (a match presumably arranged in a previous and failed attempt to create peace between the two kingdoms).

This is the turbulent background to the arrival one evening at Bardney of a carriage bearing the bones of Osthryth's uncle, Oswald. The carriage was refused entry: the monks knew, Bede explains, 'that Oswald was a saint but, nevertheless, because he belonged to another kingdom and had once conquered them, they pursued him even when dead with their former hatred'. All night long, therefore, the relics stayed outside, protected only by a tent; but all night long a miracle occurred: 'a column of light stretched from the carriage right up to heaven and was visible in almost every part of the kingdom of Lindsey'. No wonder, then, that by morning the monks had changed their minds; now they began 'to pray earnestly that the relics might be lodged with them' (III, 11). The bones were therefore washed, put into a new shrine and with all solemnity placed within the church. The water used for the washing was poured over earth which thereby acquired miraculous properties, just as had the earth at Maserfelth (possibly Oswestry in Shropshire) where Oswald had been killed.

Bardney remained of importance in the development of Mercian power throughout the eighth century. Nothing remains now of the Saxon minster, but the topography of the site is suggestive: Bardney was in effect built on an island connected to the surrounding countryside by a short isthmus. In all probability, the site already had cultic significance before the conversion, and the three churches known from the later medieval period may date back to the conversion period. The relative seclusion of the site, coupled with its proximity to the royal centre at Lincoln,[M] fits a pattern found across eighth-century England.

Folklore has it that after the momentous night when Oswald's bones were left outside, the monastery's doors at Bardney were never again shut tight; this is reputed to be the origin of the Lincolnshire saying, addressed to anyone who leaves their door open: 'Do you come from Bardney?' Behind this anecdote lies the intriguing question: what did Bede himself mean by saying that the carriage bearing the bones was left 'outside'? Did he mean outside the monastic church? Or outside the whole monastic settlement? Given the likely topography of Bardney, the latter interpretation would seem the more likely.

Though Oswald was soon accepted as a saint throughout Mercia, Queen Osthryth retained enemies and in 697 she was murdered by, according to Bede, 'her own Mercian nobles' [v, 24]. Some years later, in 704, her widower husband, King Aethelred, resigned and became abbot of Bardney, where both he and Osthryth later achieved cult status. It is likely that Bardney was their own foundation, which may account for this eventual veneration.

At the time of the Viking raids, Oswald's bones were taken to Gloucester[M] for safe keeping. Bardney was indeed destroyed: the ruins visible today are of the post-Conquest abbey.

BISLEY and the Lypiatt Cross • Gloucestershire

On the estates of the nobles and good men of the Saxon race it is
the custom to have a cross, which is dedicated to our Lord and

held in great reverence, erected on some prominent spot for the
convenience of those who wish to pray daily before it.

('LIFE OF ST WILLIBALD', IN *The Anglo-Saxon Missionaries*
in Germany, TRANS. C. H. TALBOT, SHEED AND WARD,
1954, PP. 154–5)

The Lypiatt Cross stands by the side of the road from Stroud to Bisley in Gloucestershire – so hemmed in by weeds and iron railings that it is all too easy to drive past it. Yet when it was first erected, the cross may have been as fine a monument to the new faith as could be found anywhere else in England and a salutary reminder of how much sculpture outside Northumbria may have been lost. It is now so weathered that it is not easy to reconstruct, but each of its four faces depicts a figure.

The figure on the face nearest to the road stands on a dais with a hand raised in blessing. The head is missing, as is much of the left hand. The figure wears a cloak, within whose folds are mysterious holes: these have been drilled – eight on the left and four on the right. The most likely explanation is that the cross may once have been decorated with metal strips. The 'back' of the cross is split into three panels. The main figure here carries a book, but it is clear from its surviving feet that there must have been another figure on this face. The side-faces also contain figures, seemingly linked by their posture with the figure on the 'front'.

Interpretation of the iconography is only one of the challenges the Lypiatt Cross presents. Another is the question of whether the cross was originally erected where it now stands; another, closely related, is what purpose did it serve? Did it mark a boundary? Was it a focal point for processions? What relationship did it have with the minster of Bisley? There is no written record of Bisley until 896, but the likelihood of it being a much older minster site is high. The similarities between the cross and those at Ruthwell[N] and Bewcastle[N] have tempted suggestions of Northumbrian influence such as Oftfor (educated at Whitby[N]) might have brought when he became bishop of the Hwicce sometime in the late seventh century. But the most certain fact about the cross is that currently it is lamentably neglected.

BREEDON-on-the-HILL · Leicestershire

In the year of our Lord 731, Archbishop Berhtwold died of old age... In the same year Tatwine was made archbishop in his place. He was from the kingdom of Mercia and had been a priest in the minster of Breedon. [v, 23]

It's a steep climb to reach Breedon: founded c.680 on the site of an Iron Age hill fort, it occupies a commanding position. Archaeological evidence suggests that the fort had stayed in use during the Roman period, but that in the fifth and sixth centuries it had been deserted. Its revived fortunes as a minster began with a colony of monks sent from Medeshamsted (today's Peterborough[M]) under the abbacy of Hedda, later bishop of Lichfield. Although there is some doubt about the authenticity of Breedon's foundation charter (because it survives only in a twelfth-century copy), it is usually considered as genuine and as such has been the subject of considerable discussion, not least because of its claim to be making provision for both a 'monastery and oratory of monks... and also a priest of honest life and good reputation who would bring the grace of baptism and the teaching of gospel doctrine to the people committed to his care'. Was Breedon, then, set up explicitly as a mission centre?

Equally intriguing is the possibility that the founder, an aristocrat by the name of Friduric, later buried at Breedon and venerated there as a saint, could be related to Frithuwold, founder of Chertsey,[E] and to Frideswide of Oxford.[M] In the eighth century, saintly genealogies helped strengthen both the cult of saints and the power of secular rulers. And Friduric, according to the charter evidence, was apparently sufficiently pleased with the success of his new foundation – and in particular with Hedda's preaching – to add further estates to the original endowment. In confirmation of his new gift, King Aethelred of Mercia and Seaxwulf, bishop of Lichfield,[M] 'at Friduric's request, joining their hands placed a turf from the land on a gospel-book before a multitude of the people and confirmed the testimony of this in writing, writing in their own hands'. This, it is now thought, is the land on which Repton[M] came to be built.

Breedon's main claim to fame is the magnificent stone carving, exhibited both in friezes and relief-carved panels, still visible in the church today. They are worth a visit, both for their beauty and for the tale they tell of the power and status of Mercia at the time of their making. But Bede was long cold in his grave when they were carved, and these creations belong to another age – the age of King Offa (of Offa's Dyke) and Emperor Charlemagne rather than to Bede's England; regretfully, then, we must pass by these particular vine-scrolls, and much more besides.

Bede mentions Breedon only in the final pages of his History, telling us that, in 731, a priest from Breedon by the name of Tatwine has been consecrated to the see of Canterbury. He then gives Tatwine his seal of approval. Tatwine was, he tells us, 'a man renowned for his devotion and wisdom and excellently instructed in the Scriptures' [v, 23]. Tatwine's surviving works – a much-used book of Latin grammar suitable for beginners and a collection of forty poems or riddles on a wide range of subjects from pen, parchment and prepositions to the virtues of faith, hope, charity – substantiates Bede's opinion. Since Tatwine died in 734, we can reasonably suppose his literary output to date from his Breedon years and to conclude that Breedon had quickly become a monastic centre of some repute.

In Anglo-Saxon England, the fashion for riddles seems to have been started by Aldhelm of Malmesbury,[W] to whom Tatwine was certainly indebted. To give a flavour of the genre, and as testimony to the hard labour necessary in the creation of Anglo-Saxon texts, here are two of Tatwine's riddles:

Alas, I am wholly cheated of my true nature by an enemy:
at one time I used to fly swiftly through the upper air;
now bound by three, I pay tribute on earth.
I am forced to plough along the levels of the flat fields
and the labour of love always forces me
to pour fountains of tears on the dry furrows.

A certain of my enemies deprived me of life,
Took away my physical strength, afterwards wet me,
Dipped me in water; thence took me again,
Set me in the sun where I soon lost
The hair that I had. The hard edge of a knife
Afterwards cut me.

The answer to the first is a quill; to the second, parchment.

BRIXWORTH · Northamptonshire

Chapter VII. That a synod shall be summoned twice yearly.
(But on account of various hindrances, it was unanimously
decided that we should meet once a year on 1 August at the
place known as Clofaeshoh.) [IV, 5]

Clofaeshoh? In 672, at the Council of Hertford, Clofesho (as
Clofaeshoh is usually now spelt) was named by the assembled bishops of England, under the leadership of Theodore,
archbishop of Canterbury, as a suitable venue for the annual
ecclesiastical councils. Events frustrated these good intentions,
but still, from time to time ecclesiastical councils were indeed
held there and in 747 Clofesho was once again chosen as the
meeting place.

But where is Clofesho? A possible candidate is Brixworth,
where the church is mystifyingly magnificent. According to the
twelfth-century historian of Peterborough, Hugh Candidus,
it was one of a number of the monastic projects initiated by
Cuthbald, abbot at Peterborough[M] from 675. Although many
architectural historians are inclined to accept this testimony of
Hugh's, the sceptics among them advocate a rather later, possibly ninth-century date for the building, though all agree that
Brixworth counts as a basilica. Basilicas – and there were not
many in Anglo-Saxon England – are defined not only by their
size (Brixworth's nave and choir is 12 x 36.5 metres (40 x 120 ft))
but also by certain architectural features such as the presence of
aisles, or subdivisions, alongside and of equal length to the main
body of the building. What is distinctive at Brixworth is the crypt
beyond the apse of the church and the presence of a separate

space between nave and sanctuary; noteworthy also is the use of Roman building stone taken from the Charnwood Forest area. There cannot have been any simple means of transporting it from there to Brixworth; Brixworth, in other words, was not built during a recession.

Of all the puzzles surrounding Brixworth, one of the most intriguing concerns the Brixworth relic. This relic is a small throat bone, discovered during restoration work in the church in the nineteenth century. No documentary evidence survives that would help identify the bone, but because we know that an altar was at some point consecrated there to the Anglo-Saxon missionary St Boniface of Nursling,[W] the suggestion has been made that the relic could have been his. The hypothesis is intriguing because it strengthens the argument that Brixworth could indeed be Clofesho.

Clofesho without a doubt was somewhere in Mercia. Both the king of Mercia, Aethelbald and St Boniface were key figures in the council's deliberations (in Boniface's case, only via correspondence as he was in Germany at the time). If – and it remains a big 'if' – Brixworth and Clofesho were indeed one and the same, then the claim that the throat bone could be Boniface's gains credibility. (Boniface was martyred seven years after the 747 Clofesho council.) In all of these puzzles, Bede for once fails us: neither Brixworth nor Boniface feature in the pages of his *Ecclesiastical History* and he offers no clue as to the whereabouts of Clofesho. But the etymology of the name (Cloven Height) fits the topography of Brixworth and no one as yet has actually disproved the Brixworth/Boniface/Clofesho hypothesis, even if the counter-claims of Peterborough[M] remain strong.

CASTOR · Northamptonshire

He [Peada] was earnestly persuaded to accept the new faith by
Aldfrith, son of King Oswiu, who was his brother-in-law and
friend, having married Penda's daughter, Cyneburh. [III, 21]

Castor, some four miles (6 km) to the west of Peterborough,[M]
can proudly boast to be the only church in the world dedicated to
St Kyneburgha. Kyneburgha (or Cyneburh) was a Mercian princess married to Aldfrith, seemingly in the 650s, in one of the
more dangerous political matches of the time; Peada, brother
of Cyneburh, married to Alhflaed, daughter of King Oswiu, was
rumoured to have met his death at her hands. Aldfrith, it seems,
was luckier, but nonetheless after the Synod of Whitby[N] of 664
he disappears from view. The founding of the minster at Castor
by and for Cyneburh probably dates to this period.

Castor had been an impressive Roman centre with much still
to show of its former glory when Cyneburh established herself
within its perimeter. Little now remains of Cyneburh's minster,
though fragmnts of Anglo-Saxon work can be found within
what is now, according to Pevsner, 'the most important Norman
parish church in the county'. Legend has given Cyneburh a sister
called Cyneswith. In 963, the abbot of Peterborough found it
possible to exhume them both, translating them from Castor to
Peterborough. Nothing else is known of Cyneswith, but it has
been suggested that Cyneburh, together with Aldfrith, is commemorated on the cross at Bewcastle.[N]

CHARLBURY · Oxfordshire

Diuma... was consecrated bishop of the Middle Angles and the
Mercians by Bishop Finan, since a shortage of bishops made
it necessary for one bishop to be set over both nations. After he
had won no small number for the Lord in a short space of time,
he died in the country of the Middle Angles in a district called
Infeppingum. [III, 21]

A late Anglo-Saxon source, listing the places where saints' relics could be found, names Charlbury as a location for a St Dioma, whom it has been suggested is none other than Bede's Diuma. No trace of any Anglo-Saxon church can now be found at Charlbury, but its commanding position above the river Evenlode suggests that it may have been the site of an important minster, and a key place in the Christianisation of Middle Anglia. This identification does of course presuppose that Charlbury was in Middle Anglia but this is not implausible; Middle Anglia was a short-lived sub-kingdom, created, it would seem, from a number of different peoples (including the Feppingas) by King Penda of Mercia for his son, Peada, as an outlet for his ambitions; its boundaries are notoriously difficult to establish and its lifespan was limited.

CHESTER · Cheshire

For later on, that very powerful king of the English,
Aethelfrith... collected a great army against the city of the
legions which is called Legacaestir by the English and more

*correctly Caerlegion [Chester] by the Britons, and made a
great slaughter of that nation of heretics.* [II, 2]

Caerlegion/Chester was a grand enough place in the seventh
century for Bede to call it a *civitas* or city as opposed to a mere
urbs or town. The position of Chester at the mouth of the river
Dee, as well as the proximity of salt mines, was always going to
make it an enviable possession and by the seventh century it had
been absorbed into the British kingdom of Powys.

The battle of Chester which Bede reports took place some
time between 613 and 616. By his victory at Degsastan in 603
against the Irish of Dalriada, Aethelfrith had already proved himself a formidable warrior; now his attention was drawn to north
Wales in the hope of securing for himself an impregnable border
from west to east. The army he had to confront was led by the
king of Powys, Selyf Sarffgadau, together with the support of the
British monks of Bangor who had turned out in force to pray for
his victory.

According to Bede, the monks had come in droves. For three
days they had fasted; now 'standing apart in a safe place', they
prayed. When it was explained to Aethelfrith who they were, he
gave orders that before the start of the actual battle every monk
was to be slaughtered, saying: 'If they are praying to their God
against us, then, even if they do not bear arms, they are fighting
against us, assailing us as they do with prayers for our defeat'
[II, 2]. In this way, according to Bede, St Augustine's prophecy
(given after Augustine's attempt to reach a settlement with
British monks had failed) was duly fulfilled. Such is the rhetori-
cal force of the passage that it is easy to overlook that Aethelfrith
and his army were still pagan, whereas the British were not,

however 'heretical' their views on matters such as the dating of Easter might be.

Aethelfrith's victory in battle at Chester did nothing to assuage his ambition but it did increase the determination of his enemies to curb his power. For some time now, Edwin (son of the former king of Deira) had been in exile, offered shelter first, it would seem, by Cadfan of Gwynedd, next by Cearl of Mercia and later by Raedwald of East Anglia. In each case the consequences would be momentous. The final triumph was Raedwald's – in c.616 he defeated and killed Aethelfrith in a battle by the river Idle and it looks as if he was then able to put Edwin on the throne of Northumbria as a client king. Many years later, in 633, at the battle of Hatfield Chase,[N] Caedwalla (son of Cadfan) found revenge for the ingratitude Edwin had shown when he had become king as a result of his persistent campaigning as far as Anglesey.

As for Chester, it gradually became absorbed into the ever-growing kingdom of Mercia. The church of St John's attributed its foundation in 689 to King Aethelred of Mercia, and from the tenth century onwards the daughter of King Wulfhere, St Werburgh (see Hanbury[M]) became Chester's much-revered saint. (Notable, however, and not readily explicable, is the absence of pre-Viking sculpture from Chester – and indeed, for the whole of Cheshire and Lancashire, with the exception of a ninth-century example from the area around the river Lune.)

Recent excavations at Heronbridge, just two miles (3 km) south of Chester, have uncovered over 120 bodies buried in a mass grave. These are most probably the dead from the battle, though whether British or Northumbrian is as yet unclear.

CROWLAND · Lincolnshire

714 In this year the holy Guthlac died

(Anglo-Saxon Chronicle, 714)

Crowland, one of the most famous of all medieval Lincolnshire monasteries, is a place never once mentioned by Bede. The reasons are not hard to find. Crowland was the home of the holy (and aristocratic) hermit Guthlac. Guthlac had been a thoroughly disreputable young man whose conversion sanctified the rise to power of a new branch of the Mercian royal house in the shape of the formidable King Aethelbald (r. 716–57), a king whom Bede acknowledged held authority over all kingdoms south of the Humber. Nonetheless, Bede pointedly refrained from including Aethelbald among his list of 'super-kings' or *bretwaldas*, an omission that did little to disguise his dismay at the ascendancy of Mercia in contrast to the increasingly enfeebled state of Northumbria.

Aethelbald had spent the reign of his predecessor, Ceolred (709–16), in exile, but since Ceolred had won for himself a reputation as a shocking reprobate destined for hell, Aethelbald had everything to gain from saintly approbation, and this Guthlac readily gave him. According to the *Life of Guthlac* (written by a monk named Felix), the hermit assured Aethelbald during one of his visits to Crowland of his future destiny: 'O my child,' said Guthlac, 'I have asked the Lord to help you in his pitifulness and he has heard me; and granted you to rule over your race and has made you chief over the peoples; and he will bow down the necks of your enemies beneath your heel and you shall own their possessions.' A year after Guthlac's death, Aethelbald indeed became king. In thanksgiving, he continued to venerate Guthlac, both by embellishing his shrine at Crowland and by choosing Repton as his own mausoleum, for it was at Repton that Guthlac, before he became a hermit, had been professed as a monk.

Guthlac himself died in 714; Felix's *Life* is thought to have been written in the 740s. It is likely therefore that Bede had died some years before the *Life* was written. Nonetheless, Bede and Guthlac were still contemporaries and it stretches credulity to think that Bede knew nothing of him. Felix's *Life* borrows heavily from Bede's *Life of Cuthbert* and it is hard not to detect rivalries that were probably at work even in Bede's lifetime. Bede is similarly silent in his *History* about Botulph of Iken/Icanhoe.[EA]

But despite Bede's reticence, Guthlac's cult was immediately successful. His early life as a treasure-seeking brigand, his conversion and the spiritual trials he endured in the fens had spectacular appeal (the trip he made to the gates of hell is particularly spine-chilling). Particularly notable are the two vernacular pre-Conquest poems (known as *Guthlac A* and *Guthlac B*), which further described Guthlac's life at Crowland; neither is complete but both evoked further the horrors and tribulations of the eremitical life, at the same time as proffering the hope of final glory with Christ.

Crowland, in Guthlac's day, was a remote fenland island, approached via the southern bank of the river Welland. Felix describes with relish how dismal a site it was: 'In the midlands of Britain there is a very dark fen of huge expanse... reaching as far as the sea, covered now with swamps, now with pools, sometimes with black mist-covered water.' After Guthlac's death, and particularly after the discovery a year later that his body was incorrupt – comparable therefore to St Cuthbert of Lindisfarne's (*see* page 48) – intrepid pilgrims flocked in boat-loads to his shrine.

But despite the claims of later chroniclers, anxious to stress its antiquity, it is unlikely that any monastery was built at Crowland before the late tenth century; both Guthlac and his sister, Pega, are clearly described as living as hermits rather than in communities, though their solitude was not absolute. Guthlac shared his hermitage with at least one other, a fellow hermit called Beccles, while Pega lived some seven miles (11 km) away, most likely at Peakirk; Beccles' journey to see Pega to tell her of Guthlac's death forms a particularly moving scene in *Guthlac* B.

Beccles, it may be noted, had not always been so loyal: at one point, according to Felix's *Life*, it had occurred to him that he might kill Guthlac in order, interestingly, that he would 'afterwards live in Guthlac's cell and also enjoy the great veneration of kings and princes'. The remark is telling since it makes very clear that Guthlac had patrons in high places, both from Mercia and from East Anglia (whose territory abutted onto the fens). It seems to have been Tatwine from Breedon[M] (the later archbishop of Canterbury) who first took Guthlac 'in a fisherman's skiff' to show him the spot where he might set up his hermitage; Haedda, bishop of Lichfield,[M] who some years later ordained him a priest; and an otherwise unknown East Anglian royal abbess who secured for Guthlac the lead coffin and linen shroud in which he would be buried.

The monastic ruins visible at Crowland today date from the twelfth to the fifteenth century. Attempts to discern the location either of Guthlac's shrine or of his cell should be treated with some caution. What does seem certain is that Crowland (like many other early Christian sites) was a place that already had cultic significance. The 'mound built of clods of earth' where Guthlac is said to have built himself a hut is likely to have been a place that had enjoyed veneration long before the coming of Christianity.

GLOUCESTER • Gloucestershire

In this year Cuthwine and Ceawlin fought against the Britons and killed three kings, Conmail, Condidan and Farinmail, at the place which is called Dyrham; and they captured three of their cities, Gloucester, Cirencester and Bath.

(Anglo-Saxon Chronicle, 577)

The *Anglo-Saxon Chronicle*'s entry for 577 may record an actual battle, or no more than a folk memory. The three cities mentioned were of course all major Roman cities. Gloucester, in its guise as the Roman town of Glevum, had been a centre of considerable importance and it is possible that some form of Christian worship continued there long after it ceased to be economically viable as a city. Excavations on the site of the church of St Mary de Lode suggest that a small wooden structure was erected on the site of a Roman villa which had been deliberately pulled down; westward-facing burials there possibly indicate signs of Christian practice but the evidence is far from conclusive.

Whatever may have happened between the supposed battle of 577 and c.679 is likewise very uncertain, but there seems no reason to doubt that c.679 Osric, king of the Hwicce, founded a minster at Gloucester dedicating it to St Peter. The minster looks like a dynastic foundation, designed to help preserve

Hwiccan identity in the face of the growing power of Mercia. The foundation charter records how Osric bought land from his overlord, King Aethelred of Mercia, with permission to build a minster which he could then hand on to his heirs. The first abbess was Osric's sister, Cyneburh; next came her kinswoman Eadburh (formerly Wulfhere of Mercia's queen). Cyneburh and Osric were duly buried in front of an altar dedicated to Petronilla (Petronilla being the supposed daughter of St Peter), flanked by Eadburh and Eafe. This is almost certainly the same Eafe once married to Aethelwealh of the South Saxons (*see* introduction to the Kingdom of the South Saxons or Sussex, page 229); after Caedwalla's slaughter of Aethelwealh, a return home and a safe haven as abbess of Gloucester would have been an appropriate solution for Eafe. Whoever she was, Abbess Eafe certainly added considerably to the minster's holdings, acquiring two of Droitwich's salt furnaces and land far into the Cotswolds so she could 'drive her sheep there'.

In the late ninth century, Gloucester became an important centre of operations against the Vikings when a new minster was built to which were brought the relics of King Oswald from Bardney.[M]

HANBURY • Worcestershire

... nine years after her burial, at the suggestion of the people of Hanbury, it pleased King Ceolred, who at the time ruled Mercia, to have [Waerburh's] sacrosanct body lifted from the tomb... [and] the virgin was found to be quite intact, as if sleeping in a soft bed.

(*Goscelin of Saint-Bertin: The Hagiography of the Female Saints of Ely*, ED. AND TRANS. ROSALIND C. LOVE, OXFORD MEDIEVAL TEXTS, 2004, P. 49)

Nikolaus Pevsner's guide to Worcestershire describes the church at Hanbury as occupying 'an elevated position'. He mentions the quality of the medieval arcades but for the most part notes only eighteenth- and nineteenth-century work. There is no hint here of the pre-Conquest origins of the church, no clue that the 'elevated' position might indicate that here was once a Roman-British hill fort. But this indeed seems to have been the case – the name means 'high fort' and a field survey has confirmed its character as such.

The original abbot, Colman, may have been Irish, but nothing is known about him, and by the ninth century the foundation belonged to the bishop of Worcester. By that time Hanbury was distinguished by its possession of the relics of St Werburgh. Werburgh would later become the major saint of Chester,[M] but in her lifetime her allegiances seem much less certain. Bede never mentions her, but there seems little doubt that she was the daughter of Wulfhere of Mercia and Eormenhild of Kent, and that at some point she was a nun at Ely.[EA] Seemingly, she was then summoned to Mercia by King Aethelred and placed in charge of all communities of religious women within Mercia. She died in the monastery of Threckingham but was buried at Hanbury. After nine years her body was found to be incorrupt, though by the time it was taken to Chester it had disintegrated.

The late eleventh-century *Life of Werburga* is attributed to Goscelin of St Bertin. It contains the much-loved legend of how Werburgh persuaded a flock of wild geese to desist from eating her crops, of how she had detected the theft of one of these geese, and of the misery this had brought to the flock until she had tracked down the missing bird and set it free to rejoin the others. Her other reported act of kindness was to a hermit-herdsman. His name was Alnot; he suffered at the hands of a cruel bailiff and in the end was killed by robbers. But during his lifetime he had a reputation as a saint, and his story was perhaps one of many that could have been told about an eighth-century hermit.

HEREFORD

... and Wealhstod is bishop of the people who dwell west of the river Severn. [v, 23]

As archbishop of Canterbury, Theodore was faced with a dire shortage of bishops. When he arrived in 669, there were not enough sees and only at Dunwich[EA] was there a canonically consecrated bishop. Three years later, at the Synod of Hertford, it was agreed that in principle the number of bishops should reflect the increased number of believers. Nonetheless, it took time to implement this plan, and when and how the peoples known as the Magonsaete finally got a bishop, based at Hereford, is a tangled story.

In 676, Aethelred of Mercia launched so fierce an attack on Kent that Putta, bishop of Rochester (*see* page 18), left his devastated see and went to Mercia seemingly to ask for some sort of compensation from the bishop of the Mercians, Seaxwulf (whose see was based at Lichfield[M]). If we follow Bede, we must then imagine a sympathetic Seaxwulf giving Putta a church and a small estate, and in return a contented Putta, a man with no great ambitions, happily became an itinerant teacher of a much-valued skill: church music. However, the Old English episcopal lists (of Mercian origin) tell a different story; here, Putta figures very clearly as the first bishop of Hereford, appointed in 676. What are we to make of this?

One solution is to imagine two Puttas – though the reality may be more complicated. The late seventh-century Bishop Putta may in fact be an invention of Offa's. In the time of Bede there was, to be sure, 'a bishop of the peoples who dwell over the river Severn to the west' and his name was Walhstod. 'The peoples' Bede mentions were the Magonsaete ('the frontier folk'), who formed one of the kingdoms which the Mercians, seemingly over the course of the seventh century, swallowed up.

A poem by Cuthbert, Walhstod's successor as bishop (and from 740 archbishop of Canterbury, *see* page 7), names, apart from Walhstod, two earlier bishops for whom Cuthbert had erected a spectacular funerary chapel, to be shared with appropriate Magonsaetan royals. The poem makes no mention of Putta. Moreover, the cathedral at Hereford is dedicated to St Mary and St Ethelbert, in reparation for Offa of Mercia's assassination of the king of Kent, Aethelbert, in 794; tradition has it that the murder took place at the royal palace of Sutton Walls, just four miles north of Hereford, and it has been suggested that it was this murder and the necessity for conspicuous atonement that occasioned the move of the see from Leominster[M] to Hereford.

The cathedral is, however, unlikely to have been Hereford's earliest church. There is some evidence for a cult of St Guthlac of Crowland[M] at Hereford from the early eighth century, and recent archaeological investigations suggest there may have been a seventh-century church and cemetery close to the river Wye. If this is so, it is likely to have been a church serving British Christians. Anglo-Saxon domination of this area was slow and uncertain. The name 'Hereford' means 'army-ford', an eloquent testimony to the strategic importance of the city and to the likelihood of frequent conflicts and contested territory – as late as 760, the Welsh annals were recording a battle at Hereford between Welsh and Anglo-Saxon forces. Given Bede's antipathy (as well as lack of knowledge) about the British church, his silence about Hereford is then less surprising than might at first appear.

INKBERROW · Worcestershire

... some contention was made between Bishop Heathored [of Worcester] and Wulfheard son of Cussa concerning the inheritance of Hemele and Duda which they had nominated to pass to Worcester after their death, that is, Inkberrow... and Bradley... wherefore Wulfheard wished, if he could to divert that piece of land from the aforesaid church in Worcester, through ignorance and foolishness.

(P. H. SAWYER, *Anglo-Saxon Charters*, ROYAL HISTORICAL SOCIETY, LONDON, 1968, CITED IN P. SIMS-WILLIAMS, *Religion and Literature in Western England, 600–800*, CAMBRIDGE UNIVERSITY PRESS, 1990, pp. 237–8)

Inkberrow, in Worcestershire (thought to be the model for 'Ambridge' in BBC Radio 4 serial *The Archers*) has also been identified as the likely site of a foundation created by Oshere, king of the Hwicce, for Abbess Cuthswith in the last decade of the seventh century. Nothing remains now of Cuthswith's monastery – even by the early ninth century it looks as if it was being appropriated by a local nobleman as a desirable place for him 'to live honourably and have his dwelling'. In Abbess Cuthswith's day, however, there was a very different story to be told. In c.705, Cuthswith expanded the holdings of her monastery; at the same time, the abbess seems to have had the resources to buy, or perhaps just the prestige to acquire, a fifth-century Italian copy of Jerome's commentary on Ecclesiastes.

The Jerome manuscript later found its way to Germany, but the inscription in it clearly states that it had formerly belonged to Cuthswith. It is highly probable that the MS came to Cuthswith via Oftfor, bishop of the Hwicce at the time of the foundation of Inkberrow. Oftfor had been one of the five monks from Hilda's monastery of Whitby to become a bishop. Bede comments on his love of scholarship and how, after leaving Whitby but before becoming a bishop, he had gone to study under Archbishop Theodore at Canterbury, and then had visited Rome; this trip to Rome would, of course, have provided plentiful opportunities for book buying.

But whether this was, or was not, the route whereby Cuthswith acquired her manuscript, she clearly made good use of it: some of the original leaves were missing and these were replaced by an English scribe, practising as he or she did so the new art of word separation. This way of writing we take now for granted, but it was being introduced for the first time into Europe in Cuthswith's day because it made it easier to study texts with closer attention than was possible when one word ran into the next. Inkberrow was, then, clearly at the cutting edge. The manuscript may subsequently have reached Germany with Bishop Mildred of Worcester[M] when he went to visit Boniface.

Inkberrow's history after Cuthswith illustrates the ways

in which small monasteries might either become the property of laymen or be absorbed into the holdings of the see. In Inkberrow's case, it was decided that Wulfheard might keep Inkberrow (and nearby Bradley) during his lifetime, but that the estates were indeed then to pass to the bishop of Worcester.

LEOMINSTER · Herefordshire

the king began to tell his dream like this:
'Night wore on, with me asleep
on my easy bed,
    when I seemed to see
two dogs.
Monstrous and terrifying,
    Grab me by the throat;
But from somewhere a certain person with a venerable
    appearance,
With his hair tonsured from ear to ear...
Came to my aid,
And with a golden key... he plucked me
mightily from the teeth of the dogs.

('THE LEGEND OF ST ETFRID, PRIEST OF LEOMINSTER',
ED. HUGH PAWSEY, The Early Church in Herefordshire,
LEOMINSTER, 2001, p. 23)

Anglo-Saxon Leominster was unusually rich and powerful. Tradition has it that its minster was founded in c.660 by King Merewalh of the Magonsaete, son of King Penda of Mercia and also the founder of the minster at Wenlock,[M] in response to a vision.

A fearsome dream of two dogs (clearly hounds of hell) had

so terrified the king that without hesitation he had welcomed the appearance, and the preaching, of the missionary St Etfrid (Eadfrith) of Northumbria: in this way, the king, once himself as fierce as a lion, now became as meek as a lamb. His foundation of Leominster (the 'monastery of the lion') marked this miraculous conversion. But was Merewalh in fact simply appropriating a British cult centre (it is hard otherwise to know how an arm of St David came to be venerated at Leominster) or was Merewalh, as some have suspected, himself of British origin (his name possibly means 'the famous Welshman') before being adopted, or co-opted by Penda? Or was he perhaps the son of Penda by a British woman?

To such questions there can be no certain answers; much about both Merewalh and Leominster is likely to remain a mystery, and whether it will ever be possible to detect, decipher or describe the influence of British Christianity in Mercia is highly doubtful. Nonetheless, there are clues which do at least support the historicity of Eadfrith's mission. Thus while nothing has survived of the fabric of Merewalh's church, the nature of the site is highly suggestive: the minster appears to have been well enclosed, bounded to the north and east by the river Lugg and its tributary the Kenwater, and protected on its south and west by a huge earthen bank – comparisons with Northumbrian houses would not be hard to find. Furthermore, the preservation of two prayers attributed to Columba of Iona in an Anglo-Saxon prayer book that seemingly belonged to Leominster, points strongly to Northumbrian links. (For the arrival of missionaries from Iona in Northumbria, *see* Lindisfarne, page 43.) St Columba thus remained a saint commemorated at Leominster long after his cult had been forgotten elsewhere in England.

If the guess some historians have made is correct – that Hereford's[M] first bishops had their seat at Leominster rather than at Hereford itself – then we have every reason to imagine eighth-century Leominster under Cuthbert, bishop of the Magonsaete (and possibly thereafter, from 740, archbishop of Canterbury), as a place of sophistication and splendour. Cuthbert built an impressive funeral chapel for previous bishops of the see, together with their lay patrons, and completed work on the magnificent banner ('a veil of gold and silver for Christ's sacred cross') which his predecessor, Walhstod, had begun. Both chapel and banner are described in poems Cuthbert himself wrote and then circulated to his friend at Worcester,[M] Bishop Mildred.

The abrupt end to Leominster's pre-Conquest history with the abduction in 1046 of its abbess by one of the brothers of Harold (of Hastings fame – *see* Bosham[S]) was an ignominious fate for a community that may well have been home to Cuthbert and all of Hereford's bishops for most of the eighth century.

LICHFIELD · Staffordshire

At this time King Wulfhere was ruling over the kingdom of Mercia and, since [Bishop] Jaruman was dead, he asked Theodore to provide him and his people with a bishop; as Theodore did not wish to consecrate a new bishop for them, he asked King Oswiu to give them Bishop Chad who was then living in retirement in his own monastery of Lastingham. [IV, 3]

Lichfield Cathedral, unusually, can boast three spires. Despite this distinction, the building is unlikely to top anyone's list of favourite medieval churches. Yet for those with an interest in

Anglo-Saxon history, Lichfield has special claims. Here was a see which, during King Offa's reign, succeeded, albeit for only a short spell, in rivalling the claims and prestige of Canterbury by achieving metropolitan status and thus the right to have its own archbishop. In the time of Bede, all this was, of course, yet in the future, but even before the appointment of Chad to the see, Lichfield had been singled out as a suitable place for a bishop's residence.

Lichfield thus replaced the Mercian see that had been set up some ten years earlier at a place generally identified as the former Roman city known now as Wall. Why the move was thought desirable is unclear, but the new site, according to Stephen's *Life of Wilfrid*, 'was highly suitable for an episcopal see' (possibly because it had long housed a community of British Christians whom it now seemed appropriate to absorb – or maybe supplant).

By the time of his appointment, Chad had already had a distinguished career, first as abbot of Lastingham[N] and then, after the Synod of Whitby,[N] as a bishop. As Bede portrays him, Chad practised an exemplary humility, in the manner of his master, Bishop Aidan of Lindisfarne (*see* page 43). One manifestation of this was Chad's insistence on undertaking his preaching missions on foot in imitation of Christ's apostles. This, Bede tells us, was a custom to which he was deeply attached and it took direct action by Theodore of Canterbury to encourage him onto horseback for the long journeys that made him change his ways: 'the archbishop lifted him onto the horse with his own hands since he knew him to be a man of great sanctity and he determined to compel him to ride a horse when necessity arose' [IV, 3]. Chad also followed Aidan's practice of taking retreats. Near his new cathedral at Lichfield, he had built, according to Bede, a separate oratory, 'a more retired dwelling-place... in which he could read and pray privately with a few of his brothers, that is to say, seven or eight of them' [IV, 3]. (This retreat was perhaps on the site of the present St Michael's Church or else a few miles away, at Stow.)

Chad had been bishop of Lichfield for only a few years when plague struck his community. Bede's account of Chad's own death bears all the hallmarks of a much-lamented and much-commemorated event. As reported by Bede, the main witness was Owine, a man who had originally been a member of Queen Aethelthryth of Northumbria's entourage, but who had given up this status and, bearing just 'an axe and an adze', had asked to join Chad's community. On the day in question, Owine was working outside while Chad was at prayer in his oratory. Suddenly Owine heard descending from sky, from the southeast, the sound of 'sweet and joyful singing'. The sound entered Chad's oratory. Half an hour later the sound flew back, whereupon Chad opened the window of his oratory, called in Owine and asked him to fetch the seven brethren who were in the church. To them he broke the news that he would soon die; to Owine he explained that what he had heard was an angelic host who had come to tell him he would die within a week (as indeed he did).

Years later, the story was confirmed by none other than Egbert, later of Iona, who knew that the angels who came to fetch Chad had been accompanied by Chad's brother, Cedd, who had died some years before at Lastingham,[N] but had always kept a watchful eye over Lichfield. The provision of an angelic escort was especially important because of the belief that the soul on its way to heaven might be intercepted by malignant spirits who would try to drag it to hell.

Chad, meanwhile, was first buried outside, close to the church of St Mary, and then, when Lichfield's second church, the church of St Peter, had been completed (on the site of today's cathedral), his body was translated to a new tomb, described by Bede as 'a wooden coffin in the shape of a little house, having an aperture in its side, through which those who visit it out of devotion can insert their hands and take out a little of the dust. When it is put in water and given either to cattle or men who are ailing, they get their wish and are at once freed from their ailments and rejoice in health restored' [IV, 3]. Bede gives no specific examples of Chad's cures, but what he does provide us with is a vivid account of Chad's sense of God's presence in the world, notably during tempestuous weather:

> ... if [Chad] happened to be reading or doing something
> else and suddenly a high wind arose, he would at once
> invoke the mercy of the Lord and beg him to have pity upon
> the human race. If the wind increased in violence he would
> shut his book, fall on his face, and devote himself still
> more earnestly to prayer. But if there were a violent storm
> of wind and rain or if lightning and thunder brought terror
> to earth and sky, he would enter the church and, with still
> deeper concentration, earnestly devote himself to prayers
> and psalms until the sky cleared. When his people asked
> him why he did it he replied, [quoting Psalm 17] 'Have
> you not read, "The Lord also thundered in the heavens and
> the Highest gave his voice. Yea, he sent out his arrows and
> scattered them, and he shot out lightnings and discomfited
> them?... and so said [Chad] '... as often as [God] disturbs
> the sky and raises his hand as if about to strike, yet spares

us still, we should implore his mercy, examining the
innermost recesses of our hearts and purging out the dregs
of our sins... that we may never deserve to be struck down.'
[IV, 3]

Medieval belief in Chad's own powers of intercession were
amply confirmed by the dramatic discovery in 2003, during
building work in the cathedral, of three pieces of a limestone
carving thought to have formed part of the gable end of a stone
shrine built to cover Chad's original wooden coffin. The carving
is of an angel, clad in a bright-yellow robe, poised in such a way
as to suggest he has just alighted. The work is dated to the late
eighth century and as such is a further testimony to the glories
of Mercian art under King Offa. That so much care was lavished
on Chad's tomb helps to substantiate the view that the St Chad
Gospels, displayed now in the treasury at Lichfield, were indeed
made locally and in Chad's honour – perhaps at the same time
as the new shrine – rather than being, as was once imagined, a
gospel book of continental origin that had just happened to find
its way to Lichfield.

LINCOLN · Lincolnshire

Now Paulinus also preached the word in the kingdom of
Lindsey, the first land on the south bank of the river Humber,
bordering on the sea. His first convert was the reeve of the city of
Lincoln, called Blaecca, he and his household. [II,16]

Lincoln, the chief city of Anglo-Saxon Lindsey, had been a prosperous and well-defended Roman town, its identity so well

established that its Roman name survived even after the legions had left. This might suggest continued fifth-century occupation, though there is scant archaeological evidence for this, but it does reflect the importance of the city and its geographical position.

Then, as now, the river Witham on which Lincoln lies gives access to the sea; Ermine Street runs through it all the way to London, while the Fosse Way leads to Bath and Exeter. Small wonder, then, that in the early seventh century, Paulinus, bishop of York, put Lincoln on his itinerary. His first convert in the city was a certain Blaecca, described by Bede as a *praefectus*. Whatever the exact nature of this office, it is clear that Blaecca was a figure of importance and that Bede knew of no king in Lindsey whom Paulinus should have approached instead. Whether Lindsey had ever had its own kings remains an unsettled question, but it certainly had its bishops. Where such bishops were based is another mystery, though it is highly likely that *Syddenis civitas*, the name given to Lindsey's see, was indeed Lincoln itself.

After Blaecca's conversion, Paulinus, according to Bede, erected a church of stone 'of remarkable workmanship'. Political upheavals subsequently took their toll – Bede reports that the church's roof had fallen in 'through long neglect or by the hand of the enemy', but that it had remained a cult centre where 'every year miracles of healing took place'.

A number of mysteries nonetheless surround this church. It has been plausibly argued that it is in fact most unlikely that Paulinus would have immediately erected a stone church for Blaecca's baptism. More probably he put up a wooden church (as he had done at York[N] for Edwin) and a stone church then followed, possibly in time for the consecration at Lincoln, by Paulinus, of Honorius as archbishop of Canterbury in c.633.

This stone church, St Paul-in-the-Bail, was built within the former Roman forum. To the west of the city, a further Anglo-Saxon church was built some years later, dedicated to St Peter. The relationship between these two churches is uncertain, but it is probable that they came to share between them the functions and needs of an episcopal city.

Further 'outreach' work had been provided in the waters of the Trent: this we know from Deda, abbot of Partney,[M] who reported to Bede how Paulinus had baptised many there in the presence of King Edwin. Deda's story recalls Paulinus's earlier baptismal ceremonies in the waters of the rivers Gale and Swale but the Lindsey occasion may have gained added force by their performance on the eastern banks of the Trent at a time when Mercian ascendancy over the area was still in the future and the Mercians were still pagan.

Lincoln's importance under both Vikings and Normans may explain why so few traces of early Anglo-Saxon Lincoln have survived. A rare find during excavations at St Paul-in-the-Bail in the 1970s was a seventh-century hanging bowl, of fine design and in excellent condition; it can now be viewed in the cathedral treasury. But it should be noted that an even grander hanging bowl, made of silver, and of a slightly later date, was found in the river Witham in Lincoln in 1816. In 1868 this bowl was put on show; thereafter it disappeared. Whatever the exact function of these hanging bowls may have been (and the jury is still out), they are undoubtedly objects of enormous value and splendour. Treasure hunters should keep searching...

One of Bede's lost epigrams (mentioned but not transcribed by the antiquarian John Leland) seems to commemorate the building of a cathedral at Lincoln by Bishop Cyneberht. Cyneberht had provided Bede with information about Lindsey while he was writing his *History*. The epigram was perhaps inscribed on the walls of the new cathedral.

OUNDLE • Northamptonshire

... at Oundle where he had once dedicated a church to the Apostle Andrew, Wilfrid was seized by a sickness, and knew that the end of his life was at hand.

(STEPHEN OF RIPON, *Life of Wilfrid*, CHAPTER LXV)

Notable people that appear should you Google Oundle are William Laxton, William Abell, Rowan Atkinson, Louise Mensch and Ebenezer Prout. No mention here of St Wilfrid – a shocking omission. Oundle, after all, was where Wilfrid spent his last hours, and there can be no doubt that he died as he had lived – in style. Wilfrid had arranged for the disposition of all his treasures and offices and now he took to his bed. His followers gathered around to sing the Psalter and when they reached verse 30 of what is now Psalm 104 – 'Send forth thy Spirit and they shall be created, and thou shalt renew the face of the earth' – Wilfrid died. At that moment, wrote Stephen, 'They were all amazed, for at that hour they heard the sound as it were of birds approaching.'

For Wilfrid's exequies a great crowd gathered. An abbot by the name of Bacula spread out the winding sheet and here was laid Wilfrid's body. Again, the sound of birds could be heard 'settling down with a sound and flying away again into the sky, their wings making sweet melody'. 'Wise men' explained that without a doubt angels led by St Michael had now come to take Wilfrid's soul to Paradise. Meanwhile a tent was set up so the body could be washed before being escorted for burial to Ripon.[N] On Bacula's instructions, the winding sheet was sent to an abbess to look after until Bacula could come and fetch it, but that she was not to wash it – yet she did, and the water proved to have healing powers.

Some time after Wilfrid's death, the minster at Oundle was the object of an arson attack. The miraculous preservation of the one building in which Wilfrid died and of the wooden cross that marked the spot where his body had been washed made an immense impression on Stephen. His readers today may be more likely to notice the incidental information that the attack provided about the minster: it was surrounded by a substantial thorn hedge and the building that Wilfrid died in was thatched.

Nothing remains now of Wilfrid's Oundle minster. It is thought to have been sacked by Vikings.

OXFORD · Oxfordshire

Then King Didan built a church in the town of Oxford and had it dedicated in honour of the Holy Trinity, the spotless Virgin and All Saints. Reverend Frideswide asked her father, the same King Didan, to give her the church, and he gave her the church.

('A LIFE OF ST FRIDESWIDE' IN JOHN BLAIR (ED.),
Saint Frideswide, Patron of Oxford, PERPETUA PRESS, 2004)

St Frideswide has had a chequered history – sequentially persecuted, revered, reviled, forgotten, doubted, then rehabilitated. Her story as preserved in the twelfth century is this: she was the daughter of a certain King Didan (a ruler possibly connected in some way to Deddington in north Oxfordshire), who, in her strenuous attempts to avoid being married off to her father's successor, was forced to leave the community which – with her father's blessing – she had set up in Oxford. Her escape route took her along the Thames (a river thick with minsters), but she finally returned to Oxford in time to die.

The likelihood that a minster had been founded in Oxford in the eighth century must be high, for although nothing remains now of any such foundation that could have been Frideswide's, it is clear that by then an important settlement had already developed around the crossing of the Thames near what is now Salter's boathouse. Further, by the early eleventh century, if not well before, there was a monastery, dedicated to Christ, which claimed to hold the body of St Frideswide.

After the Norman Conquest, ambitious canons, anxious to maximise the potential of Frideswide's sanctity, decided to make sure they knew where the body lay and proceeded with appropriate excavations and the expected results. The new shrine which the triumphant canons then built has now been magnificently reconstructed and placed within Christ Church Cathedral, Oxford.

PARTNEY • Lincolnshire

Some time afterwards, when Queen Osthryth was staying in the monastery a certain a certain reverend abbess named Aethelhild, who is still living, came to visit her. The abbess was the sister of two holy men, Aethelwine and Ealdwine, the former of whom was bishop of Lindsey while the other was

abbot in the monastery known as Partney, not far from which
Aethelhild's monastery stood. [III, 11]

Nothing remains now of Anglo-Saxon Partney, but as with
Bardney[M] (with which it had close links), the site itself is of interest as an example of another island foundation. In the case of
Partney, the minster was established on an island in the middle
of the river Lymn. Bede was evidently in contact with the abbot
of Partney, Deda, for it was through Deda that Bede gained his
memorable description of Bishop Paulinus of York: an old man
whom Paulinus had baptised in the river Trent had told Deda
(who in turn told Bede) that Paulinus was 'a tall man, with a
slight stoop, black hair, a thin face, a slender aquiline nose...
[a man] at the same time... both venerable and awe-inspiring in
appearance' [II, 16] and there can be little doubt that this, too, is
how King Edwin found him [II, 12].

Partney seems to have been one of a network of minsters, not
all of which can now be traced. This much is evident from Bede's
story concerning the visit paid by the neighbouring abbess called
Aethelhild to Bardney at a time when Queen Osthryth was staying
there. Aethelhild was evidently a well-connected woman: one of
her brothers, Bede tells us, was bishop of Lindsey; another, the
abbot of Partney. Her role in Bede's story is to further authenti-
cate Oswald's sanctity and miraculous powers. Osthryth gives
Aethelhild some of the wonder-working soil impregnated by
the water that had washed Oswald's bones (*see* Bardney[M]). Some
time later, the relic cures a visitor to Aethelhild's minster of
what sounds like an epileptic fit. The description of the com-
motion caused within the minster by the seizure makes it clear
that Aethelhild's community housed both men and women, but

where exactly it stood we do not know. We can tell only that it was both near Partney and sufficiently close to Bardney for Aethelhild to have seen the miraculous light that shone in the sky on the night when Oswald's bones arrived.

PETERBOROUGH · Huntingdonshire

Theodore consecrated as bishop Seaxwulf, founder and abbot of the monastery known as Medeshamstede in the land of the Gywre. [IV, 6]

Seaxwulf, its first abbot, founded Peterborough or Medesham-stede, as it was known until the tenth century, during the years before he became bishop of Lichfield in *c*.675. Bede tells us that the minster was founded in territory belonging to the Gywre, a name seemingly meaning 'marsh people' because of the boggy nature of the terrain. Apart from this brief mention in Bede, much of what is now known about Peterborough's early history comes from the twelfth-century account by its monk, Hugh Candidus. Hugh was lyrical in his praise of the marshiness of the place (though by the time he was writing it was probably much less wet than in Bede's day as a result of changes in sea levels). It is indeed likely that one of the initial attractions of the site was its 'island' quality, and the sense of isolation this gave, combined with the reality of its position near major routes (the Fen Causeway and Ermine Street).

Despite some doubts about Hugh Candidus' reliability, it is very clear that the picture he draws of Medeshamstede as a key minster in Mercia is substantially true. The minster was richly endowed and although it is no longer thought to have headed

any sort of confederation of Middle Anglian houses, its position on the border between Mercia and East Anglia undoubtedly
made it a key foundation for the Mercian royal house. It was
heavily patronised by Offa, who may well have had a palace in
the vicinity (as well as a family minster at nearby Castor[M]) and it
is not impossible that Peterborough was where the great reform-
ing Synod of Clofesho was held in 747 (though Brixworth[M] also
has its claims).

Medeshamstede/Peterborough was sacked by the Vikings in
963, plundered by Hereward the Wake in 1070, and burnt to the
ground (but for the dormitory and chapter house) by a fire in
1116. Given this tale of destruction, it was assumed that nothing
could be known about the earliest monastic buildings until late
nineteenth-century excavations uncovered evidence of Saxon
work underneath the floor of the present nave and transept.

A number of carved stones, including grave slabs, were thus
added to the two already well-known pieces of sculpture: the
so-called Hedda shrine, displayed in the southeast of the chancel, and a stone depicting two (unidentified) figures now built
into a wall in the south transept. These sculptures belong to the
age of Mercian supremacy rather than to the Age of Bede, but
it is worth noting the possible relationship between the Hedda
shrine and Chad's tomb, as described by Bede. Chad's tomb at
Lichfield,[M] so Bede tells us, was shaped like a little house, as is
the Hedda shrine, though the former was made of wood and the
latter of stone. But who is actually buried in the Hedda shrine
remains a mystery. It was for long thought to house the remains
of the abbot Hedda, martyred by Vikings in the late ninth century, but such a view is no longer tenable given the current views
of its dating.

REPTON · Derbyshire

When this same man of blessed memory, Guthlac... [had]
abandoned his weary limbs one night to their accustomed rest...
suddenly, marvellous to tell, a spiritual flame...
began to burn in this man's heart... leaving everything
he possessed, he came to the monastery of Repton, in which
he received the mystic tonsure of St Peter, under an abbess
whose name was Aelfthryth.

(Felix's *Life of Saint Guthlac,* ED. AND TRANS. BERTRAM
COLGRAVE, CAMBRIDGE UNIVERSITY PRESS, 1956,
pp. 83–5)

Repton was already in the late seventh century a sufficiently prestigious house to be chosen for his new vocation by the aristocratic
Guthlac as he turned away from his life of freebooting. (Guthlac
later became the renowned hermit of Crowland.ᴹ) Most probably
founded in the 670s on land granted to the abbot of Breedon-on-
the-Hill,ᴹ the community Guthlac entered was led by an abbess
named Aelfthryth. We know nothing about this abbess beyond
her name, and her reception of Guthlac, but it is not impossible
that she was a founding figure. Bede here is no help – he never
once mentions Repton – but extensive archaeology over several
decades has amply demonstrated the importance of the house
for Anglo-Saxon Mercia, before it was sequestered by a Viking
army as its quarters for the winter of 873–4.

The earliest Christian building that survives at Repton is a
sunken chamber or crypt of the mid-eighth century, an embed-
ded coin dated 715 providing at least one certain date. This
chamber was about 2 metres (6½ ft) deep, lined with masonry,

with niches on the north, east and south wall and a stepped entrance via the west end. It is possible this space was used both as a baptistery and as a place of burial; it may even be the mausoleum of Aethelbald, king of Mercia from 716 until 757 (when he was murdered by his bodyguard). Such burial chambers were well known on the Continent and it has been suggested that in eighth-century England they might have had particular appeal as a Christianised version of a barrow burial; from such a grave Aethelbald could have overlooked and guarded the floodplain of the river Trent.

When, some hundred years later, the Mercian house acquired a saint in the person of St Wystan, the Repton crypt was then adapted to promote his cult. Embellished and incorporated into an extended church, it is this ninth-century version of the crypt that can be visited today.

Despite's Bede silence about Repton, he does acknowledge Aethelbald as the most powerful king south of the Humber. It is just possible that we have a portrait of Aethelbald on a piece of sculpted stone found during the Repton excavations. The stone depicts a mounted warrior, armed with shield, sword and curved knife. This combination of a classical pose with Germanic weaponry suggests a form of authority Bede would readily have recognised; it is not hard to imagine that it will have been bitter to him that its seat had slipped southwards from Northumbria.

ST ALBANS · Hertfordshire

*The blessed Alban suffered death on 22 June near the city of
Verulamium… Here when peaceful Christian times returned,*

a church of wonderful worksmanship was built, a worthy
memorial of his martyrdom. [1, 7]

The story of England's conversion to Christianity is remarkably free of tales of martyrs; only with the advent of the Vikings is blood shed with any regularity in the name of the new faith. But there are exceptions: most notably that of St Alban of Verulamium (and cf. Bishopstone[S]).

St Alban was already being venerated as saint and martyr in the early fifth century. Alban belongs then, in the first instance, to the Christianity of the Roman Empire, but his story is important for Bede's day, partly because it mattered to Bede himself and also because it serves as a reminder that there are likely to be more vestiges of the Christianity of the Roman Empire in England than can ever be uncovered.

St Alban's 'crime', according to Bede, was to shelter a Christian cleric during the period of the Diocletian persecutions of the late third century (though there is some evidence that Bede's information may not be quite accurate and that St Alban in fact may have been martyred some decades earlier). So impressed was Alban by the fortitude and faith of the cleric that he adopted his faith and even took his place when orders for his arrest came. Wearing the cleric's cloak, Alban openly defied the judge who ordered him to return to pagan worship or face the consequences. Alban remained steadfast, withstood torture and prepared himself for execution. He was led to the river that ran by the city walls; so packed was the bridge with spectators that it took a miracle – the drying up of the river – to make it possible for Alban to get across. This miracle so moved one of the executioners that he promptly converted to Christianity; the other executioners meanwhile dithered while Alban himself resolutely went on up the hill to a spot close to the arena. Despite the grim fate ahead, which Alban, along with the newly converted executioner, was to suffer, the hill itself is paradoxically described in the most lyrical of terms – it was 'fair, shining and beautiful, adorned, indeed clothed, on all sides with wild flowers of every kind' [1, 7] and so many further miracles followed the executions that the judge felt compelled to order the persecutions of Christians to cease.

In Bede's own day, so he tells us, healing of the sick and other miracles were still taking place on the spot where Alban had been executed and where there was now a church. Excavations at St Albans support Bede here, suggesting that, although the Roman city will have been inside the walls, a new Christian city subsequently developed outside, in proximity to St Alban's shrine.

Some time later (and there is much debate as to how much later), the reputation of St Albans was further enhanced by the alleged discovery by King Offa of Mercia of St Alban's bones. Whatever the truth behind this story, it circulated widely in the thirteenth century and supported St Albans' perception of itself as England's premier abbey.

The present abbey was built soon after the Norman Conquest by Abbot Paul, nephew of the new archbishop of Canterbury, Lanfranc. Abbot Paul's use of red Roman brick taken from the remains of the Roman city of Verulamium to build his new abbey added considerably to the perception, already fostered by Bede, of unbroken Christian worship on the site ever since the martyrdom of Alban.

WENLOCK · Shropshire

*To the blessed virgin and best-loved lady, Eadburga... you
have asked me, my dear sister, to describe to you in writing
the marvellous visions of the man who died recently and came
to life again in the convent of the Abbess Milburga...*

(FROM *The Letters of Saint Boniface*, TRANS. E. EMERTON,
COLUMBIA UNIVERSITY PRESS, 1940, p. 3)

Wenlock (meaning, perhaps, 'the white place') is the site today of the spectacular ruins of an eleventh/twelfth-century monastery, but it has a much older history, one which the Norman newcomers, builders of the new edifice, were themselves keen to appropriate. These monks had not been at Wenlock long before they unearthed the 'holy, beautiful and luminous bones' of St Mildburg (or Milburga), seventh-century abbess of the house which, suitably enshrined, quickly began to work miracles. However fabulous some of the miracles may appear to be, the account of the discovery of these precious relics, together with a *Life* of Mildburg, contains much about the origins of the house which may be authentic.

According to these sources, Mildburg was the daughter of Merewalh, a son of King Penda of Mercia and king himself of the Mercian sub-kingdom of the Magonsaete. Some time around 600, Merewalh converted to Christianity as the result of the preaching of a Northumbrian missionary (*see* Leominster[M]). He then married into the Kentish royal house and thereafter established Wenlock as a community of men and women, with his daughter Mildburg at its head.

Wenlock under Mildburg's rule has been made famous by the

survival of a letter from Boniface of Nursling[W] to a nun named Eadburh (possibly of Wimborne[W]). This was a response to her request for details she believed Boniface had received from Hildelith of Barking[E] concerning the visions of the afterlife that a brother at Wenlock had experienced. The request thus provides a vivid glimpse of a busy eighth-century monastic grapevine, though, as it turns out Boniface had heard of the visions from the brother himself. The brother had indeed been instructed when he 'returned to his body' to tell believers what he had seen ('scoffers' he could ignore) and in particular to warn a woman who was living some way away about her sins and to tell her how she could make atonement. The brother himself was to confess any of his unexpiated sins to a priest named Begga and to let him know about all his visions.

The brother (he was probably but not certainly a monk) had already been taken for dead when he returned to life. What he had seen can be compared with other such visions (cf. Fursa of Burgh Castle,[EA] Guthlac of Crowland[M] and Dryhthelm of Melrose[N]). Scenes of hope thus alternated with those of despair. In the Wenlock vision, both vices and virtues came forward 'as if in person with their accusations' – 'I am falsehood'; 'I am the idle errand' – and their commendations – 'I am the service of the weak'; 'I am the psalm which he chanted before God to atone for the idle word'. The scenes of hell are suitably terrifying – 'In the lowest depths, as if in a deeper hell, he heard the awful weeping and wailing of sorrowing souls, terrible beyond the power of words to describe. And the angel said to him, "The lamentations and weeping which you hear in the depths comes from those souls to whom the mercy of God will never come. But everlasting flame will torture them without end".'

But the brother was also shown a lesser hell, from which, on the Day of Judgement, souls would be rescued, their sins by then having been purged. The brother was likewise given a sense both of Paradise, where those who had committed only 'trifling sins' were being purified, as well as of the heavenly Jerusalem where truly holy souls lived in perpetual joy. In the final part of the brother's vision, living individuals were singled out: here, guardian angels successfully protected the virtuous while devils gleefully egged on sinners. And among the sinners, notably, was the Mercian king himself, Ceolred. Ceolred – he had a bad press too, in the *Life of Guthlac* – is captured by demons and 'harassed and torn with infinite tortures', while the angels in despair accepted defeat and withdrew the help they had been giving him. Ceolred did in fact die soon after this vision was reported and, if we are to believe Boniface, was even then an unrepentant sinner. Boniface described his death some years later (in an admonitory letter to King Aethelred of Mercia) in particularly lurid terms: the king here had been sent mad by a malignant spirit and so 'without repentance and confession, raging and distracted, conversing with devils and cursing the priests of God, he departed from this light without a doubt to the torments of hell'.

Ceolred's accession to the throne of Mercia and his death are both mentioned by Bede; but neither Wenlock nor Boniface figure in the *History*. Such gaps remain puzzling. But even without Bede's help, the brother's vision of the afterlife spread far and wide, both in England, where it was translated into the vernacular, and abroad, where a version was still available in fifteenth-century Italy.

Boniface's letter recounting the vision is likely to have been written c.716, shortly before he left for Frisia, since he signs himself by his original name of 'Wynefrith'. Added to the letter is part of a poem; its style gives some indication of the way in which, as a young man, Boniface had been influenced by the illustrious Aldhelm of Malmesbury.[W] The wordplay is striking: *Vale, vere virgo vite/ut et vivas angelice...* ('Farewell, maiden of true life, may you live like an angel...').

WIRKSWORTH · Derbyshire

The priests were Cedd, Adda, Betti and Diuma, the last of whom was as Irishman while the others were English... After these priests had come with the king [Peada] into his kingdom, they preached the Word and were listened to gladly. [III, 21]

In the wall of the north aisle of Wirksworth church has been set a red sandstone slab, discovered during restoration work in the nineteenth century. This slab is thought to be the cover of a sarcophagus/shrine originally kept within the church itself. It is richly decorated with carvings of scenes taken, in the main, from the New Testament and from the Apocryphal gospels. The iconography is striking, not least since its depiction of the procession that attended the death of the Virgin is otherwise not found in England until the twelfth century. Who was buried in the sarcophagus is unknown, but the priest Betti has been suggested as a possible candidate.

Peada's missionaries came to his kingdom following his marriage to King Oswiu's daughter, Alchflaed. (She was later suspected of having murdered her husband, shortly after the battle of the Winwaed in 655; *see* Leeds.[N]) Betti is never mentioned again by Bede, but Diuma goes on to become a bishop, based perhaps at Charlbury,[M] while Cedd can be found at Bradwell-on-Sea[E] as bishop of the East Saxons. Adda's claim to fame, in Bede's eyes, was that he was the brother of Utta, abbot of Gateshead. No trace of Utta's monastery has survived and Bede never mentions Gateshead again. However, he devotes a whole chapter to the journey Utta made in order to fetch King Oswiu's bride, Eanflaed, from Kent. In it he describes how the abbot of Gateshead succeeded in calming a storm by using oil that had been blessed by Bishop Aidan of Lindisfarne (*see* page 43).

WORCESTER · Worcestershire

The text of the decisions of the synod is as follows:
Chapter IX: That more bishops [are to be] created as the
number of the faithful increase. (This chapter received general
discussion, but at the time we came to no decision on
the matter.) [IV, 5]

In 672–3, with a few years of his arrival in England, Archbishop Theodore summoned a national council that met at Hertford. Among the items on the agenda was recognition of the need for more bishops and, by the end of the decade, if not before, the people of the Hwicce had acquired a bishop of their own, based at Worcester. The first candidate, Tatfrith, had been a pupil of Abbess Hilda at Whitby.[N] However, Tatfrith died before he could be consecrated, whereupon Oftfor (*see* Inkberrow[M]), also from Whitby, succeeded to the see.

Despite this evidence of strong Northumbrian influence, Christianity in Worcester was probably built on a much older base. The see corresponded with the territory of the Hwicce and it is highly likely that the Christianisation of the kingdom owes as much to the indigenous British Christians as to any missionary work from Anglo-Saxons. Bede had described the outcome of the meetings between St Augustine and British bishops 'on the borders of the Hwicce and the West Saxons' as a disaster, but it looks nonetheless as if British Christianity had continued to thrive and to spread among the Hwicce. An example Bede himself gives, albeit incidentally, is of Eafe, the princess of the Hwicce, in the mid-seventh century, 'baptised in her own country, the kingdom of the Hwicce' [IV, 13], who had then married Aethelwealh of the South Saxons, taking her faith with her (*cf.* Gloucester^M).

Archaeological evidence supports the possibility that Worcester cathedral was built on an already Christianised site; the excavation of a sixth/early seventh-century grave unearthed what looks like a Christian priest still wearing his stole. Furthermore, the dedications of three early churches within the city are highly suggestive. These are to St Helena, allegedly the British-born mother of Emperor Constantine; St Alban, Britain's most celebrated martyr (*see* St Albans^M); and St Margaret, probably Margaret of Antioch, a saint found already in seventh-century British litanies. The topography of these churches to the north of the cathedral makes sense if they all pre-date it and certainly St Helen's continued to act as a major parish church long after the establishment of the cathedral. It may even be this strong Christian presence at Worcester that had encouraged the choice of that city as the centre of a new diocese in the first place, rather than the seemingly more prestigious city of Gloucester.^M

There may also have been economic factors to consider: Worcester's bridge across the Severn and its proximity to the brine springs at Droitwich should not be overlooked. Droitwich brine was enormously salty and therefore extremely profitable. It should be no surprise, therefore, that an early charter from the reign of King Aethelbald, dated c.716/17, suggests an already well-established connection between the minster and salt-works, with both king and minister vying for the profits of the salt trade.

Nor were Worcester's trading links merely local. In 743, Aethelbald granted Mildred, bishop of Worcester, 'and to all his holy community... remission of all dues on two ships exacted by the tax-gatherers in the harbour of London'. Anyone who challenged this exemption would be excommunicated: 'excluded from the body and blood of our Lord the Saviour Christ... and severed and sundered from all the fellowships of the faithful'. Alliances between trading centres and sacral sites were, as ever in Bede's England, of benefit to both and worthy of the most serious safeguarding. Quite how precious salt was can be gauged by the calculation that 36 tons of salt could cure 1,290,000 herrings.

Mildred was a remarkable scholar as well as a shrewd administrator. He was a friend of Lull of Malmesbury[W] and had evidently been to Germany to visit Boniface of Nursling[W] just the year before his death. The letter of consolation he wrote to Lull on the occasion also reveals the circle of book-borrowing of which many hints can be found elsewhere: 'I do not send the book of Porphyrius's poems because Bishop Cuthbert [of Canterbury, see page 7] has so far delayed in returning it.'

THE KINGDOM
OF THE
SOUTH SAXONS
or
SUSSEX

So [Wilfrid] turned to the kingdom of the South Saxons,
which stretches south and west from Kent as far as the land
of the West Saxons and contains 7,000 hides. At that time it
was still in the bonds of heathen practices. Here Wilfrid taught
them the faith and administered the baptism of salvation.

[IV, 13]

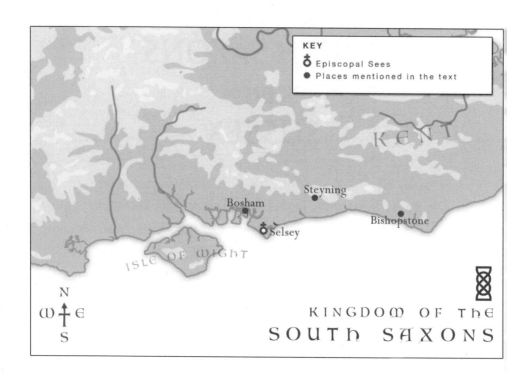

KEY

⚲ Episcopal Sees
● Places mentioned in the text

KENT

Steyning

Bosham

Bishopstone

⚲ Selsey

ISLE OF WIGHT

N
W ✝ E
S

KINGDOM OF THE
SOUTH SAXONS

Aelle of the South Saxons (Sussex) heads Bede's list of 'super-kings' or *bretwaldas* and an Aelle indeed appears in the *Anglo-Saxon Chronicle*, landing in England with three sons in 477, the successful victor of a series of battles against the native Britons. But what happens thereafter to the South Saxons is something of a mystery. It is not until Bede's *History* and the *Life of Wilfrid* by Stephen of Ripon that the kingdom again comes into focus, still resolutely pagan but for a tiny community of Irish monks at Bosham,[S] whom apparently the locals all chose to ignore. How this deep-seated paganism is overcome varies significantly between Bede and Stephen's accounts.

In Stephen's version of events, the paganism of the South Saxons is brought into high relief by Wilfrid's chance encounter on his return journey from Gaul, where he had gone for his episcopal consecration shortly after the Synod of Whitby.[N] The tale rivals any heroic saga: Wilfrid's flotilla is caught in a storm; the wind howls; waves lash the boats – it's just like being on the Sea of Galilee, says Stephen. The shore comes closer. Assembled along the beach are hordes of pagans, eager for booty. But Christian magic and militancy outwit all pagan curses. A Christian-blessed stone, hurled from a sling, kills the pagan priest. Battle is joined. Wilfrid is on the point of victory when the tide turns, whereupon Wilfrid sails off for Kent. Despite the drama of the tale, Stephen makes no attempt to link it with Wilfrid's return to Sussex some fifteen years later, where he is living following his expulsion from Northumbria (*see* Lindisfarne, page 43). On this occasion, as Stephen tells the story, Wilfrid is welcomed into Sussex by the king, Aethelwealh, whom he duly converts (along with his queen). Thereafter he preaches to 'hosts of pagans' and by his eloquence he converts them by the thousand. In gratitude, the king gives him Selsey.[S] Stephen, without missing a beat, goes on to report how Wilfrid then allies with Caedwalla, a royal exile from Wessex who, with Wilfrid's help and support, gains the throne of Wessex. Wilfrid becomes Caedwalla's 'venerable father and dearest of all to him'.

Bede's version of the story is markedly different in a number of ways. According to Bede, before Wilfrid's arrival the whole kingdom of Sussex was still in the grip of paganism, except for its king, Aethelwealh, who had been baptised at the instigation or insistence of Wulfhere of Mercia. Wulfhere had acted as Aethelwealh's godfather and he had given him as a baptismal present the Isle of Wight (recently conquered by Wulfhere), together with a sub-kingdom (Bede calls it a province) in Hampshire. In Bede's account, the Mercian dimension of Athelwealh's conversion is further underlined by his marriage to a Christian princess from the Hwicce, a kingdom centred on Worcester and now dependent on Mercia. Only then does Wilfrid arrive. Wilfrid does indeed preach to great effect to the South Saxons. And it is not just his preaching, it is also his fishing lessons (*see* Selsey[S]) which are hugely successful – and do much to alleviate the famine from which the people had been suffering (some even driven to suicide pacts by their hunger) [V, 7].

But then, just a few years later, onto the scene comes the exiled Caedwalla, who invades Sussex, kills King Aethelwealh and moves on to capture the Isle of Wight, handing over a quarter of it to Wilfrid to Christianise. Particularly shocking to modern sensibilities is Caedwalla's ethnic-cleansing programme, his clearly expressed plan 'to wipe out all the natives [of the Isle of Wight] by merciless slaughter and to replace them with inhabitants of his own kingdom...' [IV, 16].

Bede's blithe tale of the baptism of two Isle of Wight princes prior to their execution (*see* Eling^W) will not cheer the reader either. But it is on this sombre note that Bede notes that the conversion of all England's kingdoms, including the Isle of Wight, is now complete. Did Bede himself feel something else was needed? Certainly he returns to Caedwalla much later in his *History* – and with seeming pride – to tell how he died in Rome, where an epitaph records how 'he had laid aside his barbarous rage and shame'.

As for Sussex, it struggled to retain any independence. For a while it had no bishop of its own, remaining under the authority of the see of Winchester until 705, when Selsey was recognised as a bishopric. Eadberht, a former protégé of Wilfrid, became the first bishop, but even then, politically, Sussex remained vulnerable to the overlordship of its powerful neighbours, Mercia and Wessex.

BISHOPSTONE · Wiltshire

... they looked back and both saw coming towards them
a sprightly old man to whom Balger said 'Tell me... what
minster is that which we can see, what relics does it have and to
whom is it dedicated? And the old man replied that it was the

monastery of St Andrew and that it was the resting place of the
holy virgin and martyr Lewinna.

(*Acta Sanctorum*, ED. J. BOLLANDUS AND OTHERS,
ANTWERP, 1643; AUTHOR'S TRANSLATION)

Balger (in the extract above) was a monk from Saint-Winnoc
in Flanders, who, together with a companion, happened to
find himself in Sussex, his ship having been blown off-course
(the intention had been to land at Dover). The source is late –
eleventh century – but the story it tells is sufficiently intriguing
to warrant inclusion. The lost Balger was especially anxious to
find a church, because by now it was Easter Sunday, but having
perchance arrived at St Andrew's he was so taken by the alleged
virtues of its resident Lewinna (the Latin version of Leofwynn)
that he hit upon a plan to take her relics home with him, and with
considerable stealth and ingenuity he managed, leaving behind
only a few small bones.

The whole episode was written up by a fellow monk of
Saint-Winnoc, whose account includes the story of Leofwynn's
miracles as told on the parchment sheets that apparently had
been hung around her shrine. Her reliquary, moreover, had a
label attached that explained that Leofwynn, martyred during the
time of Archbishop Theodore in the seventh century, had been
translated to her present shrine by Bishop Ealdhelm of Selsey in
the latter part of the tenth century.

How much of Leofwynn's life is apocryphal we will never
know, but recent archaeological investigation has made it very
clear that Bishopstone – at least from the eighth century – was
a place of quite some importance, though whether it was actually a minster site or not remains a matter of some controversy.

Its present church may date only from the tenth century; it has been suggested that it was perhaps rebuilt on the occasion of the translation of Leofwynn's relics. Whatever kernel of truth may lie behind the story of the Leofwynn herself, it is worth remembering those pagans who had so militantly approached St Wilfrid when he, too, had landed on the shores of Sussex (*see* introduction to the Kingdom of the South Saxons or Sussex) rather than those of Kent.

BOSHAM · Sussex

There was, however, in their midst a certain Irish monk named Dicuill who had a very small monastery in a place called Bosham surrounded by woods and sea, in which five or six brothers served the Lord in humility and poverty; but none of the natives cared to follow their way of life or listen to their preaching. [IV, 13]

For many, Bosham has earned its place in medieval history through its appearance in the Bayeux Tapestry. As stitched there, it is the place from which Harold, later king of England, sets sail on the fateful journey to Normandy which led to him (allegedly) swearing fealty to Duke William, thus setting in motion the drama that ended only in 1066 at the battle of Hastings.

The church in Bosham dates in the main from the eleventh century and proudly displayed in it is the spot where Harold is said to have prayed before his embarkation. There is no sign of any earlier church at Bosham, but there is in Bede a tantalising reference to 'a very small monastery in a place called Bosham', inhabited by an Irish monk, together with five or six companions.

No evidence has survived for any other Irish monasteries along the south coast and Bede is himself dismissive of the influence of the Bosham community – 'none of the natives cared to follow their way of life or listen to their preaching' [IV, 13] – but can this really be so? As it happens, a clue to the influence of the Bosham monks may lie in the admittedly late story of St Cuthman of Steyning.[s]

SELSEY • Sussex

*At this time King Aethelwealh gave the most reverend bishop
Wilfrid eighty-seven hides of land to maintain his exiled
followers. The land was called Selsey, that is, the island
of the seal. [IV, 13]*

Selsey, 'the island of the seal', was given by King Aethelwealh to Bishop Wilfrid and those who had followed him into the exile imposed by King Ecgfrith of his native Northumbria, c.680. On this peninsula – only a tiny strip of land stopped it from being an actual island – Wilfrid founded a monastery 'chiefly consisting of the brothers he had brought with him, and there he established a rule of life'. Bede describes the territory as sizeable and already under cultivation; it included 'fields and stock' and as many as 250 slaves, all of whom Wilfrid converted and set free (this is a much rosier picture of conversion than Bede gives for the nearby Isle of Wight: *see* Eling[W]).

The inroads of the sea on the one hand, and extensive draining on the other, have changed considerably the topography of Selsey since Bede wrote his description. Even making allowances for such changes, it still seems as if something is not quite right: could Selsey ever have been quite the size Bede suggests? What are we to make of the rather different description given in the *Life of Wilfrid* which suggests that, as well as Selsey, King Aethelwealh gave Wilfrid 'his own estate in which he lived, to be an episcopal see'? It now seems likely that Wilfrid was indeed given Selsey, but that the royal grant included further estates. Moreover, it is highly probable that the residence he was given was for his own personal use (rather than as a see), since there is no evidence that Wilfrid intended to stay in Sussex longer than he needed – though for the five years he was there, he did indeed carry out episcopal duties.

Church Norton in Selsey still boasts a chapel dedicated to St Wilfrid and there are reasons for thinking that this chapel is close to where Wilfrid built his monastery. The archaeological evidence is meagre, but it includes the fragment of a gold ring of seventh-century date. The Northumbrian origins of the foundation account for the miracle Bede relates of the Selsey child, who had fallen victim to one of the bouts of plague that affected Anglo-Saxon England throughout the seventh century: the child has a vision of St Peter and St Paul who tell him that, although everyone else stricken by the plague will recover, he will not, but that through the intercession of King Oswald (whose feast day it was – this could apparently be checked by a glance at a calendar which recorded such things), upon his death he would be taken straight to heaven where he would see Christ. It is an evocative vision; so, too, is the presumed site of the monastery as Kipling's poem 'Eddi's Service' (quoted in the Preface; *see* page x) amply shows.

The plague apart, Sussex also suffered during the time of Wilfrid's mission from a severe drought – and as a consequence from terrible famine – but Bede gives an account of how 'on the very day on which people received the baptism of faith, a gentle but ample rain fell, the fields once more became green and a happy and fruitful season followed' [IV,13]. This would suggest a particular day which marked the conversion. 'The people' were also very impressed by Wilfrid's fishing skills, because until he had arrived they had apparently only known how to catch eels: these tales of better living standards under Christianity are of particular interest as Bede is likely to have learnt of them from Daniel, bishop of Winchester and we know that Daniel himself (in his letter to Boniface of Nursling[W]) thought it very important to impress on pagans that Christianity could bring material prosperity as well as spiritual happiness.

After the Norman Conquest, the see was moved from Selsey to Chichester.

STEYNING · Sussex

> ... after numberless privations he [Cuthman] came with the
> Lord's guidance to the place which we now call Steyning...
> He looked around and saw that the place would suit his needs.
>
> (Life of St Cuthman, ED. AND TRANS. JOHN BLAIR, SUSSEX
> ARCHAEOLOGICAL COLLECTIONS, VOL. 135 (1997),
> p. 175)

The Life of St Cuthman as we have it probably dates from the mid-eleventh century, but there can be no doubt that it contains much older material. Cuthman may well have belonged to the Irish community which Bede tells us was settled at Bosham,[S] because his Life contains traits common in Irish hagiography

(Cuthman, for example, hangs his gloves on a sunbeam, which is where St Bridget of Kildare used to put her clothes).

Cuthman, like many an Irish saint, undertook a period of wandering (in his case, all the while pushing around his aged mother in a makeshift invalid chair) before finally settling at Steyning, at the time, according to the *Life*, a place that was uncultivated and secluded. There Cuthman built a church. On the whole he had friendly neighbours who used to bring him food, but it was just as well not to cross him since he knew only too well how to show his anger: when two young men stole his oxen, his first response was to yoke the youths to his plough; their mother's remonstrations did her little good – she was blown sky-high: 'a wind... blew her aloft over the high downs, and dropped her down to earth, which opened its mouth like a gaping cavern and swallowed her'. The sons, however, were set free.

Cuthman was buried at Steyning. Although evidence for the church he founded there is sparse, the fact that Alfred the Great's father, Aethelwulf, was buried there in 858 suggests that it had flourished. But Aethelwulf was later reinterred in the Old Minster at Winchester; and the Normans rebuilt the church at Steyning so thoroughly that nothing is left now of the Anglo-Saxon minster.

THE KINGDOM
OF THE
WEST SAXONS
or
WESSEX

About this time the West Saxons, who in early days were called the Gewisse, received the faith of Christ during the reign of Cynegils through the preaching of Bishop Birinus. The latter had come to Britain on the advice of Pope Honorius, having promised in the pope's presence that he would scatter the seeds of the holy faith in the remotest regions of England, where no teacher had been before. [III, 7]

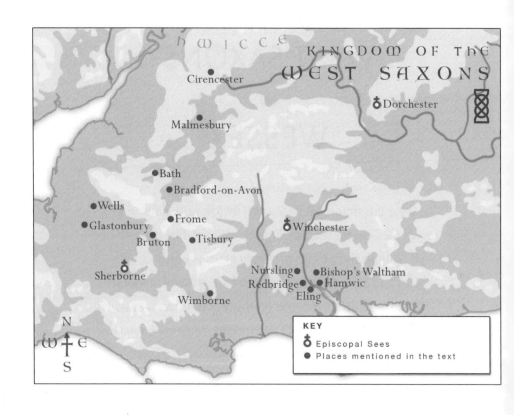

In the ninth century, after decades of Viking invasions and conquests, Wessex alone out of the seven kingdoms of Bede's England remained in Christian hands. As a consequence, Wessex came to develop an impressive sense of its place in the story of Christian salvation and English identity. In the eighth century none of this, of course, could have been foreseen, but it still comes as something of a surprise to realise both how tortuous and precarious was Wessex's rise to power (despite its seeming pre-eminence in the sixth century under King Ceawlin) and how little Bede has to say about its history.

Bede's relative silence is all the more surprising since he had a source in his contemporary Daniel, bishop of Winchester, whom he thanks in his preface for sending him 'something of the history of the church in his own kingdom, as well as of the neighbouring kingdoms of Sussex and the Isle of Wight'. Seemingly, Daniel gave out only selected information, but Bede would also have known about Wessex from Benedict Biscop – indeed, he almost goes as far as to suggest that it was serendipity rather than design which took Biscop and his wealth to Northumbria rather than to Wessex. In his *Abbots of Wearmouth and Jarrow*, Bede writes:

On entering Britain [Benedict] thought he should confer with Coynwalh [Cenwalh], king of the West Saxons, whose friendship he had relied on and whose kindnesses had helped him more than once before. But Coynwalh [Cenwalh] was snatched away at precisely this time, dying unexpectedly, so Benedict at last went back to his native people, to Ecgfrith, king of the region beyond the Humber, turning his steps to the land where he was born.

Links between Northumbria and Wessex had not always amicable, as the attempted assassination of King Edwin in 626 clearly shows, but the Christianisation of both kingdoms provided an opportunity for the fostering of new bonds. The first Christian king of Wessex, according to Bede, was Cynegils, converted by the Italian bishop, Birinus, whom Pope Honorius (625–38) had sent to England to further the mission. At Cynegils' baptism, his godfather was none other than King Oswald of Northumbria. God-parentage in Anglo-Saxon England tended to cement already unequal relationships. Cynegils thus became Oswald's spiritual son and would have been expected to act with appropriate filial loyalty. Oswald, meanwhile, proceeded to behave in a thoroughly lordly way, bestowing, albeit together with Cynegils, Dorchester[W] on Birinus as his episcopal see. Such a peace would have been further sealed by the marriage, proposed at the time of the baptism, between Oswald and Cynegils' daughter; given the threat the pagan Penda of Mercia by now presented to both Wessex and Northumbria, an alliance between them made sense.

The power of Mercia was a constant threat to Wessex and it may lie behind the establishment during the reign of Cenwalh, Cynegils' son and successor, of a new West Saxon bishopric at Winchester,[W] further away than Dorchester-on-Thames from the dangerous frontier with Mercia. Cenwalh's relations with his bishops were stormy, nonetheless, but eventually a new bishop was appointed for the Winchester see, while Dorchester did indeed pass for a while into Mercian hands. Wessex thereafter remained fragile as a kingdom, unsteady in its adherence to Christianity and beleaguered by Mercia. When Cenwalh died in 672 (the date given by the *Anglo-Saxon Chronicle*), the unity of the kingdom fell to pieces, though it seems to have been reassembled during the last years of the reign of King Centwine (d. *c.*685).

Centwine was an active patron of the church who ended his days in a monastery, though whether by choice or coercion is not clear. His successor, Caedwalla, (*see* the introduction to the Kingdom of the South Saxons or Sussex, page 229) was still a pagan when he became king, but after an enormously successful, ruthless and rapid series of battles against his rivals in 688, he abdicated and went to Rome to be baptised. And there he died, still, according to Bede, in his baptismal robes.

Caedwalla was followed as king by Ine (688–*c.*726), who likewise abdicated and died as a pilgrim in Rome, but not before he had established a new see for Wessex at Sherborne[W] and promulgated a set of laws that spelt out the obligations which now fell upon everyone in Wessex in consequence of the adoption of the new faith. Baptism now became mandatory within thirty days and no one was to work on Sundays. Churches could exact a tax (church scot) and from 704 they benefited even further from Ine's privilege in that they were to be 'free from the obstacles of secular affairs and... tribute of fiscal business so that they might serve God with fixed minds... and... offer prayers for the condition and prosperity of our reign'.

By the reign of Ine, Christianity in Wessex was thus secure and in Aldhelm, abbot of Malmesbury[W] and then bishop of

Sherborne,^W it had a remarkable champion. Bede is full of praise for Aldhelm, not least because of his staunch defence of the 'Roman' dating system for Easter in preference to that which was still in use by certain Britons living in the west of England. Here we find a rare reference by Bede to this particular group of British Christians. His distaste for Britons in general is evident throughout the *Ecclesiastical History*; whether it is enough to account for the huge gaps in the *History* about certain monastic foundations is extremely hard to tell. For whatever reason, Bede, for instance, seldom if ever casts his eye as far as what is now Devon. This is particularly strange given the achievements and stature of Boniface of Nursling^W and his circle. Boniface was a missionary of extraordinary achievements by any standard, friend and colleague to precisely the kind of holy women and men whose deeds and sanctity Bede was generally keen to praise, and a fearless critic of the sinner. Many explanations for Bede's silences are possible; few seem satisfactory. All anyone can do as she or he visits the seven kingdoms is to be alert to those places that are not on Bede's mental map, but which are undoubtedly landmarks in any wider ecclesiastical history of the English.

In Wessex, Bede's omissions are especially startling, both in respect to Boniface and to the British Christians. By way of compensation for the former, we have a remarkable correspondence of some 150 letters and a number of *Lives* of missionaries, for the latter, early inscribed Christian memorial stones dating from the years before 700. Historians' attention is increasingly being drawn to the fact that Saxon expansion in the West Country (as in the north) was made at the expense of British Christians; the evidence is tantalising and elusive, but many of the holy wells of the southwest may indeed bear witness to the practices and beliefs of early Christian communities and to their contacts with Wales and Ireland. As late as the ninth century, Cornwall had a bishop with the British name of Kenstec. The fact that he was making an episcopal profession of obedience to the archbishop of Canterbury does indeed suggest that Cornwall was now an accepted part of an 'English' church, but the profession remains distinctive: Kenstec describes himself as elected 'to an episcopal seat among the people of Cornwall in the monastery which in the language of the Britons is called Dinurrin' (possibly Bodmin).

In the tenth century, the rise to dominance of Wessex led to a building programme which did much to obscure the record of earlier centuries. A church (not included in this gazeteer) that has perhaps the best-preserved Anglo-Saxon work in Hampshire, and which may date from as early as the eighth century, is St Peter's at Titchfield – for which little documentary evidence remains. No church, for instance, is mentioned in the Domesday Book, though a charter of 982 mentions 'the community of Titchfield'. It would seem highly likely, especially given its position at the head of the river Meon, that Titchfield was once a prosperous minster, and one of many whose history it is now difficult, if not impossible, to trace. Thus Titchfield can stand as a reminder of the particular problems there are in any reconstruction of Bede's Wessex.

BATH · Somerset

Such great profit for the good of souls did the Lord bring to pass through her [Bertila] that even those faithful kings from the parts of Saxondom across the seas would ask her through trusty

messengers to send them some of her followers for teaching or
sacred instruction.

(Vita Bertilae, ED. WILHELM LEVISON, TRANS.
P. SIM-WILLIAMS, IN *Anglo-Saxon England* 4 (1975), p. 4)

Bede alerts us, early on in his narrative of the conversion, to the exodus of women from England to Gaul to join religious foundations because a sufficient number of such communities had not as yet been founded in England [III, 8]. What he does not tell us is of any women coming across the Channel in the other direction in order to help remedy this situation. However, Bath may well be one such community. Bath's foundation charter survives only in a twelfth-century copy, but none of the details it gives are improbable.

The abbess named in the charter is a certain Berta. The name is undoubtedly Frankish. At the time of the date given for the foundation, 675, Bath belonged to the Hwicce, but Frankish influence might well have been mediated through the nearby Frankish bishop of Wessex, Leuthere, who indeed is listed among the witnesses of the foundation charter.

Berta was possibly succeeded by another abbess, but thereafter the community seems to have been made up only of men. By the end of the eighth century, King Offa was claiming Bath (and had set about completing the absorption into Mercia of the kingdom of the Hwicce). It is probable that Offa, who liked to think of himself as the equal of Charlemagne, felt that Bath's Roman past added to his own imperial pretensions. Recent archaeological evidence suggests Offa may even have had a palace at Bath that included two of its hot springs. Given Charlemagne's fondness for the hot baths at Aachen, it is not hard to imagine that such springs would indeed have given Offa particular satisfaction.

BISHOP'S WALTHAM · Hampshire

So his parents set out and took Willibald to the monastery
which is called Bishops Waltham. There they handed him
over to the venerable abbot Egwald, offering him as a novice,
because of his age, to be obedient in all things.

(HUNEBERC [HYGEBURG]OF HEIDENHEIM,
The Hodoeporicon [ADVENTURES] *of St Willibald, bishop*
of Eichstätt, TRANS. AND ED. C. H. TALBOT, SHEED
AND WARD 1954, p. 155)

Bishop's Waltham is most usually remembered today as the place where Henry, bishop of Winchester in the twelfth century, built himself an exceptionally fine palace. But already in the eighth century it had a minster and a famous alumnus in the person of the missionary Willibald.

Willibald's account of his early life and of his travels we owe to Hygeburg of Heidenheim, who was a nun at Heidenheim during the time when Willibald's sister, Walburg, was its abbess. Willibald by then was bishop of either Eichstätt or of Erfurt (the evidence is inconclusive). In the summer of 778 he relayed his adventures (and Hygeburg is very precise): it was on 20 June, the day before the solstice, and Hygeburg 'as a humble relative' thought she should put into writing what she had heard.

According to Hygeburg, Willibald, aged three, had contracted a serious illness. In response, his anxious parents 'offered him up before the holy Cross of our Lord and Saviour'. Particular interest attaches to this episode since Hygeburg reports that this cross was not in a church because, as she explains, 'on the estates of the nobles and good men of the Saxon race it is a custom to have a cross which is dedicated to our Lord and held in great reverence, erected on some prominent spot for the convenience of those who wish to pray daily before it'. In southern England, in comparison with Northumbria, very few such crosses have been found, though the Lypiatt Cross (near Bisley[M]) might be one such and undoubtedly there will have been others. In any event, Willibald recovered, and two years later his parents, in honour of the promise they had made, took Willibald to Bishop's Waltham, where the abbot accepted him as a novice and where he received a monastic education. But what really attracted Willibald was the idea of pilgrimage, and once he was old enough, he persuaded his father and his brother, Winnebald, to join him. And off they set from Hamblemouth, near Hamwic,[W] landing near Rouen.

Willibald's journey is, to say the least, epic – and fraught. His father dies; in Rome both brothers catch the plague; Winnebald goes no further, but Willibald continues his adventures and does indeed reach the Holy Land. He loses his sight but then recovers it; smuggles out some balsam (needed to make incense); moves on to Greece; and after seven years he returns to Italy and becomes a monk at Monte Cassino. But in 739 the pope tells him, 'in a serious and unmistakable tone', that he is to join Boniface in Freising. Willibald obeys. He is ordained as a priest by Boniface and a year later he becomes a bishop. He now worked once more with his brother, Winnebald, (who had already been in Germany for some time) and helped him to establish the monastery of Heidenheim where, on Winnebald's death in 761, the brothers' sister became abbess. Willibald himself died c.787

and was buried at Eichstätt, which claimed him as the founder of the see.

DORCHESTER · Oxfordshire

The two kings [Oswald of the Northumbrians and Cynegils of Wessex] gave the bishop [Birinus] a city called Dorchester in which to establish his episcopal see. After he had built and dedicated churches and brought many to the Lord by his pious labours, he went to be with the Lord and was buried in the same city. [III, 7]

Dorchester was an important Roman city on the river Thames, fortified initially by an earthen rampart and ditch and then by a stone wall. Much archaeological work has been carried out on the site, but despite this no conclusive evidence either of a pagan temple or of the presence of Romano-British Christianity has been found, even if both had been expected. An excavation nearby (at Long Wittenham) has, however, recently revealed a late Roman body, accompanied by a beaker decorated with Christian symbols. But whether Christianity survived the arrival in the area of Germanic settlers in the sixth century must remain uncertain.

The arrival of Bishop Birinus in the region seems to have been part of Pope Honorius' mission to continue the work of Pope Gregory the Great in the evangelisation of England. Birinus was consecrated bishop in Italy at the pope's command and, according to the *Anglo-Saxon Chronicle*, he had reached England by 634, though there is no evidence that he had received a formal invitation to any English kingdom. Bede tells us only that, having arrived in Wessex and finding everyone there to be heathen, he saw no reason for going elsewhere and began his work of evangelisation with such success that before long the king, Cynegils, together with 'all his people', was baptised. Oswald of Northumbria took part in the ceremony, standing as Cynegils' godfather; Cynegils thereafter married a daughter of Oswald's: all this, in Bede's eyes, seemed 'lovely and well-pleasing to God'. (But church rulings from at least the eleventh century onwards, and much earlier on the Continent, would have forbidden such a marriage, since god-parentage had come to be regarded as creating kinship bonds quite as close as those of blood.)

Birinus built his cathedral at Dorchester outside the Roman wall, most probably on the same site as the present abbey, close therefore to the Thame (and the Thames); both rivers were perhaps used for baptisms. The other churches built by Birinus which Bede mentions are likely to have been within Dorchester itself. But once Cynegils had died, in c.643, Birinus's position cannot have been easy; Cynegils' successor, Cenwalh, had remained a pagan and moreover he had antagonised Penda, king of Mercia, who promptly invaded Wessex. Cenwalh was forced to flee to East Anglia, where he became a Christian; by 648 he had recovered his kingdom. If we can trust this date of 648 (cited by the *Anglo-Saxon Chronicle*), then Birinus probably lived to see Cenwalh's restoration, but by 650 at the latest he had died.

Birinus' successor as bishop was the Frankish priest and scholar Agilbert. Cenwalh, who allegedly 'only knew the Saxon language', grew tired of Agilbert's 'barbarous speech' and decided after some ten years that he wanted a second bishop. He therefore appointed Wine at Winchester[W] around 660. Agilbert, in his displeasure, left Wessex, spending some time in Northumbria (he was present at the Synod of Whitby[N] of

664) before returning home to Paris, where he became bishop.

Dorchester by now was in danger of being absorbed by Mercia, so to keep him safely within Wessex, Birinus was dug up and taken to Winchester. (None of this, however, would prevent the Augustinian canons, who in the thirteenth century refounded Dorchester as their abbey, from claiming that they still had Birinus's body. In their determination to honour him, they built a magnificent shrine which, in its restored state, can be seen in the abbey today.)

ELING · Hampshire

I must not pass over in silence the fact that among the first fruits of the island who believed and were saved were two young princes, brothers of Arwald, king of the island, who were specially crowned with God's grace. [IV, 16]

The conquest by Caedwalla of Wessex of the Isle of Wight, as Bede describes it, is likely to strike the modern reader as exceptionally brutal, Caedwalla's plan being to 'wipe out all the natives by merciless slaughter' and give a quarter of the island to Bishop Wilfrid (even though Caedwalla was not yet himself a Christian). Such a reader is also likely to be taken aback by the unfolding of the narrative, not immediately grasping that the 'two young princes' are in fact killed: following the death of their brother, the two had fled in fear of their own lives, hiding at a place usually identified as Stoneham. There they were betrayed and condemned to death. Enter Cyneberht, abbot of the minster of Hreutford (Redbridge), who successfully pleaded with Caedwalla to allow him to baptise the boys so as to assure at least eternal life for their souls.

No trace survives of any minster at Hreutford, but it has been suggested that Cyneberht's establishment was in fact at Eling, where traces of Anglo-Saxon work can still be seen in the church. (As mentioned in the introduction to the Kingdom of the West Saxons or Wessex, much finer work, thought to date to the seventh or eighth century, can be seen at Titchfield, some 20 miles (32 km) away, but here the documentary evidence dates only from the late Saxon period.)

To modern sensibilities the episode is sickening, but the extermination of rival royal lines was very clearly not unusual in Anglo-Saxon England (nor, indeed, in the following centuries). After the battle of Hatfield Chase[N] for example, the victor, Penda, murdered the royal prince Eadfrith – in spite of an oath to the contrary.

The necessity of baptism for salvation was a source of endless speculation among theologians of the Middle Ages. Although it would seem as if exceptions were always possible – so that the babies killed on the orders of King Herod were deemed to be saved, even though their deaths necessarily pre-dated the institution of baptism – there was still considerable anxiety lest children died unbaptised or were excluded from heaven because they had been baptised incorrectly. Daniel of Winchester,[W] who became blind in his later years, was one of those suspected of having caused suffering on this account – a monk in Germany had a vision of 'a sad and mourning multitude of children' whom Daniel had somehow missed out when baptising large numbers at a time (cf. Beverley[N]).

As for Caedwalla, it is perhaps a nice irony that he himself died while still in his baptismal robes. He had gone to Rome for the occasion, because, Bede tells us, '[H]e was anxious to gain the special privilege of being washed in the fountain of baptism within the threshold of the apostles; for he had learned that by the way of baptism alone can the human race attain entrance to the heavenly life; at the same time he hoped that, soon after his baptism, he might be loosed from the bonds of the flesh and pass, cleansed as he was, to eternal joy...' [v, 7].

GLASTONBURY • Somerset

688: And he [Ine, King of Wessex] built the
minster at Glastonbury.

(Anglo-Saxon Chronicle, G VERSION)

There can be no place or person so written about from Anglo-Saxon England as Glastonbury and King Arthur – and at the same time, nowhere and nobody about whom so little can be known for certain. By the ninth century, at the latest, Arthur had become the British hero who had valiantly fought off the Saxon invaders, though it took rather longer for him to be 'established' at Glastonbury. Bede himself was resolutely silent both about Glastonbury and about Arthur, though he does acknowledge the presence in the west of England of British Christians. This is evident in his mention of Aldhelm of Malmesbury's[w] writing on the subject and in his reference to the consecration of Chad as bishop by Bishop Wine of Wessex, assisted by 'two bishops of the British race'.

Despite later objections to Chad's consecration, it nonetheless seems as if in the west of England (as, indeed, in Northumbria) there were times when relationships of various kinds were possible between 'Roman' and British Christians. Although there was no Synod of Whitby[N] to settle the disputes of the south, it looks as if, bit by bit, Roman ways prevailed and that the politics of the transition here, as indeed in the north, were highly complex and will have alternated between cooperation and conflict.

What was the role in this process of Glastonbury? Glastonbury's antiquity as a place of settlement is not in doubt, dating, according to dendrochronologists, from at least the winter of 3807–6 BC, when the wooden path known as the Sweet Track was erected across the marsh. Centuries later, the Romans settled the area in force – but who came next? Given the evidence we have for native Christianity in Ireland, Scotland and Wales in the period after AD 400, there would seem to be no reason to be sceptical about positing a Christian settlement at Glastonbury. Such scepticism has of course been engendered by the fantastic accounts that developed in the Middle Ages of the great saints who had visited and were then buried at Glastonbury (notably St Patrick) and the rich concoction of stories that featured a diverse range of people, starting with Joseph of Arimathea. (The thorn bush Joseph allegedly planted in Glastonbury was vandalised in 2010, but at the time of writing it seems to be recovering.)

A number of these stories were already in circulation when William of Malmesbury visited Glastonbury (c.1129) and wrote his history of the house, and clearly they exercised his imagination. In his *History of the English Bishops*, William keeps to a sober account, attributing the foundation of a monastery to King Ine of Wessex (688–726), acting on the advice of Aldhelm, bishop of Sherborne.[W] A date in Ine's reign fits with the marginal note (quoted at the top of this entry) and with an early list of Glastonbury abbots that names the first abbot as Haemgils. But the probability that this Haemgils was a Saxon abbot taking

over a British community should be compared with the scenario at Malmesbury[W] and makes particular sense given the
establishment of Sherborne[W] in 705 as a second see for Wessex.
Added to this is the recent identification of the dedicatee of a
dramatic poem by Aldhelm, the new bishop, to be none other
than Haemgils of Glastonbury. The poem recalls a journey made
by Aldhelm into 'awful Devon through Cornwall' when a terrifying storm struck the church where Aldhelm was praying, taking
off the roof and causing pandemonium. The tourist trade today
will not want the poem widely known, but it does raise the question of what Aldhelm was doing in 'awful Devon'. One answer
might be that Aldhelm was visiting Lyme, a place that belonged
to Glastonbury and was important for the salt it produced and
for the associated tax. The new Saxon church in Wessex, of
which Glastonbury was a key component, needed all the wealth
it could get. Bishops could be (and were) big spenders, but they
also knew how to be careful administrators. (For the importance
of salt, cf. Worcester.[M])

During his visit, William of Malmesbury was deeply puzzled
by two great pyramids, one of 5.4 metres (18 ft) and the other
of 7.9 (26 ft). William took them to be 'memorials of antiquity which can be clearly read even if not fully understood'. He
believed the pyramids marked the burial spot of those named.
On the smaller of the two he deciphered the following names:
Haeddi the bishop, Bregored and Berhtwald. Haeddi here must
be the bishop of Winchester, Berhtwald the first Anglo-Saxon
abbot and later abbot of Reculver[K] and archbishop of Canterbury
(see page 7) – but who then was Bregored? The name is British
and would seem to confirm that Glastonbury was indeed originally a British foundation.

After the death of Ine, Mercia (under King Aethelbald) seems for a while to have gained control of Glastonbury, and Mercian influence has been detected in several fragments of sculpture which are housed now in the Glastonbury Abbey Museum.

HAMWIC / Old Southampton • Hampshire

Taking with them the necessary money for the journey and accompanied by a band of friends, they came to a place, which was known by the ancient name of Hamblemouth, near the port of Hamwic.

(HUNEBERC [HYGEBURG] OF HEIDENHEIM, *The Hodoeporicon* [ADVENTURES] *of St Willibald, bishop of Eichstätt*, TRANS. AND ED. C. H. TALBOT, SHEED AND WARD, 1954, p. 157)

Extensive excavations at Hamwic – from the late 1970s, and still continuing – have shown that Hamwic was a planned settlement, created very possibly at the command of King Ine, expressly to develop the new commercial opportunities of the seventh to eighth centuries. So successful was the enterprise that it gave its name to the surrounding region – henceforth 'Hampshire'. Such new 'wics' (trading centres) of the seventh and eighth centuries were both a sign and catalyst of a new period of prosperity.

Hamwic, built as it was on the west bank of the Itchen, provided easy access to ships coming up the river from the Solent. It was a substantial settlement, housing between 2,000 and 3,000 people, with gravelled streets and carefully laid-out plots. The goods made at Hamwic were not, on the whole, luxury items; the evidence of gold-working is slight, but wares of metal, glass and cloth were plentiful. Imports included Frankish glass and quern-stones from the Rhineland, much in demand for grinding. But Hamwic was no modern industrial settlement – evidence has also been found of pigs and fowl and possibly even sheep being kept within the town.

The number of eighth-century coins found at Hamwic suggests trading was brisk.

Given the proximity of Winchester, it is worth considering the interdependence of 'wic' and 'minster'. It may not be an association Bede ever makes, but the needs of any minster were significant, precisely for the kinds of goods that could only be acquired from overseas, and fragmentary references give a sense of how prosperous, busy and monastic a world had been established around the Solent during the eighth century. Something of the excitement that the arrival of a ship and its cargo could cause has been preserved in the story told about Aldhelm by William of Malmesbury (though admittedly it is about Dover, not Hamwic). Aldhelm, having just been elected bishop of Sherborne,[W] was on the look-out in case the merchants had among their cargo anything of use for his church. And Aldhelm found they had indeed brought a quantity of books, including 'a complete text of the Old and New Testaments'. Aldhelm tries to bargain with the sailors, but they refuse to drop their price... sail off... nearly get ship-wrecked... and are saved only through Aldhelm's intervention, to whom they then offer the book in gratitude – but Aldhem insists on offering them 'a nicely judged sum'.

A church at Hamwic, dedicated to Mary, was built on the corner of the main street, looking out over the beaching area for ships. Tradition claims it was built by Birinus and that Hamwic was where he landed. Perhaps it was.

MALMESBURY · Wiltshire

Aldhelm... priest and abbot of the monastery of Malmesbury...
was a very learned man. [v, 18]

We are unusually well informed about Malmesbury because it was home to one of the greatest of the Anglo-Norman historians, William. His histories, both of the kings of England and of its bishops, written in the early twelfth century, contain a wealth of information that would otherwise have been lost to us, and nowhere is this more evident than in regard to Malmesbury itself, since William concluded his *History of the English Bishops* with an appendix entirely dedicated to Aldhelm.

Bede, by contrast, tells us nothing about the foundation of the monastery, even if Aldhelm impressed him because he had written a 'remarkable' book, explaining to the Britons who were living under West Saxon rule the correct way of calculating the date of Easter. No such book has survived, but we do have a letter from Aldhelm addressed to King Geraint of 'the western kingdom' and to all the bishops of Devon. (This may, of course be 'the book'.) In it, the British Christians are urged to conform to the Roman Church both on the matter of Easter and on the shape of the tonsure. Aldhelm illustrates how divisive nonconformity on such matters could be by describing the behaviour of the bishops of Dyfed, across the river Severn, who seemingly treated the Roman clergy as ritually unclean and therefore refused to share either services or indeed food.

Aldhelm was probably born during the early years of Bishop Birinus of Dorchester's[W] mission to Wessex. He was almost certainly a member of the ruling house of Wessex, possibly even a son of King Centwine (reigning c.676–85), and at some point, though it is impossible to know when or for how long, he went to Canterbury (*see* page 7) to study at its revived school. Before then, Aldhelm may have gone to Ireland in search of learning and he may also have had instruction from an Irish monk, Meldum (from whom Bede claims the name Malmesbury was derived).

Malmesbury, situated on the borders of Wessex and Mercia and close to the Roman Fosse Way, had long been a site of strategic importance, once an Iron Age hill fort, and it is probable that when Aldhelm became its abbot (probably in the early 680s) he was in fact taking over a British monastic community that could well have had an abbot named Meldum. As abbot himself, Aldhelm became renowned both for his learning and his building projects. These were the virtues which William of Malmesbury extolled, praising the fact that whereas Meldum had only had a 'very little church', Aldhelm had built two more (as well as rebuilding Meldum's church). In addition, Aldhelm established further minsters along the Somerset/Wiltshire border, at Frome, Bradford on Avon and Bruton. Nearer home, on the opposite side of the Fosse Way from Malmesbury, stood a minster known as Tett's, which, it has been suggested, may have been a community presided over by one of Aldhelm's sisters.

Already in William's day (or so he tells us), much of Aldhelm's work had come to naught: the monasteries at Frome and at Bradford had 'relapsed into nothing'. At Malmesbury, however, the main church still stood 'larger and fairer than any old church that was to be found anywhere in England'. Inside was displayed a chasuble Aldhelm had worn in Rome (where miraculously it had hung on a sunbeam). William describes it lovingly as 'of the most slender thread, that has drunk its hue from the juices of shell-fish;

and on it black roundels contain within them pictured peacocks'. Aldhelm's stay in Rome is believed to have secured papal privileges for Malmesbury, and the sacristans of Malmesbury treated the chasuble with the utmost reverence. Neither the chasuble nor any other of Aldhelm's treasures has survived, though there was still, when William was writing, a fine marble altar at Aldhelm's foundation at Bruton which Aldhelm had been able to bring back home from Italy with the help of a camel (or was it, wonders William, some different but equally unfamiliar animal?).

But nonetheless Aldhelm left a legacy of immense importance, namely his writings, both in prose and verse. These are testimony to a dazzling intellect and to a scholar whose influence was certainly not confined to Wessex. His surviving works include a treatise dedicated to Aldfrith, king of Northumbria (for whom he stood as sponsor at his baptism), and we know from a letter that is partly preserved by William of Malmesbury that Aldhelm did not hold back from expressing his views on events in Northumbria. The letter has no date but it urges Wilfrid of Ripon's[N] clergy to stand by their prelate and to share, if need be, in his exile. The picture Aldhelm paints gives a strong flavour of the bonds of love and loyalty which should, and possibly did, exist within ecclesiastical communities: 'what toil is so hard and cruel as to divide and shut you off from the bishop, who, nourishing, teaching, reproving, raised you in fatherly love from the very beginning of your first studies...'

Aldhelm also wrote two works on virginity for the nuns of Barking.[E] The 'Bugga' for whom he wrote a poem to honour her new church – describing its dazzling beauty – may have been a sister. New churches, it seems, expected such dedicatory pieces – Bede wrote some too – and despite their length they were often incised on stone panels. The intention, no doubt, was for the inscriptions to be declaimed on suitable occasions. Aldhelm also enjoyed, and set a fashion for, the writing of riddles (cf. Breedon[M]). But word games apart, Aldhelm also knew how to captivate an audience who knew nothing of Latin. Here we have to rely on the testimony of William of Malmesbury's description of his vernacular preaching, but given all we know of the vitality of Anglo-Saxon oral culture, there is no reason to mistrust it – and the description recalls, of course, the achievement Bede attributed to Caedmon of Whitby.[N]

The scene, as William paints it, is the bridge at Malmesbury leading out from the city to the country. It is packed with people, 'heedless of the word of God... running off home' the instant the service of mass in church is over. In response:

> The holy man took his stand on the bridge and barred the
> way, playing the part of the professional minstrel. After
> he had done this more than once, the common people
> were won over and flocked to listen to him. Exploiting
> this device, he gradually started to smuggle words from
> Scripture into the less serious matter, and so brought the
> inhabitants round to sound sentiments. If he had thought
> fit to deal in stern words and excommunication, he would
> assuredly have achieved nothing.

This story William claims he got from a book that had belonged to King Alfred. There would seem to be no reason to disbelieve him.

The school at Malmesbury continued to flourish long after Aldhelm's death in 709 and its influence spread into the missionary work in Germany. One of the Anglo-Saxons who joined the mission in Germany and who (in 754) succeeded Boniface as archbishop of Mainz was Lull; Lull is reminded in a letter by an otherwise unknown monk of the friendship the two had shared at Malmesbury under the loving care of Abbot Eada (for Boniface, *see* Nursling[W]). The friendships that Lull maintained through correspondence and prayer are a particularly marked feature of the Anglo-Saxon missionary circle of the eighth century, as is the involvement of kin-groups. Lull seems to have persuaded his aunt and her two children to join him in Germany, and two of his allies in the field, Denehard and Burghard, may have been his brothers.

NURSLING (Nhutselle) · Hampshire

... he [Wynfreth] went to the monastery which to this day is called Nursling. There, attracted by the desire for learning he became a disciple of the venerable Abbot Winbert, of blessed memory and joined the community of the brethren who dwelt there with him in the Lord.

(WILLIBALD, *Life of St Boniface*, CHAPTER 2)

Nursling makes no appearance in Bede's *History*; nor, indeed, does its most famous son, St Boniface. But sometimes the gaps in Bede are so large that attempts must be made to fill them, and so it is with Boniface and Nursling.

Boniface was born around 675–80, somewhere near Exeter (traditionally at Crediton but there is no firm evidence for this.) He was christened Wynfreth and as a young boy he entered a monastery at Exeter, later moving to Nursling near Southampton (or Hamwic,[W] as it was then known). Once there was a Roman road and bridge at Nursling; traces of the road have survived, but nothing more, and there is certainly no sign of Boniface's monastery; it was possibly a casualty of the Viking raids of the ninth century.

Boniface (or rather Wynfreth, as he still was then) became head of the monastic school at Nursling; many years later (c.735) he wrote to one of his former pupils, now an abbot (it is not clear where), reminding him of the days when he was 'poorly equipped as a teacher', though nevertheless devoted to his task. Once he had reached the canonically required age of thirty, Wynfreth was ordained a priest. By then, according to his biographer Willibald, he had become a much-trusted and respected member of the community, so much so that it was he who was chosen by his abbot, as well as by the abbots of Glastonbury[W] and Tisbury (a minster near Salisbury of which we otherwise know very little) to go to Kent to seek advice from the archbishop of Canterbury on some contentious matter that had arisen. What prompted him, not long afterwards, to leave Devon to become a missionary in Germany is not known. But the Northumbrian Willibrord (whom Bede does mention: see Ripon[N]) was by then bishop of the Frisians; and Wilfrid, of whom Boniface may well have known because of the time he spent in Sussex during the reign of Caedwalla (c.685–9), had himself preached, albeit briefly, in Frisia (c.679).

Wynfreth's initial trip to Frisia was not a success, mainly on account of the political turmoil in Frisia at the time, and he returned to Nursling. He was back at home when his abbot died. His community tried to persuade him to be their new leader, but Wynfreth refused and, with the backing of Daniel of Winchester,[W]

he set off for Rome. There, in 719, he received papal endorse-
ment as a missionary and under the new name of Boniface
(after Boniface of Tarsus, an early fourth-century martyr) he
immediately set out to return to Frisia where Willibrord was now
bishop.

By 722 Boniface had himself become a bishop. His missionary work in Germany was focused first on Thuringia and Hesse,
and next on Bavaria, where he founded a number of monasteries
and reorganised the diocesan structure. In 742 he appointed the
Anglo-Saxon Burchard as bishop of Würzburg (it is not certain
from where in England Burchard had come). In the same year he
founded the monastery of Fulda; after his martyrdom in 754 in
Frisia, it was to this monastery that Boniface's body was taken
and where his cult thereafter was based.

Boniface's energy and efforts in Germany were prodigious by
any standards, but he never forgot his Anglo-Saxon origins. His
yearning to convert the Saxons of the Continent was prompted
by his firm belief that they were in some sense his cousins, and
it was this which fuelled his determination to involve Anglo-
Saxons, both women and men, in his missionary endeavours.
Boniface's team, apart from Leoba (*see* Wimborne^W), included
Willibald, Winnebald and Hygeburg (*see* Bishop's Waltham^W). At
the same time, Boniface's concern for the church of his birth and
its own spiritual health never wavered. Startling testimony to this
is the letter of coruscating criticism he, together with seven of
his Anglo-Saxon colleagues, sent to King Aethelbald in 746–7,
lamenting the king's behaviour (*see* introduction to Mercia, page
173). It is a measure of Boniface's stature that the letter produced
results, most notably in the decrees of the Council of Clovesho
(*see* Brixworth^M) in 747.

Boniface's letter to Aethelbald is but one example of his letter-writing. In all we have over thirty-eight letters he wrote, as well as thirty-two written to him. They form a remarkable testimony to the concerns of an eighth-century missionary and to the network on which he relied for help. It is all the more strange that Bede never mentions Boniface, while Boniface certainly knew about Bede, though it was not his *History* which particularly interested him but rather his works on Scripture. In one letter addressed to Abbot Hwaetbert of Jarrow some time after Bede's death, Boniface asked him for 'the treatises of that monk Bede, that profound student of Scriptures, who as we have heard, lately shone in your midst like a light of the church'. Similarly, Boniface petitioned Egbert, archbishop of York, for 'some of the works which Bede, that inspired priest and student of Sacred Scripture has composed, in particular, if it can be done, his book of homilies for the year (because it would be a very handy and useful manual to us in our preaching), and the Proverbs of Solomon. We hear that he has written commentaries on this book'. The request concludes with a hope that the two casks of wine Boniface is sending with his messenger will enable Egbert and his community to enjoy 'a merry day' together.

After Boniface's murder, letters of consolation were sent to his successor, Lull. One, from Cuthbert, archbishop of Canterbury, struck a positively patriotic note: 'We thank the ineffable goodness of God that the race of the English settled in Britain deserved to send forth from itself... such a splendid soldier of Christ'. Henceforth, Cuthbert promised, Boniface was to be revered along with Pope Gregory and St Augustine as England's special patron saint.

SHERBORNE · Dorset

When Haedde [bishop of the West Saxons] died, the
bishopric of the kingdom was divided into two dioceses. One
was given to Daniel [bishop of Winchester]... the other
[Sherborne] to Aldhelm, who presided over it energetically for
four years. [v, 18]

The creation of the new diocese of Sherborne belongs to the years 704–5. Bede fails to tell us the location of Aldhelm's see – whether because he did not know it or because he was not sufficiently interested in southwest England it is impossible to tell. The *Anglo-Saxon Chronicle*, however, is more informative; here, Aldhelm's see is described as being 'west of the wood', the wood being Selwood Forest, an area that had long acted as a natural boundary between Anglo-Saxon and British territory. The new diocese included Wiltshire, Somerset, Dorset and, perhaps, parts of Devon: in other words, much of the territory that had before made up the British kingdom of Dumnonia.

Throughout the seventh and eighth centuries, Dumnonia was constantly under attack from the kings of Wessex and its inhabitants, whether by persuasion or force, pressurised to conform to the norms of Anglo-Saxon Christianity. Aldhelm himself had long been in contact with British Christians (*see* Malmesbury[W]), which may be one reason he was considered an appropriate candidate for the new bishopric. The probability is that Sherborne had until recently been in British Christian hands – the evidence here may not be conclusive, but it is highly suggestive and it was indeed well-known medieval lore that before Sherborne became the seat of a bishopric, it had been a minster founded by King

Cenwalh of Wessex in the mid-seventh century, at the expense of those British Christians who had long before established a community there. The likelihood of this scenario is supported by the curvilinear shape of Sherborne, which corresponds closely to other British monastic sites. It is also possible that Aldhelm was himself a member of the West Saxon ruling family, possibly even a son of King Centwine, and a likely ally in its territorial ambitions.

In the tenth century, the see was divided again, but Sherborne continued to have its own bishop until 1078. According to William of Malmesbury, writing in c.1125, Aldhelm was an energetic and much-loved bishop who oversaw the building of a remarkable cathedral which William himself claimed he had seen; some Saxon work can be found in the abbey today, but nothing from as early as the eighth century. Nor have any traces ever been found of the stone crosses William reports were erected every 7 miles (11 km) along the route of Aldhelm's funeral procession. These were called bishop's stones and were believed to have curative powers. Aldhelm had died at Doulting, which was – and indeed still is – a limestone quarry, the source of the stone used for Glastonbury and for the west façade of Wells Cathedral. Aldhelm, so William of Malmesbury tells us, had died in a small wooden church at Doulting, but a monk of Glastonbury subsequently had it rebuilt in stone. And in William's own day, a stone inside the church on which Aldhelm is said to have rested as he was dying still had miraculous properties. Cures were effected with any water that had been used to wash it.

Aldhelm's successor at Sherborne from 709–10 was Bishop Forthhere. A letter from Berhtwald, the archbishop of Canterbury, to Forthhere asks him to put pressure on the abbot of Glastonbury to release from slavery a girl named Eppa (for an appropriate price). Eppa evidently had kin in Kent and Berhtwald was eager for her to be restored to them.

WIMBORNE · Dorset

In this year Ingild, Ine's brother died. Their sisters were Cwenburh and Cuthburh. And Cuthburh founded the monastery at Wimborne. She had been married to Aldfrith, king of the Northumbrians, and they separated during their lifetime.

(Anglo-Saxon Chronicle, 718)

Wimborne Minster claims on its website to be a town of 'kings, smugglers and ancient legends', but none with which the tourist is regaled date from the time of the foundation of the minster (even if a date is given). To be sure, very little is known about Cuthburh, the founder of Wimborne, but she was evidently first a queen and then a nun, having been married to Aldfrith, king of Northumbria. She was not, of course, the first Northumbrian queen to leave court to become a nun (cf. Ely[EA]), but in Cuthburh's case the circumstances are unknown.

It is possible, but not certain, that Cuthburh spent some time first at Barking[E] before returning to her native Wessex and is therefore the Cuthburh whom Aldhelm addresses in his treatise *On Virginity*. This much is speculative, but it is in any case likely that she was related to Aldhelm (since he is thought to have been one of the Wessex royal line), and since Aldhelm was Aldfrith's godfather, it is clear that there would have been many routes of communication. (Aldhelm's support for the nuns of Wessex is also known from the poem he dedicated to Bugga, who was probably a daughter of King Centwine (d. 685), to honour the dedication of her 'gleaming' church. Bugga's minster has never been identified.)

Wimborne's most illustrious daughter is, however, neither Bugga nor Cuthburh, but the missionary nun Leoba, the great associate in the mission field at Fulda of St Boniface of Nursling.[W] A *Life of Leoba* written some fifty years after her death by Rudolph of Fulda gives an arresting description of Leoba's days at Wimborne (though there is no need to accept the strict segregation which he describes, since it seems out of keeping with what we know of other Anglo-Saxon communities at the time, even if Rudolph himself found it inappropriate).

According to Rudolph's *Life*, Leoba had entered Wimborne during the abbacy of a certain Tetta. Tetta, of royal birth, was used to exercising authority when the need arose, as was proved when the young nuns jumped in glee on the tomb of a very unpopular prioress who had been an exceedingly strict disciplinarian. As the *Life* tells the story, the young nuns had seemingly sinned only because they lacked charity towards the dead woman – their grievances were considered to have been just, but they needed now to show forgiveness. A three-day fast was prescribed. By the end of the three days the grave, which had suffered from the exertions of the nuns, but to Tetta seemed also to have subsided from a sentence which God himself had imposed, had recovered and now looked its proper shape.

The story of the overzealous prioress is said to have come from Leoba herself. Leoba had been offered to the minster as a young girl in thanksgiving for her birth. Here she spent her time 'in pursuit of sacred knowledge'. She remembered herself as an industrious and serious pupil with a prodigious memory, destined, as was revealed in a vision, to work abroad; the vision had shown Leoba with her mouth full of purple thread. Try as she might to pull all the thread out, there seemed to be no end to it; eventually Leoba fell asleep. An 'aged nun' in the community was asked to interpret the dream, her expertise in such matters being well known, and she was able to explain that the thread signified 'the wise counsels which Leoba would speak from the heart' and to prophesy that Leoba would 'profit many by her words and example and that the effect of them would be felt in lands afar off wherever she went'. In fulfilment of this vision, Leoba was duly invited by Boniface, her relative, to join his mission in Germany. Tetta, extremely dismayed by the summons, nonetheless allowed Leoba to leave Wimborne and henceforth she lived abroad, becoming in time abbess of Bischofsheim in the diocese of Mainz.

Judging by the surviving correspondence, Leoba's contact with Boniface was one she herself had initiated. A letter she sent to Boniface while she was still at Wimborne recalls their kinship via Leoba's mother, as well as Boniface's former friendship with Leoba's late father. As an only child, Leoba asks if she can regard Boniface as her brother, as 'there is no other man in my family [in] whom I can put trust as I can in you'. Further, she asks Boniface to 'correct the homely style of this my letter and send me as a model a few words of your own'. Leoba then adds a poem, 'composed according to the rules of prosody', with which she also hopes Boniface will help her. Her teacher, she explains, is Abbess Eadburh.

But who was this particular Abbess Eadburh? There are several possibilities. As well as being Leoba's teacher, she could be the Kentish abbess of Minster-in-Thanet;[K] she could be the recipient of Boniface's letter reporting the vision of the monk of Wenlock;[M] or she could be the scribe, commissioned by Boniface to write out for him the Epistles of St Paul in letters of gold so as to dazzle the heathen. These Eadburhs might, or might not, be one and the same. Recent scholarship suggests that there were at least two Eadburhs, as it is highly improbable that Leoba would have gone at any point to Kent for her education. It is therefore more likely that the Abbess Eadburh who taught Leoba was the successor of Tetta and that the Minster-in-Thanet abbess was a different Eadburh. But however the Eadburhs are unravelled, it remains indisputable that nuns in eighth-century England, as on the Continent, were copying manuscripts, as indeed they did throughout the Middle Ages.

WINCHESTER · Hampshire

Cenwealh divided his kingdom into two dioceses and gave Wine an Episcopal seat in the city of Venta which the Saxons call Wintancaestir. [III, 7]

When Haedde died, the bishopric of the kingdom was divided into two dioceses. One was given to Daniel, who governs it to this day, the other to Aldhelm. [v,18]

King Cenwealh's decision to make a second see for Wessex at Winchester is usually understood to be the result of his justifiable anxiety about the proximity of Mercia to Dorchester[W] (where Wessex's first see had been founded), even if the reason Bede gives is the 'barbarous speech' of Agilbert, his Frankish bishop of Dorchester. At Winchester, Cenwealh appointed Wine, a bishop who, like Agilbert, had been consecrated in Francia but who 'spoke the king's own tongue' – though, as we shall see, this alleged concern with language is less convincing than might appear.

Before long, Cenwealh had also quarrelled with Wine who, expelled from Wessex, went off to London to become its bishop. For quite some years thereafter Wessex had no bishop at all, but then, or so Bede tells us, it struck Cenwealh 'that it was unbelief which had once driven him from his kingdom and his acknowledgement of faith in Christ which had restored him; he realised equally that a kingdom which was without a bishop was, at the same time, justly deprived of divine protection' [III, 7]. He therefore sent messages of apology to Agilbert and asked him if he would return. Agilbert, now bishop of Paris, refused but sent his nephew, Leuthere, in his stead. Leuthere was 'honourably received by king and people' and consecrated by Archbishop Theodore at Canterbury. As bishop, Leuthere was active both in the founding of Malmesbury[W] and Bath.[W] The fact that the first abbess of Bath had a Frankish name, Berta, may, given Leuthere's background, be of significance.

Excavations in the 1960s managed to uncover the ground plan of Cenwealh's Winchester minster, revealing a cruciform church with a nave just 21.9 metres (71 ft 10 inches) long, half that size in width and with two square side chapels, each measuring a third of the length of the nave. (The dimensions are notably tiny in comparison with the Winchester cathedrals that followed.) It seems reasonable to assume that the church was completed during the time of Leuthere's successor, Haedde, since it was he who arranged for Birinus's body to be brought to Winchester from Dorchester. Haedde's hand can also be seen in King Ine's

law code (*see* introduction to the Kingdom of the West Saxons
or Wessex). Bede considered Haedde to be a 'good and just
man whose life and teaching as a bishop depended more on his
innate love of virtue than on what he learned from books' [v, 18],
though this may mean no more that that Haedde was not a match
as a scholar for his contemporary Aldhelm of Malmesbury.[W] But
he was, according to Bede, sufficiently holy for the place where
he died to become a cult centre. Soil from the spot was taken to
mix with water as a drink for sick man and beast.

After Haedde's death, the see was divided between Winchester
and Sherborne.[W] The first bishop appointed to Winchester was
Daniel. Daniel is explicitly thanked by Bede for supplying him,
in writing, with information not only about Winchester but
also about the Isle of Wight and about Sussex where, for a time,
Daniel was acting bishop.

Daniel's last years were troubled by his blindness, but in his
earlier days he had been an energetic bishop and an important
supporter of Boniface of Nursling.[W] A letter he wrote to Boniface
in his early years as a missionary has, with reason, been much
quoted for the light it throws on recommended tactics. Daniel's
own diocese had recently come to include the Isle of Wight,
which, at least until 685, had remained firmly pagan, so Daniel
had first-hand experience of the task.

> You ought not [advises Daniel] to offer opposition to them
> concerning the genealogies of their gods, false though
> they are, but allow them to assert according to their belief
> that some were begotten of others through the intercourse
> of male and female, so that you may then at any rate show
> gods and goddesses born after the manner of men to have

been men, not gods and since they did not exist before,
to have had a beginning... Ask [whether] they believe that
gods and goddesses still beget other gods and goddesses ?
Or, if they do not procreate now, when and why have they
ceased from child – now have become infinite... This also
is to be inferred: if the gods are almighty and beneficient
and just, they not only reward worshippers, but also punish
those who scorn them. If they do both in the temporal
world, why then do they spare the Christians who are
turning almost the whole globe away from their worship
and overthrowing their idols? And while they, that is the
Christians, possess fertile lands, and provinces rich in
wine and oil and abounding in other riches, they have left
to them, the pagans that is, with their gods, lands always
frozen with cold in which these, now driven from the whole
globe, are falsely thought to reign.

FURTHER READING

SELECT PRIMARY SOURCES

Abbots of Wearmouth and Jarrow, ed. and trans. Christopher Grocock and I. N. Wood (Oxford Medieval Texts, 2013)

The Age of Bede, trans. J. F. Webb with an Introduction by D. H. Farmer (Penguin Books, 1965)

Bede's Ecclesiastical History of the English People, ed. and trans. B. Colgrave and R. A. B. Mynors (Oxford Medieval Texts, 1969; rev. repr. 1991)

Bede's Ecclesiastical History, An Introduction and Selection, Rowan Williams and Benedicta Ward (Bloomsbury Publishing, 2012)

English Historical Documents, Vol. I: *c.*500–1042, ed. D. Whitelock (Oxford University Press, 1955)

Felix's Life of Saint Guthlac, ed. and trans. B. Colgrave (Cambridge University Press, 1985)

Old English Liturgical Verse, ed. Sarah Larratt Keefer (Broadview Press, 2010)

SELECT SECONDARY LITERATURE

Richard N. Bailey, *England's Earliest Sculptors* (Pontifical Institute of Medieval Studies, Toronto, 1996)

John Blair, *The Church in Anglo-Saxon Society* (Oxford University Press, 2005)

James Campbell, *Essays in Anglo-Saxon History* (Hambledon Press, London, 1986)

Rosemary Cramp et al. (eds), *Corpus of Anglo-Saxon Stone Sculpture*, (Oxford University Press for the British Academy, 1984–)

Rosemary Cramp, *Studies in Anglo-Saxon Sculpture* (Pindar Press, London, 1992)

Scott DeGregorio (ed.), *The Cambridge Companion to Bede* (Cambridge University Press, 2010)

Sarah Foot, *Monastic Life in England c.600–900* (Cambridge University Press, 2006)

Catherine Karkov, *The Art of Anglo-Saxon England* (Boydell Press, Suffolk, 2011)

Henry Mayr-Harting, *The Coming of Christianity to Anglo-Saxon England*, 3rd edn (Batsford, London, 1991)

Nicholas Pevsner et al., *The Buildings of England* (Penguin Books/ Yale University Press, 1951–)

Leslie Webster and Janet Backhouse (eds), *The Making of England: Anglo-Saxon Art and Culture* (British Museum, London, 1991)

Barbara Yorke, *The Conversion of Britain. Religion, Politics and Society in Britain, 600–800* (Pearson Education, Harlow, 2006)

INDEX